Global Markets and the Developing Economy

International Finance and Development Series

Published in association with the Institute of Social Studies

General Editor: **E. V. K. FitzGerald**, Professor of Economics, Institute of Social Studies, The Hague, and Director, Finance and Trade Policy Research Centre, University of Oxford

The International Finance and Development Series reflects the research carried out at The Hague and associated centres in Europe, Asia, Africa and Latin America on the relationship between international capital flows and the process of structural adjustment in less-developed economies. The studies in this series share a common analytical approach based on the use of advanced social accounting techniques and the explicit modelling of the economic behaviour of institutional sectors, which in turn permit a new approach to macroeconomic policy design.

Titles include:

Global Markets and the Developing Economy

E.V.K. FitzGerald

Finance and Trade Policy Research Centre
University of Oxford

and

Institute of Social Studies
The Hague

First published 2003 by
PALGRAVE MACMILLAN
Houndmills, Basingstoke, Hampshire RG21 6XS and
175 Fifth Avenue, New York, N.Y. 10010
Companies and representatives throughout the world

PALGRAVE MACMILLAN is the global academic imprint of the
Palgrave Macmillan division of St Martin's Press LLC and of
Palgrave Macmillan Ltd.
Macmillan® is a registered trademark in the United States,
United Kingdom and other countries. Palgrave is a registered
trademark in the European Union and other countries.

ISBN 1–4039–1538–5

This book is printed on paper suitable for recycling and
made from fully managed and sustained forest sources.

A catalogue record for this book is available
from the British Library.

Library of Congress Cataloging-in-Publication Data
FitzGerald, E. V. K. (Edmund Valpy Knox), 1947–
    Global markets and the developing economy / E.V.K. FitzGerald.
        p. cm.
    Includes bibliographical references and index.
    ISBN 1–4039–1538–5 (cloth)
        1. Capital market—Developing countries. 2. Free trade—
Developing countries. 3. Developing countries—Foreign economic
relations. 4. Globalization. I. Title.

HG5993.F58 2003
332'.042—dc21

                                                            2003043614

10   9   8   7   6   5   4   3   2   1
12   11   10   09   08   07   06   05   04   03

Printed and bound in Great Britain by
Antony Rowe Ltd, Chippenham and Eastbourne

For Angelines, always patient and supportive

Contents

List of Tables and Figures

Tables

Figures

Abbreviations and Acronyms

BIS	Bank for International Settlements
BWC	Bretton Woods Commission
CCL	Contingent credit lines
CGEM	Computable general equilibrium model
DAC	Development Assistance Committee
ECB	European Central Bank
EMS	European Monetary System
EMU	European Monetary Union
ERM	Exchange rate mechanism
ESAFs	Enhanced structural adjustment facility
EU	European Union
FDI	Foreign direct investment
G3	Germany, Japan and the United States
G7	Canada, France, Germany, Italy, Japan, United Kingdom, United States
G10	Belgium, Canada, France, Germany, Italy, Japan, the Netherlands, Sweden, Switzerland, United Kingdom
GAB	General arrangements to borrow
GATT	General Agreement on Tariffs and Trade
GDP	Gross domestic product
HIPC	Heavily indebted poor countries
HOS	Heckscher-Ohlin-Samuelson model
IAIS	International Association of Insurance Supervisors

ICIC	International Credit Insurance Corporation
IEs	Industrial economies
IFIs	International finance institutions
IMF	International Monetary Fund
IOSCO	International Organization of Securities Commissions
LDCs	Less developed countries
LTCM	Long-term capital markets
MAI	Multilateral Agreement on Investment
MIGA	Multilateral Investment Guarantee Agency
MNCs	Multinational Corporations
MRA	Mutual Recognition Agreement
MSAF	Macroeconomic social accounting framework
NAFTA	North American Free Trade Agreement
NGOs	Nongovernmental organizations
NICs	Newly industrialized countries
OECD	Organisation for Economic Cooperation and Development
RER	Real exchange rate
ROW	Rest of World
SAM	Social Accounting Matrix
SDRs	Special Drawing Rights
SEC	US Securities and Exchange Commission
SRF	Supplemental reserve facility
STFF	Short-term financing facility
UNCTAD	United Nations Conference on Trade and Development
UNCTC	United Nations Conference on Transnational Corporations
UNRISD	United Nations Research Institute for Social Development
WTO	World Trade Organization

Series Editor's Preface

This volume is the last of ten studies in the *International Finance and Development Series* that report the findings of a major research programme on 'International Capital Flows and Economic Adjustment in Developing Countries' at the Institute of Social Studies. Our approach is based on the proposition that the response of an open economy to external shocks depends critically upon the distinct production, investment and savings decisions of specific groups of private agents (foreign corporations, domestic firms, small business and households); and thus that any rigorous approach to the evaluation of macroeconomic performance must approach the data within a well specified institutional framework. Further, we hold that any evaluation of adjustment policy must be based not only on the ability to achieve fiscal solvency and debt sustainability, but also on investment levels sufficient to ensure export competitiveness and poverty reduction.

With my colleagues Karel Jansen and Rob Vos at The Hague I have been privileged to lead this programme, although most of the credit should go to them as is evident from the authorship of the volumes in the *Series*. In addition, Karel's administrative and fundraising skills were essential to the whole project, as was Rob's creation of the Macroeconomic Social Accounting Framework (MSAF) that underpins our quantitative methodology. Two ISS colleagues – Howard White and Marc Wuyts – provided their specialized knowledge of aid and Africa to our own specializations in finance, macroeconomics, East Asia and Latin America. The three research officers on the programme – Niek de Jong, Joke Luttick and Khwaja Sarmad – made valuable contributions by systematizing large bodies of comparative data and providing a global matrix for the country studies. Six ISS doctoral students also formed part of the team: Edwin Croes, Alemayehu Geda, Philomen Harrison, Alejandro Izurieta, Luis-Carlos Jemio and Fernando Tenjo.

Their dissertations – some of which provided the basis for volumes in the *Series* – extended our approach to areas such as corporate finance, income distribution and development assistance. Last, but not least, we are indebted to the two successive ISS publications officers for the *Series*, Gary Debus and Paula Bownas, for bringing the fruits of our labour into print.

Early research funding was provided by The Netherlands Ministry of Education (RAWOO), which enabled us to establish the methodological framework. The Netherlands Ministry of Foreign Affairs (DGIS) provided resources for the case studies of The Philippines, Pakistan, Thailand and Mexico. The UN Statistical Office helped finance the construction of the World Accounting Matrix (WAM). Funding was also received from the Swedish Ministry of Foreign Affairs (SASDA) and the MacArthur Foundation. We are extremely grateful to all these bodies for their generous support.

The origins of the analytical approach developed in the *Series* can be found in three earlier books published by the team. In the preparatory phase of the research, Jansen brought together a number of the leading economists in the field for a series of public lectures at The Hague, whose different perspectives were published in his *Monetarism, Economic Crisis and the Third World*. These insights revealed the limitations of standard monetary economics in understanding the macroeconomic consequences of financial systems for growth and poverty in open developing countries. The team first addressed the task of constructing a more appropriate analytical framework in FitzGerald and Vos *Financing Economic Development*, which was one of the earliest attempts to integrate modern monetary economics with the structuralist foundations of development economics. My own *Macroeconomics of Development Finance* took these arguments a step further towards a consistent approach to the monetary aspects of the semi-industrialized economy from a post-Keynesian standpoint that allows the issues of real investment and income distribution to be integrated into financial policy design.

From these early explorations, a set of four central propositions were established as to the determination of international capital flows, the impact of these flows on developing countries, the response of domestic economies to these flows, and the policy implications of this process for sustained growth and poverty reduction. All the volumes in the *Series* share these propositions, although they apply them in different circumstances – including seven individual country case studies – and thus come to distinct conclusions. Indeed one of our strongest conclusions is just that: a 'standard' approach to financial liberalization, foreign investment and structural adjustment is misguided at best and positively dangerous at worst.

First, the determinants of the levels, variation and composition of international capital flows are to a large extent independent of the economic behaviour of the developing country that receives them. This is true for all three of the main components of these flows as classified in the *Series*. Official development assistance is constrained as a whole by the fiscal positions of donor governments, and has tended to stagnate over recent decades. Its allocation to particular countries follows largely geopolitical imperatives, although with the end of the cold war these have tended to be more closely related to humanitarian and commercial rather than military goals. International bank lending as a whole is determined by the liquidity position of major banks and the rate of interest in G3 economies, as well as by their existing level of exposure to particular regions. Bond finance – which makes up the bulk of so-called 'portfolio flows' – has tended to follow the same logic as bank lending. Finally, foreign direct investment (FDI) – that is, intrafirm asset acquisition – follows the longer-term strategic plans of multinational corporations in response to access to natural resources, cheap skilled labour and domestic markets. While macroeconomic stability is clearly a necessary condition for FDI flows, it is clearly not sufficient without one of these key attractors. In consequence, there is a strong case for regarding capital flows as largely autonomous and beyond the immediate control of local policymakers.

Second, the impact of foreign resources depends critically upon the type of flow involved. Official development assistance, foreign direct investment, international bank credit and portfolio capital flows all affect both public and private expenditure in quite different ways. On the one hand, these flows affect the resources available to different agents: aid to governments, FDI to firms, and credit to banks for instance. The macroeconomic effect will reflect the objectives of these foreign agents and the response of the domestic recipients, as well as the aggregate impact on variables such as import levels and the exchange rate. On the other hand, the 'quality' of these capital flows – in terms of price, maturity and conditions – vary considerably due to imperfections in international capital markets. In particular, official flows tend to be cheaper

and longer-term but to involve detailed and obligatory policy conditionality, while private flows are more expensive and (in the case of
bank credit and portfolio flows) of shorter maturity, but are not policy-
conditional – except in the broader sense of a pro-business environment.

Third, the response of the economy to external shocks depends
critically upon the rational yet distinct investment and savings behaviour of the domestic private sector agents, and the relationship between
them – bearing in mind that the sum of their actions must 'add up' con-
sistently with the macroeconomic constraints and thus response will
necessarily involve unexpected changes in key variables such as exchange reserves, price levels or domestic savings. The four classes of
agents that we have found both analytically useful and empirically dis-
tinguishable in these volumes are central governments, parastatal bodies, companies and households. Nonetheless, we have also distin-
guished, where possible, between the behaviours of sub-groups of
agents, particularly between rich and poor households on the one hand,
and between large (including foreign) firms and small enterprises on
the other.

Our fourth proposition follows from the previous three: that economic policy in general – and structural adjustment in particular – is as
much determined by the conditions on international commodity and
capital markets and the behaviour of the domestic private sector as it is
by ministries of finance, central banks and aid agencies. This proposition we have been able to test quantitatively because the Macroeconomic Social Accounting Framework permits financial and 'real' flows
to be integrated within a rigorous social accounting framework. The
effect of external capital flows can be traced through the balance of
payments and the fiscal accounts into the investment and savings decisions of firms and households. In this way, the functional income distribution can be linked to the flow of funds for the first time, and thus
the full implications of structural adjustment for income distribution
and economic growth be revealed. Finally, the MSAF can be used as
the basis for computable general equilibrium (CGE) modelling for examining feasible macroeconomic policy alternatives.

The *Series* itself contains ten volumes that are intended to form an
integrated whole as well as to test the four propositions outlined above.
Three of these volumes examine the international context of global
capital flows in which the case studies are located. Four case studies –

from Bolivia, the Philippines, Thailand and Trinidad & Tobago respectively – show how our methodology can be applied to the institutional specificities of individual.[1] Three further volumes address the analytical issues and present our empirical findings in a comparative context, completing the collection. In this brief discussion, these ten volumes are discussed in logical rather than chronological order.

The three international studies explore the behaviour of capital flows – both official and private – in the context of the world economy as a whole, thus lifting the 'small country' convention common to all other structural adjustment studies. This has two implications: first, that the conditions governing the supply of foreign capital can be considered, as well as for the demand for (and impact of) these funds,[2] and the consequences of allocation between host countries can be explored; and second, that the general equilibrium effects of (say) developed country interest rate changes or increased commodity exports from developing countries can be explored systematically.

In one of the most interesting volumes in the *Series*, Vos sets out to explore the functioning of international financial markets and the consequences for developing countries. In *Debt and Adjustment in the World Economy* he demonstrates not only that global capital markets are highly segmented but also that market clearing in flows towards developing countries is generally exercised through quantity rationing rather than price (i.e. interest rate) adjustment. This has been true throughout the last century even though the institutional organization of these markets has changed fundamentally. Under these circumstances, imperfect risk assessment and liquidity cycles lead to periodic overlending to and debt crises in emerging markets. Such systemic instability in international capital markets makes it very difficult for developing countries to construct sustainable long-term growth strategies, and to respond optimally to exogenous shocks from commodity markets. Vos then integrates these findings into a formal model of the world economy in the structuralist tradition that builds upon national accounting principles and adds behavioural functions for investment, savings and capital flows in the developed and developing regions. This world economic model, along with the treatment of public and private financial behaviour in our *Financing Economic Development,* provides the basis for the models used in the rest of the *Series*. Moreover, Vos' finding that an increase in aid flows may have a negative effect on growth in developing countries if they are financed from fiscal deficits that raise world interest rates and depress commodity prices is of considerable significance. In contrast, these effects would not emerge if increased aid were financed from reduced expenditure or an expansive monetary policy.

In *Accounting for the World Economy* Luttick builds on the foundations laid by Vos in order to construct a complete 'world accounting matrix' (WAM) where, for the first time world trade and investment linkages can be quantitatively measured. This logical extension of the social accounting system to the world economy effectively links not only the reciprocal current accounts between economies[3] but also their reciprocal capital accounts. The linkage between the resulting capital flows and the domestic economy is provided by integrating these two balance of payments accounts into domestic saving and investment levels. The institutional form taken by capital flows largely determines their behaviour. In this context not only the type of flow – multilateral and bilateral aid, and private direct investment and debt finance – but also the country of origin are key characteristics of the asset demand function. This volume not only provides the first consistent estimates of international capital flows by origin and destination,[4] it also makes substantial contributions to both matrix reconciliation methodology and to our understanding of the determinants of international capital flows. The construction of an international capital flows matrix[5] is complicated by the fact that each reports the flow between any two countries differently, while the sum total of inflows reported worldwide is less than the total of outflows. Reconciliation in the WAM thus requires that flows be reallocated on the basis of the relative reliability of different sources as well as the relative size of the economies concerned (i.e. 'pro rata'). Once done, these matrices permit Luttick to apply a constant market share analysis derived from trade theory in order to distinguish clearly between changes in aggregate asset demand by international investors, the asset composition of investor portfolios, and the 'attractiveness' of a particular region or country. For instance, she shows that US investment trends in Latin America can be largely explained by existing trade links and changes in the US share of worldwide investment, as opposed to the risks and returns of investing in this region rather than (say) Asia.

The third 'international' volume concerns the role of Africa as a whole within the world economy, with particular reference to finance and trade flows. Geda sets out in his *Finance and Trade in Africa* to construct a model of the world economy where Africa, with its constituent regions, is fully defined as an actor. This model explicitly draws on *Debt and Adjustment in the World Economy* and *Accounting for the World Economy* so as to integrate the effect of trade and aid flows with the impact of macroeconomic policies in developed economies on these flows. The key to a proper understanding of Africa's 'development trap' is shown to be that declining terms of trade and aid dependence have reduced the level of capital formation (both physical and human) below the level needed to stimulate rapid export growth and net poverty reduction, while generating unsustainable debt levels. That the debt problem is essentially a commodity export problem may seem fairly obvious, but it is striking that current efforts to reduce debt burdens do not address this issue directly. Moreover, the diversion of public investment away from traded production should be added to the negative effect of aid on currency overvaluation. It follows that aid could be better channelled towards investment by small export farmers rather than towards urban consumption (albeit of the poor) and that conditionality should include expansionary policies in order to keep interest rates low and exchange rates competitive. Of course, current aid conditionality is aimed almost precisely at the reverse outcome. Finally, Geda's model shows that despite its effective exclusion form international capital markets, Africa is highly vulnerable to global interest rates and liquidity levels, due to their impact on commodity prices; so that any discussion of the 'new international financial architecture' should include measures to protect Africa from adverse commodity price shocks. In sum, this volume demonstrates that rigorous economic analysis can confirm intuitions in the political economy tradition without lapsing into the platitudes of 'Third World' discourse.

The four country studies apply our analytical approach to widely different cases and, in so doing, demonstrate its flexibility and strength. Vos and Yap explore the reasons why The Philippines failed to get onto the regional growth curve in *The Philippine Economy: East Asia's Stray Cat?* This was not a question of a different government policy frame – for the policies were similar to those in neighbouring countries – but rather one of a different private sector response to investment incentives. Large firms and rich households tended to export capital, while rural producers and small urban firms were excluded from credit by the banking system. Periodic attempts to apply restrictive stabilization policies only worsened this trend and undermined the industrialization process. The construction of MSAFs at five-year intervals allows this failure to achieve structural change to be revealed in detail. It also becomes clear that low savings rate in The Philippines, which contributed to macroeconomic vulnerability to external shocks, was due to low corporate reinvestment rates rather than to household behaviour. In consequence, financial liberalization and high interest rates (caused by Treasury borrowing on domestic markets) did not stimulate private savings while depressing private investment.

In his *External Finance in Thailand's Development*, Jansen examines the Thai economy during the 1980s and 1990s in careful detail in order to establish the basis for the export growth and, by implication, its recent halt. He finds that Thailand did not have as high domestic savings rates as the other successful East Asian economies, so relied more heavily on foreign investment. However, this was deliberately switched from bank borrowing by government (which funded the necessary infrastructure) in the 1970s to FDI for the private sector in the 1980s: thus shifting financial risk the domestic fiscal sector towards the foreign private sector. However, borrowing abroad by Thai banks in the 1990s in response to high domestic interest rates after financial liberalization had the contrary effect, with disastrous consequences. The contrast between these two cases is marked: in Thailand the banks were not required to finance the government as they were in The Philippines so could fund industry; in Thailand, corporate profits were reinvested while in The Philippines they were exported; and at least until the late 1990s, Thai macroeconomic policy was the more pragmatic and stable (due to independence from foreign creditors), leading to reduced investor uncertainty and thus higher growth.

Turning to another continent, Jemio sets out, in *Debt, Crisis and Reform in Bolivia*, an alternative framework for the analysis of the numerous external shocks (including the growth of narcotics exports), stabilization policies and structural reforms in a small open economy over the past quarter-century. He argues that existing neoclassical (e.g. World Bank or IMF) and neo-structuralist (e.g. UN Economic Commission for Latin America) approaches are unable to explain the impact of external shocks on short-term macroeconomic equilibrium and long-term growth, because they are too aggregated to capture the heterogeneous nature of even in a small economy such as Bolivia. In particular, the segmented nature of markets – and thus the 'informal' sector – requires explicit modelling in his CGE framework as well as the major production sectors themselves. Further, the economic behaviour of public and private institutions changes over time due to the accumulation of assets and liabilities from previous periods on the one hand, and the learning process itself (including the influence of international agencies) on the other. In particular, Jemio's treatment of the 'coca economy' is highly innovative: he places narcotics transactions within the social accounting framework, which allows him to trace the effect not only on exports and GDP as previous authors have done, but also on income distribution (elucidating the behaviour of both the urban rich and the rural poor) and monetary balances. This latter aspect allows the increasing dollarization of the Bolivian economy to be explained and thus the reduced capacity of the authorities to maintain macroeconomic equilibrium.

Firm behaviour under adjustment policies in an even smaller economy, although none the less complex for that, is analyzed by Harrison in her study of *The Impact of Macroeconomic Policies in Trinidad & Tobago*. She takes up the central hypothesis of the Bretton Woods institutions that the post-independence state-led development experiment had failed and that sustainable growth could be better attained by a market-based strategy. She notes, however, that this hypothesis was presented as an axiom, and that little published research exists on how firms actually behave in small open economies. Further, it is necessary to distinguish between large and small firms, not only because of the employment potential of the latter but also because the linkages of the former with national and international finance. Her detailed work on business surveys shows that the affiliates of foreign firms in small developing countries are disproportionately large and have privileged access to funding; so that the domestic private sector cannot respond to the 'shock therapy' of the sudden liberalization of trade and finance because of its own technological and organizational weaknesses. In particular, capital markets remain segmented and uncompetitive even after liberalization, and thus a high degree of prudential regulation is needed in order to both prevent systemic crises and to ensure a broadly-based investment pattern based on low real interest rates, long-term credit availability and tax incentives for domestic firms. In sum, both these studies demonstrate that high domestic interest rates fail to stimulate saving while depressing investment, while the crowding out of small firms and the uncertainty caused by restrictive monetary policy reduce not only growth but also employment.

The three comparative volumes contain cross-cutting analyses of theoretical issues and comparative empirical studies. In *External Finance and Adjustment* (edited by Jansen and Vos) bring together the empirical findings of the main fieldwork project in the research programme. The original five case studies (Mexico, Pakistan, Philippines, Tanzania, and Thailand)[6] are summarized here by the lead economists from the respective country teams and their counterparts at The Hague. The task of evaluating structural adjustment policies involves – as is so often the case in scholarly enquiry – a reformulation of the question. This issue cannot be regarded as simply one of 'successful' or 'failed' domestic government policies as both the international financial institutions and their critics suppose. How the private sector reacts to external shocks and to the policy response can be equally or even more significant. The nature of this reaction cannot be taken for granted or derived from textbook economic principles. The five case studies in this volume contain detailed and comparable analyses of the relationship between the fiscal sector, the balance of payments, the financial system and the 'real economy' of households and firms. How crises developed from the way in which structural adjustment was conceived becomes clear: private sector over-borrowing abroad in Mexico; balance of payments stress resulting from the stock market boom in Thailand; failure to convert foreign capital flows into productive investment in The Philippines; fiscal constraints on private sector development in Pakistan; and destabilizing effects of aid on private savings and investment in Tanzania.

This volume also contains valuable cross-country results derived from the MSAF methodology, which allows rigorous comparison of individual cases for the first time by using CGEs based on common classifications and similar policy simulations. This allows significant results to be derived from the long-period estimation of external shocks and domestic adjustment. Specifically, it is possible to separate the initial impact of an external shock (whether through trade or finance) on the public and private sectors from the secondary effect of policy response on both sectors. The evidence that policies can either buffer or magnify the initial impact implies that intervention can be effective, but only when directed towards maintaining private investment levels and when maintained over the medium term. Above all, policy design can and should go beyond the conventional nostrums of fiscal balance and market opening to address the expected behaviour of firms and households, and construct incentive patterns and regulatory measures in order to ensure that this behaviour is consistent with macroeconomic stability.

While the main focus of the seven country case studies is private sector behaviour – in relation to both capital flows and domestic firms – the team felt that it was appropriate to address the relationship between official development assistance ('aid') and structural adjustment by using our methodology to trace the macroeconomic impact of aid through the public, private and external sectors of vulnerable aid-dependent economies.[7] The theoretical discussion and the econometric results in *Aid and Macroeconomic Performance* clearly indicate that aid cannot just be seen as a form of fiscal support, as it also affects production and consumption directly through import finance. The potentially negative macroeconomic effect of currency overvaluation can thus be countered by channelling aid (or the counterpart funds) so as to support private investment, production inputs and the export sector. In this volume, White and his collaborators show that this approach also requires policy makers to base their actions on consistent sets of national accounts, balance of payments and fiscal data through which the effect of aid flows can be clearly identified. Unfortunately this is rarely the case although the method is not complex. Aid is usually regarded as a 'balancing item' rather than as the central macroeconomic factor in least developed countries despite the fact that on average, official assistance funds half of public expenditure and a similar proportion of imports. The scope for policy improvement clearly depends on the level, composition and allocation of aid; but this is in the hands of a multiplicity of unilateral donors whose objectives are microeconomic and social, and a few multilateral donors who focus their policy conditionality on government reform rather than private investment. White argues that donor conditionality can and should be radically reoriented in order to stress debt relief, avoid import liberalization booms, focus on human capital formation, support sustainable reform programmes and promote private sector investment.

Finally, in the present volume *Global Markets and the Developing Economy*, I bring together some key background themes of the *Series*. A Keynesian analysis of global savings trends indicates that a single long-term real interest rate has emerged as major capital markets have become more closely integrated. This provides not only a single reference point for the 'cost of capital' against which all emerging markets set their interest rates in combination with the risk premium, but also provides a continuously available 'safe haven' for domestic savers. Thus traditional concepts of 'capital flight' must be replaced by one of portfolio diversification, where not only risk and return but also tax avoidance must be taken into account. However, the converse does not apply: developing countries do not have continuous access to this pool of global savings, and are periodically 'rationed out' by market sentiment reflected in international liquidity preference. The present volume goes on to draw out the implications for the analysis of open economy macroeconomics where volatility of capital movements must be considered to be both exogenous and systemic. I also attempt to generalize here our findings on the differential behaviour of distinct categories of firms in terms of their investment behaviour in the face of uncertainty and funding constraints. This approach then leads logically to a reappraisal of the effect of market opening on income distribution through the consequences of employment and wages where adjustment does not (and cannot) involve instantaneous adjustment of productive structures, but rather relies on new private investment to create the desired supply changes. If this investment is not forthcoming, then 'structural adjustment' will not be successful. The policy implications are considerable, for to the extent that capital flow shocks are exogenous and their effects on domestic firms are asymmetric, then domestic authorities should introduce regulatory stabilizers in order to reduce domestic investor uncertainty and thus promote long-term growth.

It is not really appropriate for me to assess the impact of our research programme, or the thirteen volumes in this *Series* and their precursors, on academic development economics or professional policy practice. When we embarked upon the programme, our central propositions were considered radical – if not positively mistaken – by orthodox economists associated with the Bretton Woods Institutions, because the shifting of financial resources from the public to the private sector could only increase efficiency and thus economic growth and poverty reduction. Traditional development economists associated with UN agencies were still concerned with augmenting the flow of capital to developing countries and with the public sector as the axis of resource mobilization, and thus regarded our focus on private sector behaviour and monetary policy as irrelevant to the central concerns of development policy. Now, both sides of the debate recognize that private investment decisions are what determine economic development, but that these are framed within a specific institutional context that has both domestic and international dimensions. Whether we have had some influence on this important debate or were just ahead of the trend, only the reader can judge, but our own intellectual satisfaction is hardly the point. The opening of the third millennium sees the number of the world's poor rising, persistent financial instability in emerging markets and a decline in both official and private capital flows towards developing countries. There are still many lessons that national policy makers and international development institutions need to learn about the relationship between capital flows and economic adjustment and it would not be immodest to suggest that some of these are to be found in this *Series*.

Notes

1. Case studies were also carried out for Mexico, Pakistan and Tanzania: our partner institutions published these separately. Summaries can be found in the respective chapters of Jansen and Vos (1998).

2. In my opinion this classification is misleading, and it would be more logical in economic terms to speak of the demand for assets by international investors, and the supply of these assets by host countries.

3. As, of course, the United Nations LINK Project has done for some time through reciprocal import demand determined by GDP levels.

4. It is extremely unfortunate that the UN Statistical Office has been prevented by lack of funds from putting the estimation of the WAM on an official basis, as had been originally planned.

5. Similar problems hold with trade matrices, which is why the UNCTAD uses export figures only in its estimates of the origin and destination of merchandise trade.

6. Bolivia and Trinidad & Tobago were added subsequently.

7. In this case, those of Guinea-Bissau, Nicaragua, Tanzania and Zambia.

References

FitzGerald, E.V.K. (1993) *The Macroeconomics of Development Finance: A Kaleckian Analysis of the Semi-Industrial Economy*. Basingstoke: Macmillan.

FitzGerald, E.V.K. (2002) *Global Markets and the Developing Economy*. Basingstoke: Palgrave.

FitzGerald, E.V.K. & R. Vos (1989) *Financing Economic Development: A Structural Approach to Monetary Policy*. Aldershot: Gower.

Geda, A. (2002) *Finance and Trade in Africa: Macroeconomic Response in the World Economy Context*. Basingstoke: Palgrave Macmillan.

Harrison, P. (2002) *The Impact of Macroeconomic Policies in Trinidad and Tobago: The Firm Under Adjustment*. Basingstoke: Palgrave Macmillan.

Jansen, K. (ed.) (1983) *Monetarism, Economic Crisis and the Third World*. London: Cass.

Jansen, K. (1997) *External Finance in Thailand's Development: An Interpretation of Thailand's Growth Boom*. Basingstoke: Macmillan.

Jansen, K. & R. Vos (eds) (1997) *External Finance and Adjustment: Failure and Success in the Developing World*. Basingstoke: Macmillan.

Jemio, L.-C. (2001) *Debt, Crisis and Reform in Bolivia: Biting the Bullet*. Basingstoke: Palgrave.

Luttick, J. (1998) *Accounting for the World Economy: Measuring World Trade and Investment Linkages*. Basingstoke: Macmillan.

Vos, R. (1994) *Debt and Adjustment in the World Economy: Structural Asymmetries in North-South Interactions*. Basingstoke: Macmillan.

Vos, R. & J. Yap (1996) *The Philippine Economy: East Asia's Stray Cat?* Basingstoke: Macmillan.

White, H. (ed.) (1998) *Aid and Macroeconomic Performance: Theory, Empirical Evidence and Four Country Cases*. Basingstoke: Macmillan.

Author's Preface

This book is the fruit of my research on the macroeconomics of open developing countries over the past ten years. This has been a decade marked by the liberalization of capital accounts and conservative fiscal management, matched by integration to volatile world markets. This shift has required a fundamental rethinking of development economics: the difference in my own ideas is clear if this volume is compared to my *Macroeconomics of Development Finance* published in 1993. The major change has been the extent to which world markets penetrate the national economy, so that the problem of sustainable growth and poverty reduction is no longer one of the external funding constraint on investment, but rather one of private sector behaviour in an uncertain international environment. Investment decisions, rather than savings levels, are still the fundamental problem, but capital accumulation can no longer be regarded as a national process with foreign lending as a complement. Moreover, whereas previously development finance was a matter of fiscal resources and bank lending, it is now a matter of judgements about risk and return by private investors. Inadequate infrastructure clearly limits the ability of poor countries to expand exports into global markets, but public investment is no longer the motor of development. High savings rates are no longer a guarantee of growth (because they can fund overseas assets) but they do constitute an essential buffer against external shocks.

The current disenchantment with the outcome of the financial liberalization process springs largely from the fact that the undoubted efficiency gains have been accompanied by persistent financial instability, so that the expected rise in levels of investment and growth have not been forthcoming. There is thus a growing interest in the institutional basis for more effective regulation of markets that confirms my earlier approach to development finance. However, the major difference between this book and *Macroeconomics of Development Finance* is that the concept of planning – in the sense of a deliberate development strategy which macroeconomic policy should support – appears to have passed into history. This is partly due to the official enthusiasm for market deregulation, but also to the realization that only the largest individual developing countries can conduct independent macroeconomic policies. If alternative macroeconomic policies that will increase growth and reduce poverty are to be constructed, they will necessarily be coordinated at an international level: this is after all our own experience in Europe, and is presumably valid *a fortiori* for developing countries.

Global capital markets now provide a single point of reference for emerging markets, but while the former determine the cost of capital and a 'safe haven' for domestic savers, developing countries do not have continuous access to this pool of global savings, and are periodically 'rationed out' by market sentiment reflected in international liquidity preference. The implications for the analysis of open economy macroeconomics where volatility of capital movements must be considered to be both exogenous and systemic are serious: if private productive investment is not forthcoming, then 'structural adjustment' will not be successful. This volume concludes that the role of the International Monetary Fund – as established in its constitution – of helping member countries adjust to these shocks, should take into account these systemic problems at the international and national level. In particular, it is as important to regulate lenders, as it is to regulate borrowers in an integrated global capital market – as indeed is the practice within the financial systems of industrialized countries.

The research upon which this book is based was made possible by the generosity of the MacArthur Foundation, to whom I am deeply indebted. I am particularly grateful to Ame Bergés of Lucy Cavendish College, Cambridge, who undertook the difficult task of turning my messy and inconsistent manuscript (or rather word processor files) into a coherent single text. Without her careful redrafting and constructive suggestions the book would never have been completed. Last, but not least, my thanks to the ISS publications officer Paula Bownas for her cheerful efficiency and Joy Misa for her customary typesetting skills.

Valpy FitzGerald
Oxford and The Hague

1 Introduction: Liberalization, Investment and Global Markets[1]

The extension of free trade throughout the world and greater integration of capital markets during the 1990s were thought to herald the truly 'global economy' anticipated by Keynes and his colleagues at Bretton Woods 50 years before. Official opinion held – and still holds – that this dynamic global economy should particularly benefit poor countries: by embracing the principles of liberal capitalism and establishing efficient production structures, developing countries can and will reap the economic benefits of rapid export growth and massive foreign investment. The previous decade had also seen the replacement of the post-war model of economic development (which had focused on issues of agrarian transformation, state-led industrialization and income redistribution) by a new paradigm often referred to as the 'Washington Consensus' that favoured trade liberalization, fiscal stabilization, structural adjustment, and sale of public assets.

The conduct of economic policy in developing countries during the 1990s was also transformed by dramatic changes in the nature of international capital flows. Since the 1982 debt crisis, resource transfers toward the public sector had been replaced by capital inflows to the private sector. Official development finance shifted from development projects and budgetary support towards humanitarian relief and central bank support. Government borrowing moved from bank loans to bond issues, while local banks and local firms accessed international financial markets through the issuance of securities and bank credit.

This changing scenario of international financial markets offered new opportunities and posed fresh problems for developing countries, hence conditioning their economic development strategies. On the one hand, employment and wage policies in particular were now con-

1

strained by the need to both maintain international trade competitiveness and attract foreign investment. On the other, access to world capital markets appeared to offer new opportunities to raise productive investment rates in order to support modernization and sustainable growth.

At the opening of a new century we can now see that this model – or at least the form in which it was applied – did not function as planned. Successive financial crises in Latin America, East Asia, Eastern Europe and Russia have made this plain, as has the failure of much of the developing world to make sufficient progress towards the agreed global targets of poverty reduction and welfare provision. The aim of this book is to address the question of why this was so, and what can be done about it. In the neoclassical tradition, capital markets are orderly and well behaved, clearing the supply and demand for funds in national and international markets through the interest rate. Consequently, developing countries should always be able to access the global pool of savings at a rate determined by their country risk premium over the global rate, and as long as their rate of return on investment is higher than this, then growth and employment will increase. To the extent that country risk is reduced by economic reform and sound policy, then the cost of capital is reduced and growth increased. The evident failure of capital markets to support development in this way is conventionally attributed to two systemic factors in addition to particular country problems: first, the 'shortage' of national savings from developed countries available on international markets, and second, the lack of sufficient trade and financial liberalization in developing countries. However, it is not at all clear – theoretically or empirically – that capital markets do work in this way.

Most of this book is concerned with the second problem. Chapter 2 opens, however, by exploring the relationship between national savings and international capital markets and how they are linked through interest rate behaviour. Examination of the savings trends in the major economic areas and the debate on the determinants of savings does not reveal a 'savings shortage' as such. Indeed, there is strong evidence of a converging global real interest rate which (although relatively high by historical standards, due to low rates of inflation) is relatively invariable by type of borrower. In consequence, the main characteristic of international capital markets appears to be credit rationing in response to the liquidity preferences of private lenders. Monetary co-ordination between leading world economies is probably the only form of extra-market intervention capable of overcoming these liquidity constraints, and developing countries would benefit enormously from this. However, as this is not politically feasible, credit rationing and liquidity cycles remain a central feature of international capital flows. The rest of this book is dedicated to exploring the implications of this central characteristic of global capital markets for macroeconomic policy in developing countries and for the reform of international financial institutions.

Economic doctrine plays a critical role in determining the actions of international institutions and the national elite who manage small open economies, but modern theories of international economic fluctuations persistently fail to address macroeconomic policy response from the point of view of either sustainable growth (that is in terms of investment) or poverty reduction (that is, in terms of employment and wages). This is particularly clear in the case of the relationship between domestic monetary equilibrium and international capital markets. So Chapter 3 outlines a Keynesian response to the gap between the reality of international capital markets and the 'standard paradigm' of economic theory underpinning the policy model offered to poor countries. Although recent work on imperfect markets from the 'new Keynesian' perspective has modified the standard model substantially to allow for non-price clearing, the resulting framework does not appear to have been integrated with new trade theories, while the implications of systemic volatility and credit rationing behaviour under these circumstances have not yet been theorized either. The chapter suggests that a return to Keynes' original approach to investor uncertainty and aggregate demand – but at an international level – might not only help integrate international macroeconomic theory in a plausible manner, but also contribute to the formulation of more effective policies in developing countries.

After over two decades of strenuous and socially costly attempts to implement macroeconomic adjustment policies, the hard-won achievements of narrower current account deficits, reduced government expenditure and lower rates of inflation have yet to be matched to any extent by sustained renewal of per capita income growth, let alone by industrial transformation. At the heart of the standard model lies the plausible intuition that sustainable growth is based on domestically financed private investment in traded production. At the macroeconomic level, fiscal deficits should be reduced in order to release household savings for more productive use by private entrepreneurs and for a reversal of capital flight. At the microeconomic level, commercial deregulation and real exchange rate appreciation should increase the profitability of traded production and stimulate investment demand, while higher real rates of interest raise domestic savings and attract foreign capital.

Chapter 4 scrutinizes the concept of the financial constraint on private investment that underpins this standard model more closely, to explore the implications of a more plausible account of the heterogeneous behaviour of firms ranging from multinational corporations to household enterprises. The assumptions about firms' accumulation decisions, that appear to underpin the macroeconomic models employed by the World Bank and the IMF, focus on a simple causal link between household savings and enterprise investment. However, the observed financial behaviour of the different kinds of firms that characterize semi-industrial economies reveals that their investment behaviour is highly heterogeneous. In particular, the affiliates of multinational corporations and member firms of large domestic groups are subject to few credit constraints, although the latter will have more balance sheet exposure to currency shifts, while the small firms that provide the bulk of employment are much more vulnerable to macroeconomic shocks. This heterogeneity implies that 'standard' policy rules may require radical rethinking if they are to be socially sustainable in the Keynesian sense of leading to full employment.

Trade liberalization and financial liberalization are usually closely linked in practice, it being generally agreed in principle that the former should precede the latter. The expected capital inflows should support the new investment needed in order to take advantage of integration into the world economy by increasing export capacity and making home industries more competitive. Nonetheless, standard trade theory says little about the required investment process, relying on a smooth reallocation of existing resources (labour in particular) in response to relative price incentives. However, as we have seen in previous chapters, this investment response cannot be taken for granted. The aim of Chapter 5 is remedy this gap in order to explore the consequences of economic reform for income distribution in developing countries. The standard textbook model of trade liberalization as applied to labour markets has been extended to include nontradables and human capital, but does not address investment directly, so that the familiar results of increased employment and higher wages derive from assumptions of doubtful validity. Positive outcomes depend upon the rate and form of technical change, and hence on the investment process, but recent theoretical work suggests that the effect of trade liberalization on aggregate investment is ambiguous and may well be negative if accompanied by restrictive stabilization policies, rapid financial liberalization or increases in exchange rate uncertainty. A formal framework for understanding the effects of trade liberalization on wages, employment and investment – based on assumptions that are more plausible – can be constructed, which has considerable implications for macroeconomic policy in open developing economies.

Short-term capital flows – both inward and outward – following financial liberalization have become a serious source of concern as they can bring about sudden shifts in real exchange rates, domestic interest rates, asset values and domestic credit levels. National authorities are often forced to change fiscal and monetary policy both suddenly and frequently in order to offset such shocks, while the international institutions they appeal to become even further involved in policy conditionality and last-resort lending. However, concern as to the impact of short-term capital movements should extend beyond the systemic risk to the financial system that arises from the differing maturity of assets and liabilities over the transmission of uncertain expectations from one institution or market to others. Short-term capital flows can have a negative effect on the real economy. The most frequently-cited transmission mechanism is that inflows (and subsequent outflows of capital) shift relative prices and thus distort resource allocation decisions through fluctuations in the exchange rate and the domestic interest rate. Nonetheless, abrupt fluctuations in aggregate demand in the Keynesian sense probably constitute a more important transmission mechanism. In addition, the effects of capital flows are asymmetric, so that the effect of an inflow followed by an equal outflow is not such as to leave the economy in the position it was before – particularly due to the irreversible nature of fixed investment decisions. Further, volatility in key macroeconomic variables (such as the exchange rate), even around a stable trend, increases business uncertainty and thus reduces growth.

Chapter 6 explores these 'real effects' in some depth, by examining the consequences of short-term capital-flow instability arising from the desire of investors to hold liquid assets in the face of uncertainty. The transmission mechanism towards the real economy consists of an indirect effect through price variables such as the interest rate and the real exchange rate, and a direct effect through changes in the demand for bank deposits and government bonds. The analysis then proceeds to examine the impact of short-term capital inflows and outflows on fiscal behaviour, demonstrating that the required shifts in the primary budget balance that are consistent with solvency can shift dramatically with investor sentiment and force large fluctuations in public investment expenditure. The impact of short-term capital flows on the availability of bank credit for firms is found to have a considerable and asymmetric impact on output and investment, with grave consequences not only for employment but also for long-term private investment. The impact on employment and the real wage rate of fluctuations in the real exchange rate and aggregate output are also shown to be substantial, although the extent to which the burden of adjustment falls on employment or wages depends largely on the government's macroeconomic stance.

The global expansion of free trade and the integration of capital markets in the early 1990s offered the prospect of a dynamic 'global economy' in which developing countries were expected to be the primary beneficiaries. In this context, policymakers were confident that the implementation of sound economic policies in poor countries would raise export growth and encourage massive foreign investment inflows, leading to efficient production structures and the elimination of poverty. Nevertheless, the difficulties surrounding the first multilateral trade negotiations since the foundation of the World Trade Organization (WTO) – the so-called 'Millennium Round' – revealed the lack of consensus between developed and developing countries, between developed countries (particularly the US and the EU) and the within individual countries between governments and particular sectors of civil society. The series of financial crises in the emerging markets and transition economies of Latin America, East Asia and Eastern Europe have similarly exposed the limitations of international regulatory institutions. In particular, the International Monetary Fund has clearly been unable to fulfil its statutory short-term aim of maintaining orderly exchange rates, stable capital flows and regular debt servicing, let alone its longer-term statutory objective of promoting employment and incomes.

Chapter 7 evaluates, therefore, the role of the IMF under the central criterion of the need to provide adequate institutional support for an orderly global capital market that can promote worldwide trade and investment. The experience of the post-war Bretton Woods System and subsequent practice reveal that there exist systemic problems caused by rapid expansion of global capital markets without underpinning regulatory frameworks. The interventionist approach to payments crises with corollary defence of exchange rates that is associated with the IMF is thus almost bound to fail in the modern world where fiscal deficits are no longer the drivers of currency imbalances. It may well be that the approach espoused by the Bank for International Settlements, which emphasizes the establishment of international rules for global financial markets, is a more appropriate option for a global market dominated by private actors. The implication is that the powers and procedures of the IMF, and also its place within the emerging system of global financial management and regulation, require complete revision.

Despite these reservations, capital markets continue to globalize. The second half of the 1990s saw asset deflation and currency collapse in Latin America and East Asia, raising public action issues that have also introduced broader questions of the social benefits of economic globalization in light of such extreme asymmetry between large states and firms on one hand, and small nations and the poor on the other, and by extension the type of institutions required for the smooth running of a truly global economy. Moreover, there are good reasons to believe that financial markets are inherently unstable, and have historically required strong institutions to control them. This argument is intrinsically stronger at the international level than at the national one, but international institutions for prudential financial regulation and emergency intervention are weak or non-existent in comparison with equivalent institutions at the national level.

In consequence, Chapter 8 concludes the discussion by focusing on some current policy debates about the construction of the international institutional 'architecture' from the point of view of developing countries. After addressing the global causes of emerging market volatility, its local consequences, and the failure of international financial institutions (such as the IMF) to contain it, the current attempt to extend multilateral bank regulation towards emerging markets and its limitations are discussed. It appears that the effectiveness of transborder mutual recognition agreements and the potential of international credit insurance schemes are very limited. In fact, the establishment of a binding set of rules for international investment (with logical consequences for both global capital taxation and international debt write-offs) is the only sound foundation for a long-term solution, mirroring as it does the arrangements within mature capital markets. However, the implications of the argument for the recognition of private property in international law – and thus for the concept of 'global citizenship' itself – are unexpectedly radical.

2 International Markets and Domestic Savings

2.1 INTRODUCTION

In the Ricardian tradition, savings out of profits provide a constraint on investment because the saving decision and the investment decision are the same, so that *ceteris paribus*, growth is constrained by the rate of profit. Drawing from the strict neoclassical tradition, capital markets are orderly and well-behaved, clearing the supply and demand for funds in national and international markets through the interest rate. Consequently, the failure of capital markets to clear is traced back to savings constraints that arise due to structural budget deficits and demographic trends, and drive up world interest rates. This interpretation has led the current academic, policymaking, and global market orthodoxy as embodied in the International Monetary Fund (IMF) to assert that a global 'savings shortage' lies at the heart of international macroeconomic instability:

> The critical importance of saving for the maintenance of strong and sustainable growth in the world economy, for external adjustment, and for the amelioration of the international debt problem is well recognized. Consequently, the declining trend in the saving rates of many countries, industrial as well as developing, has been a major source of concern. This decline has been associated with lower rates of capital accumulation and growth in the world economy. In addition, the substantial divergence of saving rates among countries has contributed to the emergence of large current account imbalances, especially among the major industrial countries. (Aghevli et al. 1990: 3)

This chapter is concerned with the relationship between savings and capital markets and how they are linked through interest rate behaviour.

9

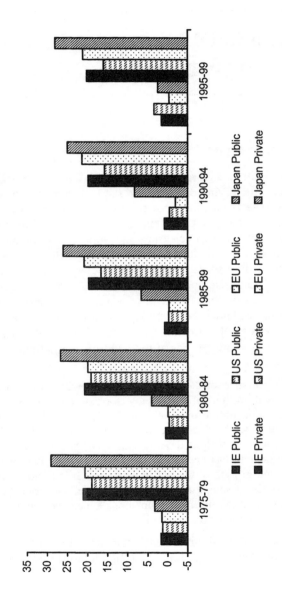

Figure 2.1 Public and private sources of saving in OECD countries, 1986–2000 (% of GDP)

Source: Table A.4 in the Statistical Appendix.

Figure 2.2 Composition of private savings in select OECD countries, 1985–2000 (% of GDP)

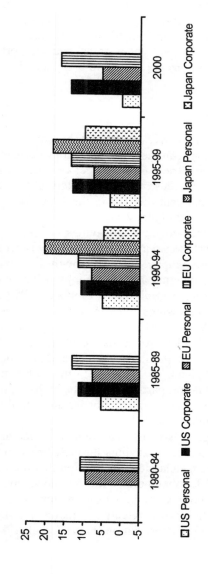

Source: Table A.4 in the Statistical Appendix.

In Section 2.2, we examine the savings trends of major economies and review the policy debate on the determinants of savings. In Sections 2.3 and 2.4 we turn to interest rate behaviour to discuss why interest rates should be high by historical standards and relatively invariable by type of borrower, how public debt overhang affects the global interest rate level, and the feasibility of fiscal co-ordination between leading world economies as an extra-market intervention to overcome liquidity constraints. Section 2.6 summarizes our conclusions and supports the proposition that financial institutions are needed to prevent and manage macroeconomic crises.

2.2 GLOBAL SAVINGS

The rise in rates of returns on new investment, largely a new development due to global deregulation, contrasts sharply with the steady decline in saving in industrial countries. From 24 per cent of gross domestic product (GDP), saving in industrial countries fell to 21 per cent of GDP in the 1980s and 19 per cent of GDP in the 1990s (see Table A.4 in the Statistical Appendix and Figure 2.3).

Most analyses of this downward trend in savings and savings behaviour tend to focus on household savings. Drawing heavily from life cycle theory,[1] they regard demography, income growth, interest rates and inflation as the principal determinants of savings behaviour (see Browning & Lusardi 1996, Engen et al. 1996, Lindbeck 1997).[2] For instance, the decline in private savings rates in industrial economies (IEs) during the 1970s and 1980s (see Figure 2.1) was attributed to an improved relative position of older groups in the population, the revaluation of the stock of wealth (particularly equities and housing), and financial liberalization (see Aghevli et al. 1990). In the 1990s, the imminent aging of OECD populations, particularly of the high-saving Japanese, has also been a source for concern (see for instance, Leibfritz et al. 1996, OECD 1998a, Nakagawa 1999).[3]

These analyses of savings behaviour determination generally neglect the role of firms as a source of savings through firms' retained profits, largely because of the neoclassical assumption that the modern corporation is merely a 'veil' for shareholders' household savings decisions. This assumption does not bear serious examination as an explanation of firm behaviour, while profit retention remains a significant component of gross saving before depreciation (Fazzari et al. 1988). To be sure, retained profits are the source of almost all funding for fixed investment undertaken by business (Goldstein & Mussa 1993), and corporate savings (undistributed corporate profits) are accounting for an increasing share of private savings in OECD countries (Figure 2.2). Furthermore, empirical evidence on the determinants of private savings behaviour is widely divergent (for surveys see Aghevli et al. 1990, Hutchinson 1992, Bosworth 1993 and Loayza et al. 2000). The effect of demographic factors on saving, for instance, varies greatly across countries for no readily apparent reason (see Hutchinson 1992).

Lastly, by generally drawing from the neoclassical tradition, these analyses rule out real interest rates as significant determinants of private savings behaviour.[4] In the standard view, declining savings rates are associated with lower rates of growth and capital accumulation in the world economy, while 'changes in inflation and interest rates seem to have had relatively small effects on saving behaviour' (Aghevli et al. 1990: 3).[5]

As to public saving behaviour, the prevailing orthodoxy assumes that the public sector deficit is at the discretion of the government, and that public sector savings 'crowd in' private savings indirectly by driving up interest rates through the public sector borrowing requirement (IMF 1987). In a closed economy, private savings may still be forced even if public savings are constrained by real balance effects through increases in the money supply. The same effect is felt in small open economies through inflows of foreign savings in the monetary approach to the balance of payments. The effects of these capital inflows on savings in emerging markets are explored further in Chapter 6.

Public saving behaviour is held to reflect mainly the fiscal stance of governments, which is partly endogenized by the differential effect of tax receipts and welfare entitlements at particular points in the business cycle (see Buiter 1988). Demographic factors also appear to be relevant, since welfare entitlements assume a demographic dimension over the longer term, while tax pressures are limited by the international mobility of the factors of production. Debt also becomes endogenized with the accumulation of fiscal deficits. In accordance with Ricardian Equivalence theory, these fiscal deficits should be balanced by an increase in private savings, which in turn provide for future tax burdens (Buiter 1988, Barro 1989).

Figure 2.3   World saving, 1986–2000 (% of GDP)

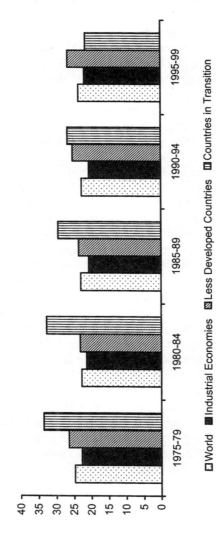

□ World ■ Industrial Economies ▧ Less Developed Countries ▦ Countries in Transition

Source: Table A.4 in the Statistical Appendix.

Empirical evidence on public and private savings in OECD countries, however, does not support this relationship. Indeed the downward trend in public savings rates in OECD countries has been accompanied by a decline in private savings rates (Dean et al. 1990, see also Figure 2.1). In these countries, the increase in real interest rates during the eighties and early nineties was linked to their large budget deficits (see Domenech et al. 2000).

The lack of compelling evidence for this 'crowding in' is complemented by indications that the origin of the deficit (whether originating from changes in the tax rate or from changes in the expenditure rate) also determine private sector response.[6] In this context, the particular composition of the tax and expenditure structure is of critical importance: tax reductions appear to generate offsetting private saving while increased expenditures do not.

In non-OECD countries, the downward trend in savings in the 1970s and 1980s (Figure 2.3) is partly explained by income outflows to oil-exporting countries or wealth adjustment savings. In the former centrally planned economies, the removal of constraints on consumption and direct state access to profits contributed to a decline in savings.

Some middle-income countries experienced high rates of private savings during adjustment in the 1980s (Figure 2.3), but this reflected the need to finance capital flights: increased consumption and falling savings rates reemerged in the 1990s. Clearly, the expected reduced budget deficits and enhanced private savings from increased real interest rates and higher profit shares through structural adjustment were not forthcoming.[7]

Nonetheless, the declining savings rates in emerging markets leading up to the crisis of the late 1990s were substantially reversed as capital inflows ceased, government expenditure cut and current account balances shifted into surplus. This is particularly marked in East Asia, and underlines the fact that savings are strongly influenced by macroeconomic factors and thus cannot be simply taken as 'structural'.

2.3   GLOBAL CAPITAL MARKETS

In principle, investment levels in an open economy should not be constrained by savings, and nor should savings have to be in equilibrium with investment: the resultant current account balance could be financed by matching international capital flows. Empirical analysis of trends in long-term international capital flows is difficult because of discrepancy in capital flow data and, by extension, in global asset/liability positions.[8] Broadly speaking, investment income flows are poorly recorded and the returns on financial assets are often underreported. Further, the observed global excess of recorded liabilities over assets, and the questionable reliability and compatibility of various sources, force the adjustment mechanism to fall onto the reduction of the initial estimates of liabilities.[9] Despite these caveats, it is clear that international capital flows have expanded much more rapidly than global output, investment or trade, and have become significantly more mobile since the late 1970s.[10] In the United States, for instance, the fiscal deficit implied by the shift in the current account from a net surplus to a net deficit position was essentially financed by Japanese householders whose savings in Japanese banks allowed those to purchase US Treasury bonds.

Contrary to the prevailing orthodoxy, international capital flows often fail to bridge the gap between global savings and investment. First, the acquisition of financial assets is subject to strong 'home bias' tendencies, with obvious implications for global capital market adjustment. Detailed studies suggest that the close correlation between domestic saving and investment within IEs cannot be attributed alone to a spurious correlation[11] or to regulatory restrictions (see Turner 1991, Frankel 1992, Obstfeld 1994). Rather, 'home bias' is more likely to arise from currency risk, agency problems and asymmetric information, among other factors. In other words, 'home bias' in financial asset acquisition appears to arise from factors that are endemic to the market itself such as currency risk, agency problems and asymmetric information.

Second, international capital markets fail to clear because capital flows are subject to a systemic rationing system. This systemic rationing system is based on market perceptions of 'sovereign risk' and an assessment of the 'quality' of a country's bonds, and hence of the country's longer-term growth potential and fiscal solvency. Market perceptions of 'sovereign risk' play a role of critical importance. Indeed, they are partly responsible for the segmentation of capital flows by portfolio flows, foreign direct investment (FDI), bank credits, and official development assistance between IEs and the rest of the world (ROW) (World Bank 1994). Differences in institutional behaviour affect asset acquisition, but country 'quality' appears to be the determining factor.

To be sure, the importance of perceptions of country 'quality' holds even when the investment and savings decisions are the same, when externalities prevent profitability from reflecting factor scarcity, particularly in the case of FDI (Lucas 1990), and when infrastructure and skills are central to location choice (UNCTC 1992). International capital flows are also segmented between country groupings (World Bank 1994). Since the early 1980s, bank credit flows from IEs to the ROW have declined, while the rise of portfolio flows in the early 1990s was confined to only a small group of upper middle-income countries. Similarly, FDI flows have been confined to relatively few newly industrialized countries (NICs) and are largely financed by the firms concerned, while aid flows tend toward the poorest countries. It is worth noting that these flows are spurred on by different concerns. For instance, whereas bank credit and portfolio flows have been essentially concerned with public sector finance, aid flows are determined largely by non-economic factors. During the early 1990s, the rise in private portfolio flows to emerging markets allowed aid flows to decline – while apparently closing the 'savings gap' – but by the end of the decade, the withdrawal of these flows revealed the difficulties of relying on external private finance for domestic capital formation.

Further, whether an increase in autonomous capital flows from IEs toward the ROW – sometimes regarded as a means to generate greater global aggregate demand – will bridge the savings gap depends crucially on how the capital flow is financed. To the extent that the capital flow is financed by increased taxation or by reduced investment or consumption in the 'North', then reduced demand in the 'North' for exports from the 'South' may have a counterbalancing effect. To the extent that the capital flow is financed by monetary expansion, it may raise world interest rates and affect international commodity prices and debt burdens.[12]

Consequently, it would appear that even if savings were to rise autonomously in one country, it may not be possible for another country to tap the savings-investment surplus because of the portfolio preferences of asset holders.[13] This has been generally the case within the IEs (certainly between the USA, Japan and the EU) and *a fortiori* between IEs and the ROW. The issuance of Special Drawing Rights (SDRs) is one mechanism for overcoming the problem of global liquidity preference. This position reveals the current orthodox position on global savings to be essentially Ricardian rather than neoclassical and draws on Keynesian theory in the strong wealth effects and weak saving by firms.

In sum, where access to global capital markets is highly segmented and the 'quality' of financial assets is determined by investors' perceptions of the country's characteristics, the market for savings and investment will fail to clear *a fortiori* for flows to the ROW. An international portfolio approach is clearly needed to reach an understanding of patterns of global savings, given that the reconciliation of desired asset positions between economies will determine the global macroeconomic equilibrium.[14]

2.4   GLOBAL INTEREST RATES

The global market for savings and investment clears through the global interest rate. Whereas national monetary authorities determine nominal short-term interest rates,[15] the capital market largely sets long-term interest rates. In turn, real (inflation-adjusted) long-term interest rates affect corporate investment decisions, the fiscal solvency of governments and the return on personal pension schemes; by contrast, nominal short-term interest rates affect exchange rates and consumer demand for credit. In this manner, the globalization of capital markets in the early 1990s has led to the emergence of a 'global' long-term interest rate that acts as an essential anchor for both national monetary policies and multinational business strategies, and affects the stability and growth of global capital markets and the sustainability of domestic monetary policies.

Despite broad equalization of yields on similar dollar bonds within the OECD since the eighties (Figure 2.4) and exchange rate adjustment to domestic interest rate differentials, which have allowed for a modest margin of risk (Turner 1991), interest rates have not cleared the international capital market and have not brought savings and investment into global equilibrium.[16]

Part of the reason lies in the increasing convergence of real long-term rates in leading industrial countries towards a high 'global rate'. Between 1960 and 1972, the long-term, inflation-adjusted, 'global' interest rate (the mean of the G7 long-term interest rate) averaged approximately three per cent per annum, the usual peacetime level for nearly two centuries. During the inflationary splurge and breakdown of the Bretton Woods system in the late 1970s, real long-term interest

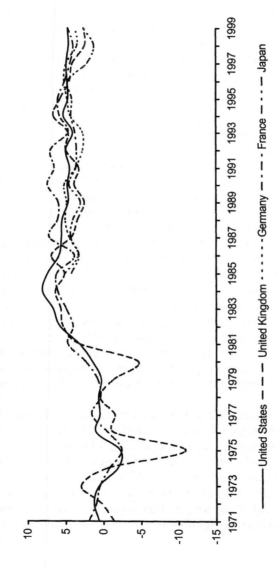

Figure 2.4   Real long-term interest rates in leading industrial countries, 1971–99

Source: Table A.4 in the Statistical Appendix.

rates collapsed and became negative. In the 1980s, real long-term interest rates returned to historic highs of around five per cent due to the US fiscal deficit and tight monetary policy. In recent years, although world inflation and short-term rates have experienced a sustained decline, real long-term rates continue to hover around four per cent (Figure 2.4). Furthermore, bond markets have enforced a uniform monetary policy independent of the divergent cyclical position of national economies, although flexible exchange rates were expected to extend greater autonomy to domestic demand management. Moreover, exchange rates do not appear to affect trade flows sufficiently or rapidly enough to adjust current account deficits and avoid asset adjustment (Goldberg 1993).[17]

As to the determining factors of long-term interest rates, ambiguity and lack of consensus result in a wide discrepancy of interpretation, market opinions and policy response to specific events. For instance, some research asserts that while growing debt to GDP ratios among the G7 since the 1980s has put pressure on short-term interest rates, long-term rates remain less affected by monetary and fiscal policy (see IMF 1995, Reinhart & Sack 2000). Other research maintains that fiscal and monetary policies explain about one-half of higher-than-historical levels of long-term rates, since these reflect risk premia generated by G7 fiscal deficits and balance of payments difficulties (see Eichengreen & Mody 1998, Ford & Laxton 1999), with financial deregulation since the eighties – which has reduced authorities' ability to contain long-term interest rates for specific market segments such as government bonds and mortgages – accounting for the remainder (Orr et al. 1995). Furthermore, while the IMF maintains that a single global interest rate has emerged, the OECD suggests that this pattern of 'convergence' is confined largely to EU members and that G3 dissonance has not been reduced significantly.

These interpretations of the determinants of long-term rates derive from two analytical approaches (Ciocca et al. 1996). The first approach sees real long-term interest rates as determined by the equilibrium of personal savings supply and corporate investment demand, and maintains that any increase in government deficit is countered by a rise in private savings in anticipation of future taxes (the so-called 'Ricardian Equivalence' theory). According to this approach, long-term nominal rates are this fundamental equilibrium rate *plus* the market's expectation about inflation.

The second approach assumes that nominal long-term interests rates reflect market expectations about the global liquidity situation and hence, the borrowing strategies of major governments. This approach pits the monetary policies of their respective central banks against the demand of portfolio managers for bonds as against equities. According to this approach, long-term real interest rates are the market equilibrium *less* the inflation that eventually ensues. Consequently, the first approach would consider the fall in personal saving rates in OECD economies[18] and the rise in Less Developed Countries' (LDCs) demand for funds,[19] forecasting a rise in long-term real interest rates. By contrast, the second approach would focus on efforts to reduce government deficits in the G3 and on the implications of the European Monetary Union (EMU), forecasting a reduction in nominal interest rates by the next decade.

Clearly, the policy implications derived from these two approaches to interest rate determination differ greatly. The first view would conclude that the only way to bring down long-term interest rates by means other than a reduction in investment demand (which would harm world growth prospects) would be to raise saving in the major economies through radical reductions in fiscal deficits and privatization of pension schemes. The second view, by contrast, would place greater emphasis on reduction of the debt overhang and better policy co-ordination as measures to improve market sentiment.

This lack of consensus regarding the underlying determinants of long-term interest rates constitutes a major problem for business strategists. Major technological investments in a multicountry strategy require corporate planners to assume a position on the long-term cost of capital that cannot be reversed once the project has been undertaken, while capital market uncertainty over global bond prices imparts a corresponding instability over long-run essential exchange rate relationships and thus over the profitability of production in different locations. The lack of clarity is not only problematic for private sector planners, but for the G3 monetary authorities as well, as they attempt to keep short-term interest rates down and sustain economic activity.

Figures for benchmark bond yields suggest that there is a wide divergence in monetary policy between the three centres of the global capital market: the US, Germany and Japan. Divergent monetary policy largely affects short-term interest rates as inflation-adjusted long-term rates have converged on a global average during recent years.

In the United States, for instance, the official US policy aimed to keep short-term rates as low as possible through the elections and raise them only if there is an apparent danger of wage inflation resulting from near-capacity utilization. Eventual budget-balancing is expected to bring down long-term rates in time, but the market clearly does not yet believe the policy entirely, which explains why short-term rates remain above five per cent, while long-term rates of over seven per cent contain an expected inflation rate of some four per cent.

By contrast, in the Euro-area, recent reduction of German short-term rates towards two per cent still leaves long-term rates at over six per cent, despite signs of economic recovery. This long-term rate approximates the global rate once expected inflation is taken into account. Finally, in Japan, short-term rates are now as close to zero as is technically possible, with monetary and fiscal expansion continuing despite the fact that output has hardly grown for a decade. By contrast, long-term rates have risen to nearly four per cent, which also approximates the global real interest rate. In this case, investor uncertainty on corporate solvency is expressed by the declining Nikkei rather than by the fall in bond prices.

Probing beyond these essentially transitional issues raises questions regarding the role of interest rates in the essential poles of the world economy (Ciocca et al. 1996), since the broad spectrum of political economies in the G3 appear to block the emergence of an orderly international bond market. These divergent political economies not only make co-ordination difficult but also generate significant uncertainty for institutional fund managers, who in turn induce destabilizing capital movements as portfolios are continually adjusted to reflect the expected moves by G3 authorities.

2.5   GLOBAL MACROECONOMIC CO-ORDINATION

With respect to global trade and economic co-ordination, the agenda of the World Trade Organization (WTO) emphasizes the mainstreaming of trade integration strategy into LDCs' development plans and poverty reduction strategies, more active co-operation with international finance institutions such as the IMF and the World Bank, and has built up useful precedents in dispute settlement. The governance of international capital markets has also gained importance in discussions on global economic issues and global co-ordination of strategies among the

G7, but reform of the international capital market poses a much greater problem than trade. First, unlike trade, full liberalization of financial flows is not possible. This situation arises because of the impact of volatile capital flows and lagged adjustment of asset and liability positions on the fragility of financial institutions. Second, financial markets are based on assets whose value depends on expectations; in other words, financial markets are inherently unstable. Consequently market integration is not simply a matter of eliminating barriers to entry, but must also involve the integration of jurisdictions. Third, government debt accounts for a significant proportion of international securities trade. Hence, the government's fiscal stance becomes a determinant of, and is subject to, international financial flows.

International regulatory reform could develop along three different tracks to eliminate current overlaps and gaps between regulatory authorities in different countries, as will be seen in Chapter 7. Because this is where both large profits and potential disasters are spawned, it is necessary to address these inconsistencies, or 'fault lines', as the Bank for International Settlements (BIS) in Basle calls them.

One option would be the extension of a dominant regulatory system from a major national market to the ROW. It comes as little surprise that this is the preferred option of the United States, although in the wake of the Mexican and the Long-Term Capital Market (LTCM) debacles, the Federal Reserve is reluctant to take on the implicit monetary responsibilities this approach implies. Furthermore, difficult issues of extraterritorial jurisdiction are likely to arise.

The second option would be the establishment of a 'convening regulator' for each international financial business group. In the event of a crisis, this 'convening regulator' would be responsible for initiating and co-ordinating the response of all affected regulators. This UK proposal would grant the Bank of England a commanding position for a number of key groups and would reflect the dominance of the City of London within Europe.

The third option would be the creation of a supranational regulatory body out of the existing capabilities of the BIS, the IMF and the OECD. Clearer rules and active participation in the regulatory body would entail considerable advantages for non-US and non-UK players in the system, not only for IEs like Japan and France, but also for emerging regional powers such as Brazil, India and China.

Reaching consensus at the G7 level is not a strictly geopolitical problem, for even if G7 leaders could come to a major new agreement on debt or, more importantly, regulatory co-ordination, they still face three outstanding difficulties. One is that the G7 leaders may be unable to carry their respective legislatures, central banks or major financial institutions with them on implementing decisions. Another is that the G3 may be unable or unwilling to comply with the high degree of fiscal discipline or to co-ordinate monetary stances between them, both of which are necessary for global financial stability. Finally, the tasked agency assigned to address global financial emergencies may lack the resources and the ability to intervene rapidly and autonomously.

To complicate matters further, the resolution of financial problems is increasingly acquiring a regional dimension. Regional co-ordination is certainly easier in terms of institutional harmonization and intergovernmental co-ordination, but leaves exposed gaps between regulatory areas that can be exploited by capital markets and may result in even greater tensions between the resulting 'tectonic plates'.

In the US, for instance, countervailing powers make coherent economic policy extremely difficult to achieve: political sources exert a sustained downward pressure on short-term nominal interest rates, while budget deficits exert a sustained upward pressure on long-term interest rates via capital markets. The principle of supremacy of a dispersed corporate enterprise means that capital markets, rather than the authorities, are the *de facto* arbiters of the most desirable economic strategy, and offers considerable flexibility to changes in business circumstances. The resultant variability in interest rates and exchange rates strongly prejudices management of the world economy, particularly given the enormous political and economic weight of the United States and its low savings rate.

In the European Union, by contrast, banking control of industry pushes for stable long-term interest rates, while centralized income policy presses for low inflation. The high concentration of corporate power and policymaking capacity have led to the 'negotiation' of economic strategy with business and labour. Once chosen, the strategy is applied firmly and supported by a strict monetary policy that implies relatively high long-term interest rates. Rather than plan the economy, the government attempts to control the conditions under which economic strategy is negotiated between banks, firms and labour. While imparting greater stability – and thus considerable predictability – to European policy, it also entails less flexibility.

Japan resembles Europe in its similar concentration of economic power, but its government undertakes a higher degree of planning. Government authorities administer capital markets directly and maintain real interest rates at low levels through market segmentation and relatively tight monetary policies. The consequences of weak asset portfolios are now well documented, but there is little argument that this system engendered the export drive that formed the basis of much of Japan's economic strength.

These three very distinct political economies attempt to incorporate national needs into their respective long-term interest rate policies. These strategies have strong international effects and require frequent modifications to prevent the resulting exchange rates and capital flows from becoming uncontainable. At the global level, there is a double confrontation, one at summit meetings of the leading countries regarding the economic policies of the three currency areas, and another between the policy line expressed at these summits and that of an increasingly integrated and liquid world financial system.

2.6 CONCLUSIONS

The problem of the failure of capital markets to clear does not stem from a global savings shortage, as the IMF and the World Bank would assert. Though low, savings rates in OECD and LDC countries appear sufficient to finance investment demand. A the heart of the problem is uncertainty in the strictest Keynesian sense regarding global asset values that translates into a problem of global liquidity preference and is made evident by the buoyancy of long-term interest rates. In the absence of a solid basis for capital market expectations, these high long-term interest rates reflect risk premia.

High real-interest rates affect private investment prospects as well as government debt solvency, and the reluctance of institutional investors to commit long-term capital discourages investment in large projects. While this presents a particular difficulty for major technological investment programs of global companies, it (unfortunately) constitutes little obstacle for global companies planning takeovers or speculative operations on financial markets. The problem is not so much the interest cost of funds as such, but rather the terms and conditions upon which they are offered, as these increasingly involve an unacceptable dilution of management control or repayment schedules that fail to consider the long lead-times involved.

In the next few years, the enormous infrastructure requirements of Asia, Latin America, and Eastern Europe will generate large bond offerings from governments and regulated private utilities. The problem that is likely to arise is not so much the real interest rate charges, which rarely exceed five per cent after inflation, but rather the risk-evaluation process undertaken by overseas investors. As will be seen in Chapters 7 and 8, the risk-evaluation process is highly volatile and relies on incomplete information. Market sentiment about a particular country or region can swing sharply, making it almost impossible to construct an efficient medium-term financing program for infrastructure.

In a global economy, the ultimate solution for high real interest rates and the shortage of long-term investment funds would presumably be a global monetary authority. However desirable, this solution is a long way off from fruition if only because a global monetary authority would have to function in crucial currencies and government bonds, which would effectively constrain macroeconomic policy in the G3. What appears to be clear is that real long-term interest rates will probably remain at their present historic high levels until new institutional conventions emerge. What form these institutional conventions take and how effective they are in addressing the problem of capital market clearing will be examined in further detail in Chapter 7.

3 International Markets and Open Economy Macroeconomics[1]

3.1 INTRODUCTION

The extension of free trade throughout the world and greater integration of capital markets after the late 1980s was thought to herald the emergence of a truly 'global economy' anticipated by Keynes and his colleagues at Bretton Woods fifty years ago. Popular opinion held that this dynamic world economy would principally benefit poor countries; by embracing the principles of liberal capitalism and establishing efficient production structures, developing countries would reap the economic benefits of rapid export growth and massive foreign investment.

The 1980s also witnessed a convergence of opinion regarding the principles of sound economic policy with respect to the developing countries. Most notably, the post-war model of economic development – which had focused on issues of agrarian transformation, forced industrialization, and income redistribution – was replaced by a new paradigm. This paradigm, which is often referred to as the 'Washington consensus', favoured trade liberalization, fiscal stabilization, structural adjustment and privatization. The post-war paradigm and the 'Washington consensus' drew from different traditions. Whereas the former evolved from the classical tradition of political economy, the latter was founded on textbook neoclassical principles and staunch convictions that market forces were superior to public action.

These convictions were no more challenged than during the 1990s, begging the question of the adequacy of the current paradigm, particularly among professional development economists. The unsatisfactory conclusion of the Uruguay Round and chronic instability in global financial markets have revealed the risks of rapid global market integration by developing countries with inadequate economic and institutional capacity, as well as the limited ability of international regulatory institutions to reduce this risk. At the same time, standard open-economy adjustment policies have been unable to help poor countries cope with growing poverty and environmental degradation. These policies may be leading toward a 'triage' marked by the stagnation or even decline of living standards of a significant part of humanity as unemployment expands and welfare coverage shrinks.

Economic doctrine plays a critical role in determining the actions of international institutions and the national elite who manage small open economies, but modern theories of international economic fluctuations persistently fail to address macroeconomic policy response, particularly of small open economies.[2] Given that developing countries account for almost 37 per cent of output, 18 per cent of trade, and 40 per cent of investment (see Table A.5 in the Statistical Appendix), the absence of adequate and realistic policy response recommendations is even more striking.

Drawing from Keynesian principles, this chapter attempts to incorporate the structural reality of poor countries into policy recommendations for global market integration and national macroeconomic management that rest on modern economic theories of international economic fluctuations. Efforts to incorporate recent work on imperfect international capital markets from the self-styled 'New Keynesian' school are examined in Section 3.2. In Section 3.3, we turn to attempts to modify the standard paradigm of open economy macroeconomics, and find that the gap between international economics and macroeconomics remains. In Section 3.4, we outline a Keynesian approach toward investor uncertainty and global demand in an effort to integrate the two topics more plausibly and contribute to the formulation of more desirable (and effective) policy positions. Section 3.5 offers some concluding remarks.

3.2   INTERNATIONAL ECONOMICS IN THE GLOBAL ECONOMY

As seen in Chapter 2, the standard paradigm holds that the world market is the most efficient allocator of global resources and that the failure of capital markets to clear is due to a global savings shortage. Mainstream analytical models of international capital markets in industrial countries continue to rely on an implicit model of independently and identically distributed random shocks and a homogeneous population of consumer-investors that differs, at most, in their risk-aversions and endowments. It is well established that capital does not flow between industrial and non-industrial economies on the scale suggested by standard theory (IMF 1991) regarding relative factor endowments.[3] They are unable to readily explain the origins of global financial instability, the rationing out of risky sovereign borrowers, or the systemic problems of international fiscal co-ordination and speculative currency crises (van der Ploeg 1994). Even the application of industrial organization theory to analysis of direct foreign investment flows requires a decidedly eclectic approach (Dunning 1992). Recent theorization of imperfect international capital markets has yet to be adapted explicitly to non-industrial economies. Neo-structuralist 'North–South' models have examined the interaction between new trade theories, capital flows and LDC growth on a global basis (see Muscatelli & Vines 1989), but capital flows continue to be treated as exogenous, save for the borrowing limits imposed by existing debt burdens. Similarly, the Heckscher-Ohlin-Samuelson (HOS) model of trade considers international capital markets and macroeconomic adjustment in developing countries as an essentially unproblematic general equilibrium problem. This contrasts distinctly the Keynesian approach to disequilibria, which derives from asset holders' expectations on international capital markets.[4]

The Keynesian interpretation challenges the Fund's view that capital markets fail to clear because of a global savings shortage. In the Keynesian approach, investment demand is able to generate the required level of savings if and when extra-market intervention addresses liquidity problems. As seen in Chapter 2, segmented access to global capital markets and investors' perceptions of the 'quality' of a country's financial assets prevent interest rates from clearing the market for savings and investment. This is Keynes' central proposition: interest rates do not clear the savings/investment balance, and liquidity demand affects the desire to hold the *stock* of bonds. Given uncertainty over asset returns and the availability of liquidity, which plague the reconciliation of desired asset positions between economies and ultimately determine the global macroeconomic equilibrium, this approach is highly relevant to understanding international capital markets.

The leading international macroeconomic policy models (van der Ploeg 1994) claim to be Keynesian because they are demand-driven. In these models, the GDP of industrial economies rises until reaching a capacity constraint or an employment/inflation corner. Asset positions enter in the consumption function (and by implication the savings function) with households essentially responsible for savings. Investment functions are simple accelerator models with various lags and minor relative-price effects. Interest rates derive from monetary policy stances and play an essential role in determining exchange rates, with income effects through the debt burden. The basic macroeconomic transmission mechanism in these models is adjusting capital flows, and the policy conclusion is that effective co-ordination between economies will increase the equilibrium aggregate level of world GDP.

3.3   MACROECONOMIC THEORY AND THE SMALL OPEN DEVELOPING ECONOMY

The application of macroeconomic theory to developing countries is based on two models of the small open economy: one set out in terms of traded and non-traded sectors (Meade 1951), and the other set out in terms of domestic adsorption,[5] which were subsequently synthesized into a single model (Dornbusch 1980).[6] The analysis of traded and non-traded sectors, excess demand from budget deficits, the role of the real exchange rate as a key policy instrument, savings (whether domestic or foreign) as the primary constraint on growth, and the positive effect of trade liberalization on employment (and hence on income distribution) now comprise the standard approach:

> ... [M]acroeconomic stabilization and fiscal consolidation are needed to reduce pressure on prices, real exchange rates, and the balance of payments while increasing domestic savings for more investment. Governments also need to press ahead with outward-oriented structural reforms that maximize competition in goods and labor markets, expand the opportunities for private enterprise, improve efficiency, and raise productivity growth. In this regard rationalization of large public sectors, trade liberalization, deregulation of investment, and reforms to create more flexible labor markets are all important. (World Bank 1995a: 22)

Despite evidence of successful monetary stabilization and an ambiguous out-turn regarding adjustment leading to export growth and poverty reduction,[7] the standard theory has come under considerable criticism from the neo-structuralist school. The neo-structuralist alternative to the standard theory incorporates the insights of the founders of development economics such as Prebisch, Kalecki, Lewis and Kaldor into a more formal analytical framework of modern open-economy macroeconomics (Taylor 1983, Taylor 1992, Dutt 1990).

Several 'stylized facts' underlie the central premises of the neo-structuralist critique, which appear to be almost diametrically opposed to the axioms of the standard theory.[8] Firstly, world market conditions place binding constraints on investment, growth and employment, although the form of this constraint depends on the specific structure of the economy in question.[9] Secondly, markets can clear through adjustments of both price and volume, but this adjustment hinges on the ability of producers to impose markups and labour's ability to negotiate wage adjustments. Thirdly, government expenditure can have positive effects on growth by 'crowding in' private investment. Fourthly, while technology may be externally imported, the factors of production are virtually unsubstitutable, so that employment depends on sectoral output rather than wage levels. Fifthly, structural rigidities ensure that exports and imports respond poorly to changes in the real exchange rate. Sixthly, fiscal and monetary variables are largely endogenously determined. Lastly, the macroeconomic resolution of *ex ante* disequilibria in expenditure plans under resource constraints determines the pattern of income distribution.

The alternative macroeconomic theory aims to provide convincing explanations of inflation, balance of payments problems and unemployment. However, the lack of an explicit definition of private sector behaviour (households and firms) remains a serious weakness, as does the absence of financial variables and analysis of the nature of interaction between macroeconomic policy and the world economy.

Certainly, defense of the standard model has led to greater sophistication. The successive inclusion of more plausible assumptions about the power of relative prices, the market equilibria and the possibility of an optimal policy response to external shock, and the structure of developing economies, have permitted the standard model to retain its core neoclassical assumptions of maximizing behaviour.[10] This model can thus still maintain that government intervention will continue to bring about market inefficiencies and 'distortions', and conclude that the removal of these government distortions will not only increase production but also improve the income distribution – albeit under somewhat implausible assumptions about labor markets (Bourguinon et al. 1989).

To its credit, the defense of orthodoxy has attempted to introduce a degree of endogenous behaviour by economic agents, and certainly, it has made a valuable contribution toward understanding domestic policy response to external shocks, including aid. Moreover, although these models generally aggregate the microeconomic 'overlapping generations' theory of household utility maximization, they have also made some progress toward endogenizing governmental behaviour (Rodrik 1989).

Despite efforts to introduce elements of endogenous determination, these models fail to come to terms with the implications of the endogenous growth theories. Indeed, these growth theories undermine many of the core assumptions of the standard model regarding longer-term growth:

> ... [A]lmost all the views on economic growth relate the accumulation of knowledge to externalities, so private decisions to save and to invest are not optimal and growth is from a social point of view too low. Naturally, this implies an active role for the government; depending on the engine of growth the government should try to support R&D [research and development], improve the channels of international communication, promote investment, maintain and expand the infrastructure, and/or invest in education. (van der Ploeg 1994: 575)

By contrast, the application of modern mainstream macroeconomic theory to industrial economies takes systemic market failure far more seriously (Blanchard & Fischer 1989). Indeed, New Keynesian theory relies on quantity-constrained models of open economies to show that imperfect markets require the application and efficacy of active fiscal and monetary policies (van der Ploeg 1994). To be sure, both the positive and welfare analyses of government policy will differ significantly from those under Walrasian equilibrium when based on more realistic assumptions regarding the maximizing behaviour of representative firms and households in markets that are characterized by imperfect competition.

The application of New Keynesian theory to issues in development economics has considerable implications for macroeconomic policy design (see for instance Woodford 1991), particularly its application to the analysis of the impact of price- and wage-formation rules on production and income distribution (Edwards & van Wijnbergen 1989, Mankiw 1991b) and to the analysis of asymmetric information in credit markets on investment and firm size (Stiglitz 1994) and on market equilibrium (Mankiw 1991a).

In spite of efforts to incorporate the economic reality of small open economies, both structuralist and New Keynesian approaches to open economy macroeconomics are severely limited. For instance, both retain implicit assumptions that the world economy is a given and stable reference point, propositions regarding maximizing behaviour constrained by known and continuous production functions and under conditions where expectations can be characterized by measurable risk. This approach takes insufficient account of the heterogeneous nature of the private sector, of the complex interactions of state institutions and civil society and of the increasing globalization of the productive and financial systems in developing countries. Surely the reality of imperfect capital market structures calls for a macroeconomic theory that can appeal to the wide variety of representative firms, from transnational corporations to peasant households, as will be seen in Chapter 4.

The textbook HOS modeling of the gains from trade continues to underpin recommendations for trade liberalization in developing countries, despite evident limitations of the model's underlying assumptions regarding scale economies, factor substitution, technological access and full employment. Furthermore, modern theories of endogenous growth (Baumol et al. 1994) suggest that a critical minimum threshold of development must be crossed in order for increasing returns at the firm level (technological scale and managerial scope) and national level (economic infrastructure and human resources) to spark catch-up and convergence between poorer and richer countries:

> A poor country tends to grow faster than a rich country, but only for a given quantity of human capital; that is, only if the poor country's human capital exceeds the amount that typically accompanies the low level of per capital income. (Barro 1991: 409)

Clearly, endogenous growth theory has radical implications for international economic theory in general, and open economy macroeconomics in particular, because an increase in trade can affect a country's long-run growth rate, and not just from a once-and-for-all effect from greater openness. Furthermore, rapid export growth depends on specific forms of policy intervention that support industrialization, rather than on strict reliance of market mechanisms alone (Grossman & Helpman 1991, Wood 1994).

An extension of the HOS model from trade to factor flows that posits that capital responds to take advantage of natural resource endowments and cheaper labor skills also underpins the proposition that greater access to international capital markets (in the form of foreign direct investment, bank loans, portfolio flows or official aid) would enhance poor countries' growth. However, as this does not happen in practice, by implication, public action is required here too.[11]

Several elements, when combined, paint an essentially Keynesian picture of the determination of aggregate investment levels, output growth and employment. First, modern microeconomic theories suggest that the effective constraints on private investment decisions are actually uncertainty and access to funds, rather than the traditional interest rate (Fazzari et al. 1988, Dixit & Pindyck 1994,). Second, developing countries depend on human capital and infrastructure provision to make significant contributions toward creating conditions of profitability. The combination of these elements completes a Keynesian picture where liquidity and expectations – rather than disposable savings net of the fiscal deficit and long-term capital inflows as in the standard model – determine the level of aggregate investment, output growth and employment.

To be sure, these arguments help explain why financial liberalization has had such perverse consequences in many developing countries. The standard model of financial repression suggested that once real interest rates were raised, private savings would increase sharply, and in consequence private investment would also increase, particularly if budget deficits were reduced simultaneously (IMF 1987). However, if, as seen above, savings do not respond to real interest rates and investment is not savings-constrained, then there is no reason to expect that the recommendations of the standard model will work.

Furthermore, in practice, financial liberalization appears to involve a combination of (i) 'disintermediation' (where banks cease to provide long-term credit to companies) which depresses investment, (ii) consumer credit expansion which depresses private savings (*net* asset acquisition) and stimulates imports, and (iii) increased reliance on volatile capital from abroad that is attracted by high real investment rates (Gibson & Tsakalotos 1994). In consequence, developing countries that opt for financial liberalization may encounter exchange rate overvaluation and balance-of-payments fragility.

3.4 INTERNATIONAL MARKETS AND OPEN ECONOMY MACROECONOMICS: Are Keynesian Economic Policies Still Relevant?

Keyne's *General Theory* presents the principle of effective demand as a theory of how investment demand and willingness to save reach equilibrium. In this case, the equilibrating force is the level of aggregate income, not the rate of interest. Further, the level of aggregate income does not necessarily correspond to full employment, and 'savings equals investment' simply because investment induces a like amount of savings. Extrapolating to the global market, even if individual countries face additional balance of payments constraints that might prevent market equilibrium at any given level of activity, global unemployment would only arise if the propensity to save were too high, rather than too low. Even then, the high savings propensity could be rectified through appropriate demand expansion by the surplus economies. The fixed savings coefficient implicit in the Keynesian consumption function, however, suggests that the Keynesian model is not entirely plausible either. Hicks' redefinition of saving (set in terms of changes in net worth) allows for wealth effects in the consumption function,[12] and offers an attractive ambiguity about the net effect of interest rates on saving. Hicks' redefinition is much more convincing empirically[13] than post-Keynesian attempts to endogenize the savings rate by making it contingent on income distribution. Nevertheless, a major shortcoming of the Keynesian model – and by extension, of the theory of effective demand – is its assumption that capital markets intermediate between saving households and investing firms. In point of fact, firms largely finance investment out of retained profits, and households are themselves major borrowers. As we have seen, the Keynesian view is, of course, diametrically opposed to this essentially Ricardian account, seeing investment demand as ultimately generating the required level of saving, given appropriate extra-market intervention to overcome liquidity problems.

Unfortunately, heterodox economists have not advanced the theory of international finance much beyond where Keynes left it fifty years ago (FitzGerald & Mavrotas 1994). Certainly, a Keynesian analysis of

international capital markets should be concerned with the reconciliation of desired saving and planned (or lagged) investment decisions.
This reconciliation should be mediated by multi-stage portfolio 'rules'
applied by the institutions of asset-acquiring countries that are based on
the perceived 'quality' of assets specific to their country of origin.
These perceptions of asset 'quality' are themselves determined by 'endogenous growth' fundamentals (particularly in the case of FDI), fiscal
stances (particularly in the case of bonds), and the 'herd instinct' generated by perceptions of other investors' expectations. In consequence,
the effectiveness of international financial intermediaries (commercial
banks, stock markets and the Bretton Woods institutions themselves)
could be judged in terms of their ability to maintain an orderly market
and stimulate real investment, growth and employment on a global
scale, where the real constraint is Keynesian liquidity preference.

With respect to volatility of international capital markets and domestic macroeconomic adjustment, crude deficit-driven demand inflation at the national level should not be associated with Keynes himself.
Keynes believed that the transmission mechanism of administered
shocks to the economy operated through an active *ex ante* response to
changing business *expectations* rather than through an *ex post* response
of output to increased consumption demand. Keynes' theory of effective demand drew from his view of the macroeconomic adjustment of
microeconomic investment and saving decisions by firms, including
decisions on stock levels, employment and capacity expansion (Asimakopulos 1991).

As Kregel (1994) points out, there is little in the *General Theory* on
policy apart from the positive impact of expenditure on output and employment under conditions of excess capacity. Indeed, the 'conventional' Keynesian policy applied during the post-war period related very
little to Keynes, and Keynesian policy priorities are currently reversed
by the priority given to balanced budgets over full employment.
Keynes' own views on inter-war policy supported reductions of the size
and cost of excess stocks to change market expectations, rather than direct price intervention. However, on post-war policy Keynes appears to
have supported a balanced budget in a special sense: a continual current
balance for reasons of efficiency and an anti-cyclical capital budget to
maintain employment balanced over time. Public investment would
imply considerable socialization of overall investment expenditure
during the reconstruction period (Kregel 1985), so that Keynes' pri-

mary concern centred on private investor confidence, which, though stimulated by public investment, would be undermined by the prospect of fiscal insolvency.

Various supposedly 'Keynesian' policy proposals may be found in the development economics literature, but all of these tend to overlook the problem of expectations and investment.[14]

One popular variant is that domestic demand should expand through deficit finance in order to use excess capacity and generate employment. Import controls should be used to overcome the foreign exchange, or in a subtler variant, increased expenditure should be focused toward non-traded goods and services such as domestic foodstuffs or road maintenance.

Another variant maintains that either the external government debt should be cancelled, or there should be an increase in official development assistance. This would permit an increase in budgetary expenditure (to raise output and generate employment) without a local currency deficit, which would otherwise have to be financed by inflationary monetary expansion or by a loss of external reserves.

A more sophisticated version of the first proposition is that government should employ a policy of wage and price controls to press for the downward redistribution of income downwards. The assumption is that the consumption pattern of the poor is more labour-intensive and less import-intensive than that of the rich, so that output and employment will rise in the externally constrained economy even without an increase in aggregate demand.[15]

Finally, a fourth variant posits reliance on deficit-financed public works. This is justified by the use of surplus skilled labour at no real resource cost to the economy and by the contribution to output growth that will generate a matching increase in national saving to balance the increase in investment.

Despite their intrinsic merits, these proposals are not truly 'Keynesian' and relate more closely to the management of a centrally controlled economy rather than of an economy where business expectations are the primary dynamic force. Ironically, the World Bank and IMF draw from the Ricardian tradition of profits as a funding constraint to analyze these proposals for their perverse effect on private investment.

A more promising line for Keynesian policy construction would be to focus on investment behaviour, where public provision of infrastructure and education stimulate private capital formation, as suggested by endogenous growth and 'new' trade theories. Differential tax and credit policies would have to be designed to affect the expectations of different firm types, from multinationals, domestic corporations and small enterprises, accordingly, as shall be seen in Chapter 4. 'Crowding in' would result from the shift in the marginal efficiency of capital schedule (or expected supply costs) rather than from the increase in aggregate demand as such. In this way, it would be more compatible with implicit Keynesian growth theory and might even allow for a revision of its explicit formalization by Harrod and Robinson which, as Asimakopulos (1991) points out, are undermined by their desire to find equilibrium solutions without any account of business behaviour.

It is now empirically clear and theoretically evident even to neoclassicals that higher interest rates do not raise savings. Although Keynes' view of household saving behaviour is not very appropriate for non-industrial economies and he overlooks corporate saving and links into banking activities – where Kalecki provides more insights (FitzGerald 1993) – Keynesian policy of low real interest rates to stimulate investment in developing countries would have a great deal to recommend it. Certainly, the motivations for high real interest rates in LDCs include financial liberalization and the desire to attract foreign capital, but the main cause is undoubtedly the reliance on local bond sales to finance large budget deficits. A Keynesian policy would require positive fiscal saving, while the nearest practical equivalent to a capital tax (or levy) would be the traditional practice of large reserve requirements on domestic banks to be held in government bonds. A Kaleckian proposal for developing countries which is rather Keynesian in logic, is the heavy taxation of luxury consumption in order to ensure macroeconomic equilibrium as well as improve income distribution (FitzGerald 1993).

A Keynesian approach would have immediate consequences for IMF-type conditionality (high real interest rates, overall budget balance, elimination of reserve requirements and so on). Certainly it would help to avoid the negative consequences of financial liberalization as undertaken by most LDCs under the tutelage of the Bretton Woods institutions, whose immediate macroeconomic consequences have included import booms as banks shift towards consumer credit, excess borrowing abroad as private corporations attempt to reduce interest charges while ignoring exchange rate risk, and destabilizing inflows of portfolio capital. Moreover, the process of 'disintermediation' – by which financial intermediaries withdraw from long-term investment finance – would thereby be prevented, a problem which Keynes would doubtless have understood. Further, effective use of public development banks would seem to correspond most closely to the Keynesian concept of the socialization of investment.

The other central element of macroeconomic policy in an open economy is the exchange rate. Nominal exchange rate anchors and currency boards (the present-day equivalents of the gold standard) are rather un-Keynesian as well as being demonstrably dangerous. Stable real exchange rates do seem to have, by contrast, a positive effect on expectations as well as on securing profitability.[16] However, such a policy would require an implicit real wage policy, which, if not achieved through the deliberate creation of unemployment, would have to involve direct negotiation with organized labour. Unlike neoclassical factor substitution, employment depends on foreign exchange availability (and thus exports) in the short run and on investment in the longer run, which implies declining real wages.

3.5 CONCLUSIONS

In sum, a Keynesian policy at the national level intended to raise employment and sustain growth would be concerned with (i) designing public investment so as to shift the capital efficiency schedule, (ii) introducing budgetary policy so as to support long-term stabilization (with low interest rates maintained by high reserve requirements), (iii) stimulating private investment by influencing differential expectations of firms, (iv) active use of luxury taxation and development finance, and (v) managing the balance of payments through real exchange rate stability and banking controls. Of course, these have specific consequences for the linkage with international capital markets.

Keynes' international policy at Bretton Woods was clearly designed to help developing countries. As will be seen in Chapter 7, the original plans for a global central bank, an international investment fund and a commodity stabilization system were not implemented in practice, but clearly the central intent was to stabilize the world economy and, by improving expectations, to raise investment and employment. Although Keynes' solution to unfettered capital movements (that is, to channel capital flows through central banks) is no longer applicable today and integrated international capital markets now constrain expansionary policy implementation by surplus governments, he remains highly relevant to addressing international market instability and open economy macroeconomics.

A modern Keynesian approach to international capital markets might draw from the three 'psychological factors': (i) propensity to consume, (ii) long-term expectations as to yields on capital assets and (iii) attitude to liquidity, that were central to Keynes' model (Asimakopulos 1991), to design appropriate institutions for both operational rules and discretionary intervention. The propensity to consume might be the subject of international tax regulation, while long-term expectations and attitude to liquidity relate to the functioning of capital markets. Furthermore, the Keynesian scheme for the domestic macroeconomy includes two crucial money values: money wages and the quantity of money. At the global level, money wages would presumably relate not only to eventual nominal exchange rate stability (adjusted for productivity) but also to labour standards enacted through the WTO. The quantity of money would relate to the volume of transactions required for world trade and long-term investment flows, as the contemporary equivalent of Keynes' commodity reserve currency ('bancor').[17]

Keynesian analysis of international capital markets should be concerned with the reconciliation of desired saving and planned (or lagged) investment decisions that are mediated by multi-stage portfolio 'rules' (Tobin 1998). Certainly, these decisions are based on the 'quality' of assets specific to their country of origin, which is in turn determined by the macroeconomic stance of IEs and 'endogenous growth' fundamentals in the ROW. However, international capital movements (and the 'animal spirits' of domestic investors by extension) are highly dependent on considerations of uncertainty (incorrectly termed 'risk') about the future value of assets that are difficult to liquidate. Thus, a Keynesian policy towards developing country access to international capital markets would presumably involve the reduction of such uncertainty by prudential enforcement of property rules and by discretionary intervention to provide liquidity where appropriate.

If expansionary adjustment of the world economy through investment recovery in deficit countries of the North may be considered Keynesian, then the popular type of 'global Keynesianism' associated with the Brandt Commission – where large amounts of aid transfers from North to South are expected to stimulate world trade and recovery somehow – suffers from a misattribution similar to that described by

Kregel (1994) in the case of the post-war US budgetary policy. Indeed, the expansionary effect depends entirely on how the aid is financed. If private investment response in the North is perverse, then aid may in fact lead to reduced world growth and terms-of-trade deterioration (Vos 1994). From a Keynesian point of view, LDC debt cancellation[18] would only have a positive effect if it increased investor confidence. There is little sign that this is the case except where the creditor's willingness to act as lender of last resort (thereby creating liquidity) is credibly signaled, as occurred with the US Treasury during the Mexican crisis.

More sophisticated 'North–South' global macroeconomic policy models, though 'demand-led' in their output determination and hence classed as Keynesian (Muscatelli & Vines 1989), cannot really be considered to be Keynesian because they do not conceptualize effective demand as the central dynamic that equilibrates investment and savings. Such models characterize international capital flows in OECD countries as a residual that automatically covers the current account deficits generated by the trade model once interest rate parities are established. By contrast, capital flows for the ROW are exogenously determined, although they may be rationed between countries based on the existing debt burden.

In sum, a Keynesian global policy relevant to developing countries would recognize that capital markets do not clear investment and savings (and thus the current account of the balance of payments) via interest rates (which relate to liquidity preference), and that expectations depend on partial and imperfect information leading to rationing behaviour by institutions. Consequently, any scheme for international monetary reform must therefore contain appropriate prudential regulations and information systems for such markets as well as discretionary intervention by an international central bank in order to provide liquidity when and where required.

An appropriate Keynesian policy for stabilization of linkages between international capital markets and open economy macroeconomics must be circumstantial and consider not only the structure of the economy and its insertion in the world economy, but also the recent macroeconomic events and prospects that sway investors' attitude. In his evidence to the Macmillan Commission, Keynes highlighted the problems caused by the divergence of the rate of interest required to attract foreign capital and finance the current account deficit from the rate of interest required to support the recovery of full-employment investment (Kregel 1994).[19] Keynes' post-war proposal for an international clearing union aimed to overcome this problem and to allow for autonomous domestic macroeconomic policy. In practice, however, the destabilizing impact on global demand of asymmetric adjustments to disequilibrium by creditor and debtor nations under a fixed exchange rate system was never directly addressed, mainly because of the position of the US under and after the Bretton Woods system. Consequently:

> In the absence of some automatic mechanism, such as a clearing union, or international policy coordination, to offset the deflationary tendency of asymmetric adjustment, conventional Keynesian policy to ensure full employment cannot be viable in one country. Ironically, in the postwar period it has fallen to the IMF to ensure that any country that attempts an independent expenditure policy will be forced to reverse it in the interests of stability. (Kregel 1994: 275)

This statement does appear to exaggerate the power of the IMF somewhat. Moreover, an essentially Keynesian 'externally constrained' accelerator model of investment that incorporates exogenous shocks, public capital, fiscal deficits and regime instability, can be constructed to be both theoretically plausible and econometrically satisfactory (FitzGerald et al. 1994) and compatible with fiscal stability. Moreover, to the extent that productive employment depends on investment levels and that investment levels are very sensitive to international capital flows in developing countries, the integration of a theory of capital market segmentation (distinguishing between direct foreign investment, development assistance and financial asset acquisition) with a macroeconomic theory of aggregate investment (that allows for the interaction of public and private investment decisions affected by capital flows), will have significant implications for domestic and international regulatory policy (FitzGerald & Mavrotas 1994). Consequently, what would require modification are not so much IMF views on fiscal prudence and exchange rate management, but rather IMF views on capital market regulation and interest rates.

In conclusion, Keynesian policies – once properly understood – are clearly relevant to the problem of open macroeconomies that lie on the periphery of the global capital market. However, relevant policy design for those economies today must be based on a Keynesian view of the world as it is, learning as much as possible from the mainstream rediscovery of imperfect markets, rather than relying on the hermeneutics of documents written fifty years ago under the unbearable pressure of those contemporary events.

4 Firm Behaviour, Private Investment and Structural Adjustment

4.1 INTRODUCTION

After over two decades of strenuous and socially costly attempts to implement macroeconomic adjustment policies in middle-income countries[1] inspired by the World Bank and the IMF, a remarkable degree of consensus has been attained (or rather re-attained) on the virtues of budgetary balance, on the need for a strong real exchange rate to promote exports, and on the conduciveness of market signals to firms for microeconomic efficiency. However, the hard-won achievement of narrower current account deficits, reduced government expenditure and lower rates of inflation has yet to be matched to any extent by sustained renewal of per capita income growth, let alone by industrial recovery. During these decades, this same model, with surprisingly little modification, appears to have been employed by the Bretton Woods institutions as the basis for the design of macroeconomic policy appropriate to the transition from centrally-planned to market economies in Eastern Europe and to address a series of financial crises in the latter half of the 1990s.

At the heart of this 'standard model' lies the proposition that sound recovery is based on domestically financed private investment in traded production. At the macroeconomic level, fiscal deficits should be reduced in order to release household savings for more productive use by private entrepreneurs and for a reversal of capital flight. At the microeconomic level, commercial deregulation and real exchange rate appreciation will increase the profitability of traded production to raise investment demand, while real rates of interest raise domestic savings and attract foreign capital. Despite the standard view that rising real

44

exchange rates and falling real wages implies increased profit and private savings rates in many cases, evidently adjustment efforts and the reallocation of resources have not been converted into new productive capacity formation, at least on the scale or at the pace expected.[2] It is essential, therefore, to examine more closely the concept of the financial constraint on private investment that underpins the standard model and to explore the implications of a more plausible account of the heterogeneous behaviour of firms ranging from multinational corporations to household enterprises.

This chapter has three elements. Section 4.2 sets out the assumptions about firms' accumulation decisions that appear to underpin the macroeconomic models employed by the World Bank and the IMF, focusing on the link between household savings and enterprise investment. Section 4.3 proposes an alternative approach based on the observed financial behaviour of the different kinds of firms that characterize semi-industrial economies, while Section 4.4 explores the relation of this 'proto-model' to the so-called 'new theory of the firm' in industrial economies. Section 4.5 draws some preliminary conclusions regarding the possible impact of 'standard' policy rules.

4.2   PRIVATE INVESTMENT IN THE STANDARD POLICY MODEL

The standard macro-policy models used by the Bank and the Fund[3] treat private savings and investment at the aggregate level as independent activities. However, the Bank and the Fund approach private savings from two different angles. The Bank, on the one hand, views private savings as the inverse of the consumption function, and hence essentially dependent on GDP growth. The Fund, on the other hand, views private savings as the demand for money balances, and hence essentially responsive to interest rates and inflationary expectations.

The Bank and the Fund also differ in their approach to private investment. The Bank, for instance, approaches private investment by maintaining that the private sector budgetary balance constrains capital expenditure at the aggregate level; in other words, capital expenditure is constrained by the sum of disposable income less consumption (and tax) plus foreign investment less net domestic borrowing by the public sector. The Fund, however, pursues a monetary approach to the balance of payments, so that net private demand for financial assets (or the difference between deposits made and credit received) is a stable function of national income. Hence, private investment varies directly with private savings.[4]

Where the Bank and Fund models appear to diverge significantly is in private sector access to external capital markets.[5] Whereas the Bank presumes that private sector access to external capital markets is limited, the Fund maintains that the private sector can replace domestic credit either through foreign borrowing or by running down reserves. Consequently, while the Bank concludes that increased domestic borrowing by the government will crowd out private investment, the Fund concludes that monetary authorities should control government borrowing carefully so as to allow the private sector to meet its credit requirements from domestic sources.

The microeconomic underpinning of the standard approach is the textbook theory of household savings and enterprise investment that virtually equates private savings with personal savings (Gersovitz 1988). Consequently, the Bank and Fund views lead to an emphasis on consumption patterns (where savings are the residual) and on the role of financial asset (or liability) acquisition as a means of changing the flows of income and consumption over time. This model is based on that for developed economies and can include structural factors such as education, longevity and taxation as well as income levels (Bryant, 1990). For developing countries additional structural factors such as minimum consumption levels for low-income groups can also be included (Lluch et al. 1977). However, this approach inevitably produces a relatively stable private savings rate over time, which is inconsistent with the aggregate time series data. Not only is the stability of the Bank and the Fund approach admittedly questionable in theory, but the relationships also lack depth. Firstly, the emphasis on consumption patterns effectively excludes the scope for consideration of the household as a unit of production in its own right, and by extension, household participation in the process of physical capital formation. Secondly, the emphasis on financial asset (or liability) acquisition as a means of changing income and consumption flows over time effectively excludes consideration of corporate savings as a macroeconomically significant category, and by extension, rules out all firm types, save the owner-managed firm.

However, the opposition of income and substitution effects means that neoclassical theory is unable to provide an unequivocal expectation regarding the direction of causality between interest rates and household ('personal') savings, which creates complications for the standard theory of financial intermediation. Consequently, for policy purposes, the modelling of the private savings function becomes in practice the inverse of some variant of the personal consumption function (see for instance Khan et al. 1990).

The theory of private investment assumes that entrepreneurs behave in the neoclassical fashion, and are thus willing to borrow up to the point where the rate of return on the marginal project is equal to the effective cost of debt (Gurley & Shaw 1960). Whereas households are considered net savers, firms are assumed to constitute the only investors and considered net borrowers. Furthermore, firms' demand for funds originates from requirements of fixed investment and working capital, the latter of which may vary according to capital stock and capacity utilization. This demand is met from two sources, particularly in developing countries. One source is firms' limited stock of reinvestible profits. The other source is bank borrowing. Equity markets are generally thin in developing countries, particularly given the dearth of private pension funds. Certainly, the high levels of self-financing in small firms and the reduced role of equity funding in large firms, commonly observed in semi-industrial economies, are adduced as evidence of lack of capital market development. The high levels of bank borrowing by corporations are held to reflect a weak savings capacity in industrializing countries.

The essential issue is, of course, how households and particularly firms respond to financial market deregulation. According to standard theory, the combination of misguided policy and government's desire to minimize the fiscal cost of domestic borrowing results in low (or negative) real interest rates, that in turn reduce the level of household savings and generate an excessive demand for funds by firms. Excess demand for funds subsequently forces banks to ration credit on criteria other than the marginal productivity of investment, or, in an even worse scenario, to fund the budget deficit. Raising the rate of interest achieves two things. First, the market will clear at a higher level of savings, given that household and foreign savings are at best inelastic to interest rates (IMF 1987). Second, the rate of investment that firms can actually undertake will rise, with the added advantage that the marginal (and thus the average) rate of return on private investment will be higher than under 'financially repressed' conditions. Moreover, the rise in the rate of interest should make smaller firms better off in three principal ways. First, the rise in the real rate of interest coupled with the lower capital intensity of small firms should increase their relative competitiveness as compared to larger firms. Second, their access to credit would no longer be constrained by rent-seeking discrimination by branch bank managers. Thirdly, market unification might even lower absolute borrowing rates for small firms below borrowing rates of informal ('kerb') lenders (World Bank 1988).

Once financial markets are liberalized and able to clear through interest rates rather than credit rationing, the issue of investment funding itself disappears. According to the classical Modigliani-Miller approach to financial policy, the financial structure of the firm is irrelevant to both its value and its operating decisions (Greenwald & Stiglitz 1990), although the process of industrialization (Goldsmith 1975) should spur the process of financial 'deepening' (measured by the growth of quasi-money as a proportion of aggregate income). Indeed, this phenomenon is held to be the case in industrial economies.

Dailami & Giugale (1991) integrate the macro and micro aspects of this theory by assuming that the owner-managed firm must resort to limited retained earnings (which is a concave function of capital stock) and to bank credit in order to fund capital expansion. The objective of the firm is to maximize the present value of the future stream of cash flows (which is determined by tax-adjusted profits less debt service, plus new loans less new investment) over an infinite time horizon. The solution to this optimization problem is the familiar equalization of the real cost of equity (represented by the owner's particular discount rate) with effective debt cost, so long as credit is unconstrained. However, as macro-financial fluctuations affect the aggregate credit level, banks allocate funds in proportion to the net worth of firms. As firms' net worth depends on previous investment decisions, they can improve their future credit position by investing more now. Given availability of portfolio investment opportunities and a lower cost of debt relative to the firm's discount rate, the level of investment will depend on interest rates and on credit market conditions (Dailami & Giugale 1991).

In all fairness, 'neo-structuralist' efforts to provide alternative (and more empirically plausible) macroeconomic formulations of the private investment functions in terms of the process of capital stock adjustment, 'crowding-in' by public provision of infrastructure, and aggregate import constraints (Taylor 1983, Taylor 1988, Bacha 1990, Fitz-

Gerald & Vos 1989) cannot claim to be based on a properly specified microeconomic model either. Indeed, it is the object of this chapter to contribute to such an endeavour.

4.3 FINANCIAL CHARACTERISTICS OF FIRMS IN THE SEMI-INDUSTRIALIZED ECONOMY

Central to this chapter is the view that the process of capital accumulation in the typical semi-industrial economy would be better understood as the combination of investment and savings activities of various kinds of firms rather than as the result of mutually exclusive categories of entrepreneurs who invest and households that save. Indeed, the 'structure-conduct-performance' paradigm (Sawyer 1985, Clark 1985) used for analysis of industrial organization suggests four main structural stylized facts. Firstly, the control and finance of registered companies is not separated as assumed by the neoclassical paradigm (Leff 1978). Secondly, the household sector plays an important role in trading, production and direct investment (Ellis 1988, Kirkpatrick, Lee & Nixson 1984, Lydall 1979). Thirdly, all firms rely heavily upon retained profits for fixed-investment financing (Kitchen 1986). Finally, private investment depends heavily upon public investment for essential infrastructure provision.[6] As regards to the 'conduct' of firms, focus is primarily on the nature of firms' expansion decisions, and particularly on the validity of the financial constraint on private investment.

Our analysis of firm behaviour focuses on four kinds of 'firm': (i) parastatal corporations, (ii) multinational affiliates, (iii) private companies, and (iv) micro-enterprises. Certainly it would be possible to add other categories of firms and dispute category distinctions according to other criteria such as size or technology. However, the above classification is drawn corresponding to more intuitive ideas about financial behaviour. Clearly the relative importance of, and relationship between, these types of 'firm' varies according to factors such as the degree of industrialization, the nature of the leading production sectors, institutional history, and so forth.

4.3.1 Parastatal Corporations

Although ownership and control are not separated in parastatal corporations and multinational affiliates, they cannot be considered 'owner-managed' firms. Parastatals' investment decisions, which are 'private' to the extent that they are not part of the central government budget, are made by state managers whose primary objective is the maximization of the total size (gross assets or sales) of the firm in the short or medium term rather than profitability. Parastatals face two principal constraints on expansion. One is the avoidance of fiscally unacceptable operating losses, which depends largely on pricing policy. The other is the credit limit imposed by creditors. This latter constraint depends largely on the government's own policy regarding the overall public sector borrowing requirement (in the case of domestic credit), but more importantly it depends on foreign borrowing for the acquisition of capital goods and technology. Furthermore, this access to foreign borrowing depends more on the sovereign risk rating of the government on international capital markets rather than on the profitability of the parastatal enterprise.[7] In the case of joint ventures with foreign investors, at most the specific conditions attached to the individual project will be relevant. Given these determinants of parastatal investment, the adjustment programmes, often designed with the specific intention of increasing parastatal profitability and hence parastatal non-budgetary savings, are unlikely to increase parastatal non-budgetary investment. Indeed the financial effect of privatization is a reduction in government net assets and in private net assets, an outcome that is reflected in the national accounts as private dissaving.

4.3.2 Multinational Affiliates

Like parastatal corporations, multinational affiliates also cannot be considered 'owner-managed' firms. Multinational affiliates' decision to expand forms part of an international corporate strategy,[8] particularly where intra-firm exports are concerned, although the head office may permit more autonomy with respect to local markets. Concerning exports, expansion decisions will depend on (dollar) production costs, resource title and reliability of supply. Concerning local markets, however, expansion decisions will depend on demand growth and competition from other foreign firms. In both cases, however, the tax system, labour regime and currency convertibility may be more important than local profitability, but in any event, firms in this category are often preferential borrowers from local banks and enjoy access to international capital markets through their head office. Local managers presumably seek to maximize the size of their affiliate within the corporate strategy established by the head office, the latter being presumably a manager-controlled firm. Whatever the corporate strategy may be, expansion decisions are unlikely to be constrained by local financial conditions, although other components of adjustment policy such as privatization and deregulation may have some influence over their investment decisions.

4.3.3 Private Companies

Private companies are defined as firms that are constituted as legal entities – for instance, registered accounts, tax subjects, licensed and owned by domestic residents. In long-established market economies, firm ownership is privately held and concentrated in the hands of one (or few) families; even if the company's shares are quoted on the stock market, it is still closely held, such that going public does not affect control. In transitional economies, management 'buyouts' may well represent the first stage in this process. Furthermore, for all intents and purposes, these private companies can be considered to have professional management, although this may very well entail an owner or a family member, and to have long-term objectives that are expressed in terms of sales or asset growth.[9] These firms are relatively 'large' in that they are one of few firms of any size in a particular branch (or region) of production, and thus can be presumed to apply full-cost mark-up pricing in non-traded sectors, benefit from specific incentives or concessions from the government in traded sectors. Fiscal incentives, inflation effects and inadequate reporting tend to lower the effective taxation burdens on corporate profits of such firms. It is commonly observed (Drake 1980, Kitchen 1986) that even though the degree of self-financing of fixed assets seems quite high, private companies in industrializing countries have low equity-to-asset ratios, which is often attributed to the absence of proper stock markets. However, it seems more plausible to argue that high rates of gross profit and profit retention, and close relationships with banks affect private companies' ability to finance fixed investment or service loans where necessary, particularly for private companies belonging to a 'group' that is connected to a specific bank (Leff 1978, Drake 1980) and hence benefits from preferential access to cheap credit for purposes of working capital.

Private companies as defined here[10] may therefore be considered to experience no binding financial constraints on expansion. Thus other factors are more likely to determine investment decisions, such as expected market growth (home as well as foreign) for existing products at a known profitability, new opportunities arising from access to natural resources or foreign technology, and the risk of asset depreciation (or loss) in the foreseeable future.

The acquisition of variable assets as working capital corresponds not only to the production process itself but also to the provision of trade credit to smaller clients and to the finance of inventories, particularly when imports are costly or foreign exchange is not readily available. However, once an attractive investment opportunity is identified, the quantity or cost of finance, at least from domestic sources, is seldom an obstacle. So long as credit is easily obtained, reinvestment is not constrained by required dividends to shareholders nor is it constrained by fear of stock-market takeover. Further, bank borrowing is more likely to be constrained[11] by the interest charge on earnings[12] than by gearing ratios on asset–liability structures as a whole, particularly under inflationary conditions. Once distributed to the respective 'rentier' household (which is not involved in production), dividends are partly consumed but also used to acquire financial assets (including real estate) both at home and abroad, and appear to correspond to the familiar model of net wealth adjustment (see Tobin 1982).

Under these conditions, neither real interest rates nor aggregate credit controls will have a significant effect on fixed investment. Firstly, even if private companies tend to be closely held, they nevertheless have recourse to equity financing through retained earnings or access to 'inside' funds of the group. Secondly, although higher interest rates might discourage debt financing and lead to a lower gearing ratio, the increased interest costs can also be passed on to consumer through mark-up pricing in the non-traded sectors, thereby permitting higher self-financing (Dutt 1990-1).

Trade liberalization is not likely to have a very strong effect on exporters in this category, but import-substituting companies may be severely affected and possibly shift from production for the non-traded to the traded sector. Real exchange rate appreciation is likely to have a positive effect on the profitability of private companies in both traded and non-traded sectors. Essentially, the effect of the real value of profits on depends on the growth of markets.

Where banks confront limited credit demand from prime borrowers, either because of low investment rates or because such firms have already reached their own corporate indebtedness limits, they appear to prefer to accumulate excess liquidity or lend to the government rather than to smaller firms.

4.3.4 Micro-enterprises

Micro-enterprises are firms where the activities of the enterprise are integrated with those of the respective household, both in terms of the financial 'structure' and the organization of labour, and possibly in terms of the location of production. Micro-enterprises are characteristic of peasant agriculture, artisan industry and 'informal' services, and are located in highly competitive sectors with few entry barriers and little product differentiation. Rudimentary technology and family labour make it difficult to further reduce costs, so that as price-takers, micro-enterprises enjoy minimal profitability, while alternative portfolio opportunities are few. However, there are no market constraints to the expansion of an individual firm and the risks are large but known.

According to the standard model, private savings are essentially a residual after consumption, or derive from the optimization of income and expenditure streams over time. However, micro-enterprise financial savings may be viewed as the working capital of the micro-enterprise, where increased profits resulting from relative price changes[13] or from demand growth allow existing firms to expand or new ones to enter the market. Evidence from household surveys seems to point to the correlation of savings rates with property and self-employment income rather than with wages – in other words, with the retained profits of the micro-enterprise.[14] In fact, micro-enterprise investment in land improvements, house building or human capital formation such as education and health is more frequently funded by an increased labour effort than by reduced consumption, while the acquisition of fixed assets usually entails adequate access to credit for the purchase of transport equipment, additional landholdings or simple machinery. Empirical observation in many countries suggests that rather than registered companies, households account for the bulk of savings-bank deposits. These deposits are more likely to reflect 'working capital' held against micro-enterprise risk of bad harvests or collateral for bank credit rather than savings for retirement, the latter of which is far more likely to take the form of land, gold and even (male) progeny.[15]

Unlike parastatal corporations, multinational affiliates, and private companies, the micro-enterprise can be considered financially constrained. However, micro-enterprises are not financially constrained in the textbook sense of having a given time-preference rate for consumption that weighs the rate of interest when making borrowing decisions. Indeed, profit retention capacity is determined by earlier investments, market fluctuations, desired borrowing limits and the proportion of total family income that can be safely allocated to debt service. Consequently, even though micro-enterprises' desired 'gearing ratio' between own assets (fixed and variable) and bank credit may not be reached, the 'service ratio', which is highly sensitive to the interest rate, is of critical importance. As is well documented, credit is difficult for micro-enterprises to obtain. Financial repression and the shortage of loanable funds certainly comprise one problem, but even with an abundance of loanable funds, the high unit costs of such loans to banks, lack of suitable collateral and difficulty of collection make micro-enterprise access to credit very limited. Therefore, micro-enterprises are generally more willing to 'over-invest' unless interest rates are very high, and this response to profit rates will be quite elastic.

Under these conditions orthodox financial reform can have skewed and unexpected effects. First, an increase in interest rates will sharply reduce profitability and micro-enterprises' capacity to borrow. This effect would be further exacerbated by bank deregulation involving the elimination of government special schemes for small business, so that reduced government borrowing may well not increase funding to this sector. Second, while trade liberalization may be expected to have a positive effect on prices received by small exporters, its effect on import-substituting micro-enterprises will be negative. Real exchange rate appreciation should increase the profitability (and hence investment) of micro-enterprises in traded agriculture but reduce it in non-traded services. Micro-enterprises face the added difficulty that any financial burden such as lack of trade credit or higher costs absorbed by larger firms will be passed on to smaller ones in oligopolized branches. Third, even the orthodox 'repression' model predicts[16] that financial liberalization will lead to the reallocation of funds from small 'informal' towards large 'formal' firms as the 'kerb' market shifts its portfolio towards higher-yielding bank deposits, treasury bonds, and so on.

4.4 THE IMPLICATIONS OF 'NEW THEORIES OF THE FIRM'

The 'theory of the firm' that underpins the standard macropolicy model fails to account for different kinds of firms with particular behavioural characteristics in semi-industrial economies. The behavioural characteristics identified hardly constitute an alternative theory of the firm, and there is no logical reason to believe that such a general theory is even possible or desirable. However, recent analytical advances in the long-established field (Penrose 1959, Baumol 1967, Wood 1975) of non-neoclassical 'managerial' theories of the firm in industrial countries might be usefully adapted to the analysis of firms in semi-industrialized economies.

Specifically, four topics might be fruitfully explored. First, the work of Williamson (1975, 1985), which conceptualizes firm behaviour as an efficient nexus for minimization of the costs of economic transactions, has revolutionized the theory of firm behaviour. This approach, which extends from the 'contract' paradigm, has already been applied to the study of agricultural organization in LDCs, and to some extent to the 'principle-agent' problem in public enterprises. This transactions-cost approach is also highly applicable to analysis of profit retention within private companies (which is not a freely disposable asset) and the disposition of dividends among financial assets, both home and overseas. Furthermore, measurements of self-financing ratios net of accumulated equivalent financial assets reveal that these ratios are also very high in industrialized countries, which undermines the standard argument that such ratios are high in LDCs because of underdeveloped capital markets[17] and financial repression. However, Mayer's (1987) comparison of the relationship between German and Japanese banks and their industrial clients and that between US and British banks and industrial clients[18] concluded that:

> ...[F]inancial systems that can internalise the externalities associated with information collection and the coordination of control are likely to be able to sustain higher levels of external funding. Internalisation will usually require financial intermediation in the provision of both equity and debt capital. (Mayer 1987: iii)

Consequently, the idea of a 'governance structure' would also appear to be relevant to the 'group concept' identified by Leff (1978).

Second, developments in the theory of the firm associated with the work of Stiglitz have converged toward exploration of the economic implications of imperfect information, characterized by asymmetries of information which exist between the outside investors who provide capital and the inside managers who control its use. These analyses have modified the theory of how firms acquire and deploy capital and, by extension, how firms react to external environmental and policy changes (Greenwald & Stiglitz 1990), and called into question the validity of the neoclassical model of the firm. In one case, the asymmetric distribution of information between buyers and sellers of financial instruments may lead to a breakdown in financial markets; free access to capital assumed in the neoclassical model of the firm does not obtain and is effectively replaced by credit rationing. In another, asymmetric distribution of information between the decision-makers (agents) and the presumed beneficiaries of those decisions (principals) affects the reward functions that govern firm decision-making, preventing convergence to simple marginalist equilibrium solutions with unambiguous implications for the effect of policy instruments that derive from neoclassical assumptions. Indeed, Stiglitz (ibid.) argues that firms' decisions regarding 'productivity improving activity', which range from R&D, overheads to improve efficiency, to fixed capacity formation, are a direct reaction to firms' financial circumstances and to conditions of uncertainty in the economy at large, even if macroeconomic conditions (such as high inflation or unstable government policy) appear unlikely to increase systematic risk. Further, the 'new' view of employment, which considers stable wages and rationed access to jobs, has broad implications for the orthodox choice-of-technique position that higher interest rates promote labour-intensive investment. The orthodox view, which informs standard credit-market clearing, maintains that lenders' risk is fully reflected in the interest rate differential, and that the interest rate differential fully reflects the gains and losses from default. However, where unable to establish the risk for individual borrowers, lenders will charge a fairly uniform rate and ration credit according to various rules of liquidity assessment and access to collateral (Stiglitz & Weiss 1981, Stiglitz & Mathewson 1986), and this appears to be *a fortiori* true in semi-industrialized economies. What is more, the higher the real interest imposed by the monetary authorities, the lower the 'quality' of the remaining pool of borrowers, so that overall risk is even higher. In other words, even when capital markets are in equilibrium, asymmetries in information between borrower and lender will create the need for credit rationing.[19]

Third, developments in the empirical analysis of corporate finance in the industrialized countries have confirmed early speculative 'managerial' theories of the firm, further undermining the neoclassical model (Edwards, Franks, Mayer & Schaefer 1986). Mayer (1987) attributes the deficiency of serious research on the relationship between financial deregulation and firm-level performance in industrial economies to two factors. One factor is the continuing dominance of the Modigliani-Miller theorem, which maintains that apart from distortions introduced by corporate taxation, the real performance of a firm (reflected by its market value) is independent of how it chooses to finance its investment or distribute dividends. The other factor is the assumption that deregulation reduces transactions costs and makes investment more efficient *ex hypothesi*. Despite empirical experience to the contrary, real activity is presumed to be dominated by considerations such as technology, productivity, factor endowments and the structure of demand, while the financial system itself has no role to play other than as a channel between savers and investors. The 'group' model corresponds closely to Mayer's observation that internalization of externalities helps financial systems sustain higher levels of external funding. 'New' firms that have not established relationships with banks will have to self-finance a more substantial proportion of investment, and their growth will be more sensitive to profitability through the adjustment cycle (on the USA see Fazzari, Hubbard & Petersen 1988). This phenomenon applies *a fortiori* to industrializing economies, where there have been few attempts to construct a connection between the financial structure and the process of industrialization, with the notable exceptions of pioneering work by Goldsmith (1975) and McKinnon (1973).

Finally, there is broad scope for reformulation of microeconomic theory of the firm to include the relationship between post-Keynesian corporate financial structures and macroeconomic conditions (see Odagiri 1981, Davidson 1986, Chamberlain 1990, Skott 1988) and neo-Keynesian private-sector dynamic wealth-adjustment behaviour in a macroeconomic reconstruction with substantial modification of the simple multiplier-accelerator model (Tobin 1982, Godley & Cripps 1983). Clearly, reformulation of the theory of the firm along these lines would interpret the direction of causality from investment to savings in a more Kaleckian than Keynesian nature, based on profit creation and allocation rather than on levels and distribution of aggregate income.[20]

There have been a number of attempts to integrate microeconomic theory of firm behaviour to macroeconomic conditions and corporate financial structure. For instance, Bourguinon et al. (1989) attempts to integrate the firm with dependent-economy macro-models. They build a very simple company sector with fixed gearing ratios and physical capital formation determined as a proportion of personal savings into a computable general equilibrium model (CGEM) separately from households in order to distinguish the productive from the distributional implications of adjustment packages. The more flexible framework presented by Cohen & Tuyl (1991) develops a methodology for reconciling micro-firm data within the macroeconomic constraints of the social accounting matrix (SAM) for the case of The Netherlands, while Lydall (1979) considers the effects of firm size in income distribution.

The standard macroeconomic model used to formulate structural adjustment policies continues to draw from the 'old' neoclassical model. However, recent work on 'new' theories of the firm in the advanced industrial countries offers better analytical elements than the 'old' neoclassical model for understanding firm behaviour in the enterprise structure specified above. These new theories of the firm offer a number of important observations:.

First, neither high real interest rates nor reduced public investment can be expected to stimulate private investment or foreign direct investment.

Second, real exchange rates may be more effective in stimulating higher savings and investment levels than real interest rates due to their respective effects on firm profitability, and require joint management of nominal wage and exchange parities for real exchange rate management.

Third, sustained growth of home and foreign markets, credible tax policies and asset security weigh more heavily in the investment decisions of multinational affiliates (Brewer 1993) and private companies than low wages (which may reduce risk) and exposure to world price fluctuations (which may increase it).

Fourth, the self-financing rules of firms have important consequences for aggregate private savings behaviour and hence for responsiveness to fiscal policy. In the standard model, budget deficits 'crowd out' private investment. This may be demonstrated using a very simple model where households save a given amount of income in the form of bank deposits (D_h). A portion of (D_h) is lent to the government (L_g) and the balance lent to firms (L_f) by banks, so that

$$L_f = D_h - L_g \qquad (4.1)$$

Firms have unsatisfied investment demand (I) *and* limited profit retention possibilities (R). Total private saving (S), which is stable, is given by:

$$S = D_h + R \qquad (4.2)$$

Private investment will be given by:

$$I = R + L_f \qquad (4.3)$$

Substituting (4.1) in (4.3), private investment is given by:

$$I = R + D_h - L_g \qquad (4.4)$$

so that budget deficits 'crowd out' private investment $(dI/dL_g = -1)$.

However, if firms raise their retention ratios in response to credit restrictions and their investment demand is limited by market growth, then the reverse obtains. Assuming I is exogenous, private saving is given by:

$$S = D_h + R \qquad (4.5)$$

Substituting (4.3) for (R) in (4.5), private savings is determined by:

$$S = D_h + (I - L_f) \qquad (4.6)$$

Given (4.1), then

$$S = I + L_g \qquad (4.7)$$

and budget deficits 'crowd in' private saving (or $dS/dL_g = 1$).

Fifth, given constrained external finance, the combination of tight monetary policy and a sustained fiscal deficit will 'crowd out' investment by small rather than large firms due to the latter's preferential access to bank credit and greater self-financing capacity within a 'group' (see also FitzGerald 1990).

Sixth, strict prudential regulation of the financial sector is probably necessary when product markets are deregulated in order to prevent overlending to (and tax evasion by) large firms and to compensate for market bias against small firms.

Lastly, the choice of technology by firms (and thus employment creation) may not be closely linked to relative factor prices, but rather to considerations of capital structure, because technological advance involves both scrapping (including the bankruptcy of inefficient firms) and long-term expenditure on 'learning by doing'.

Moreover, an additional priority is the collection of more reliable and more micro-level financial data. Although the United Nations National Accounts methodology requires the disaggregation of institutional sectors in all the balances, from which firm behaviour would become evident, such complete accounts are rarely available. Even the more detailed Social Accounting Matrix exercises tend to focus on the disaggregation of production sectors or income groups and leave the financial variables at an aggregate level.[21] The systematic acquisition and compilation of more micro-level financial data on firms in industrializing countries is also essential. Although micro-level financial data is not available from international sources, a number of useful sources exist at the national level, including official data from censuses, tax returns, stock-market regulators, case studies of individual firms in the context of technology transfer, and sectoral studies of small farmers.

4.5　CONCLUSIONS

This chapter draws four main conclusions. First, the implicit theory of the firm that underpins the standard model for macro-policy in middle-income economies lacks organizational specificity and is implausible as regards investment and savings decisions by the private sector. Second, parastatal corporations, multinational affiliates and private companies cannot be considered to be financially constrained in the neoclassical sense, while it is more useful to regard households as firms rather than as consumption units. Third, a fresh approach based on 'new' theories of the firm should provide a better microeconomic basis for macroeconomic policymaking in semi-industrial economies. Finally, the macro-policy implications of such an approach would probably be significantly different from those of the 'standard' model.

Meanwhile, the question remains: why do the theory of the firm and the practice of company behaviour – factors identified above as salient to private sector investment and savings behaviour – continue to exert such limited influence on the standard policy models used to design structural adjustment policies? The fact that analyses of industrialized countries also neglect to consider them is hardly consolidation. Until 'economic theory' begins paying greater attention to the findings of 'business studies' about market behaviour (Kay 1991), standard policy models and structural adjustment policies will continue to leave out the central character, with predictable and disappointing results.

5 Investment and Labour Markets under Trade Liberalization[1]

5.1 INTRODUCTION

A keystone of modern development strategy in general, and of structural adjustment policy in particular, is trade liberalization. Derived from familiar trade theory, liberalization aims to achieve productive efficiency and international competitiveness, enabling a more rapid rate of growth than under the previous strategy of protected industrialization. The evident welfare gains of free trade to the global economy are accompanied by increased aggregate income for those developing countries that become integrated to the world market.

However, the effects of trade reforms on employment and wages are largely established *ex hypothesi* in standard trade theory, leading economists to focus on the behaviour of labour markets to explain empirical observations of unemployment and wage dispersion. In this respect, 'new trade theory' offers a more critical and relevant view of the relationship between trade openness and industrialization to the problem of unemployment and wage dispersion. Nevertheless, it has yet to be extended formally to derive robust employment and wage results. In addition, the analysis of the dynamic relationship between trade and domestic labour demand requires an appropriate formulation of aggregate investment behaviour, which trade theory often neglects.

The object of this chapter is to explore this lacuna in the literature in the hope of clarifying the consequences of economic reform for income distribution in developing countries. Section 5.2 outlines the standard textbook model and basic model of trade liberalization. Sections 5.2.1 and 5.2.2 examine the basic model of trade liberalization and recent extensions to include nontradables and human capital aspects, while

Section 5.2.3 focuses on the short- and long-term effects of liberalization. Section 5.3 reviews extensions of the standard model to labour markets and investment, and identifies the main weaknesses of this approach in Section 5.4. Indeed, the familiar results of increased employment and higher wages derive from highly specific assumptions that may not obtain even within the standard model.

In Section 5.5, we examine new trade theory as an alternative framework to the standard textbook theory, and derive its implicit employment and wage consequences of liberalization. Though these implications are not presented formally in the literature, it is evident that positive results depend upon the rate and form of technical change, and hence on the investment process.

In Section 5.6 we focus on the macroeconomic dimension of trade liberalization. We find that recent theoretical work on the effect of trade liberalization on aggregate investment is ambiguous and may well be negative if accompanied by orthodox stabilization policies, rapid financial liberalization or increases in exchange rate uncertainty. Section 5.7 considers the weaknesses of the standard model and the micro- and macro-dimensions of trade liberalization. In this section, we also specify a formal framework for understanding the effects of trade liberalization on wages, employment and investment based on assumptions that are more plausible. Section 5.8 offers some concluding remarks.

5.2   THE STANDARD MODEL OF THE EFFECT OF TRADE LIBERALIZATION ON EMPLOYMENT AND WAGES

5.2.1   The Basic Model

The most obvious point from which to begin an analysis of the consequences of trade liberalization on employment and income distribution is the standard HOS model. This model was developed formally by Samuelson (1948), Samuelson (1949), Jones (1956) and Jones (1965) from the framework originally set out by Ohlin (1933). As a general equilibrium model, HOS permits rigorous examination of the repercussions of changes in goods markets on factor market equilibria. The model presents a comparative statics analysis of the impact of liberalization and makes the case that, so long as adjustment is instantaneous and costless, liberalization stimulates the response of the economy in the long run.

Because macroeconomic equilibrium is assumed, simultaneous structural and stabilization policies are not considered in the HOS model.

According to the HOS model, liberalization involves the reallocation of resources between sectors that leads to a higher Pareto-efficient equilibrium. The change in the relative price of commodities creates intersectoral factor reward differentials that encourage shifts in capital and labour until the differentials are eliminated. However, the most salient results that the HOS model can offer refer to the effects of liberalization on sectoral employment and income distribution, but not on aggregate employment. This is the case because, by definition, the assumptions that underlie the HOS model[2] rule out the possible effects of policy-induced price changes on aggregate unemployment.

In its simplest form, the HOS model simulates the behaviour of an economy in a two-country world, with two goods (importables and exportables) and two factors (capital and labour). In a developing country, the importables sector is assumed capital-intensive, while the exportables sector is labour-intensive. Further, the economy is assumed to be positioned on the international production possibility frontier (PPF) and is not subject to distortions other than those created by the tariff. Consequently, a tariff cut that reduces the domestic relative price of importables will stimulate a shift from an import-substitution to an export-oriented strategy.

Given these assumptions, the HOS model (Corden 1993) is able to make unambiguous predictions regarding the direction of changes in aggregate and sectoral employment and factor prices. Output increases in the exportables sector and decreases in the importables sector as instantaneous adjustment takes place along the PPF. Given that the exportables sector is more labour-intensive than the importables sector, then the shift in the composition of output towards exportables increases the aggregate demand for labour and reduces aggregate demand for capital so that capital rental falls. The equilibrium real wage rises because aggregate employment does not increase along with the demand for labour, since labour supply is rigid and there is no prior unemployment. The increase in wages (and decline in capital rental) encourages producers to adopt more capital-intensive techniques in both sectors, which mitigates – but does not reverse – the initial shift in factor demand and prices.

Further, if prior to liberalization distortions such as multiple exchange rates or import controls existed, which artificially reduced the cost of capital and favoured the capital-intensive importables sector, then reform may well lead to the adoption of more labour-intensive techniques. In this case, the demand for labour will increase as a result of both output composition (income) and the substitution effects (Krueger 1990). Extensions of the basic model to include more factors, goods and countries also yield complex implications for sectoral employment and income distribution. However, as these extensions do not involve any relaxation of the underlying assumptions, aggregate employment is not affected.

5.2.2 Extending the Basic Model

Kenen (1965) enriched the factor-endowment analysis by assuming that production uses the services of many different capital assets rather than directly embodying available capital in the final product. Land and other resources, or 'natural endowment', are specifically included among capital assets. If exportables are more land-intensive than importables, then liberalization redistributes income from capital-owners to landowners, but the impact on wage-earners depends on sectoral labour-intensity as before. Keesing (1966) also contributed to the basic model by introducing human capital. If human capital (skilled labour) is assumed complementary to physical capital, then liberalization not only improves income distribution through the redistribution of income from capital-owners to workers but from skilled to unskilled workers as well.

Komiya (1967) introduced nontradables as a third sector, an approach further developed by Edwards (1988). In this case, the outcome of the model depends on the assumptions regarding the factor intensity of nontradables and the response of their relative price to trade liberalization. As predicted by Stolper-Samuelson, if nontradables are less capital-intensive than importables, then a reduction in the relative domestic price of importables will cause an increase in the relative demand for labour and a corollary increase in real wages. As in the basic model, output of and employment in the exportables and importables sectors increases and decreases respectively due to relative price shift. Output in the nontradables sector increases due to the reduction of the relative domestic price of importables and the overall increase in real income. However, the actual magnitude of the change depends on the relative price-elasticity of demand for nontradables.

The attractive ambiguity of relative price-elasticity of demand for nontradables means that the output of and employment in this sector will increase if the relative price of nontradables rises. However, the reverse may also be the case: the direction of the change depends on the relative importance of the income and substitution effects. The reduction in the relative domestic price of importables raises real income and increases demand for all goods, while shifting consumption towards importables. As demand for exportables is determined abroad and is perfectly elastic, the production of exportables is unaltered. In contrast, the production of nontradables depends on the shift in domestic demand: if the substitution effect is stronger than the income effect, then demand for nontradables may decrease, with a corresponding effect on that sector's output and labour. However, if the income effect is stronger than the substitution effect, then demand for nontradables (and subsequently output of and employment in that sector) may increase. As in the basic model, regardless of the effects on sectoral employment, there is no aggregate unemployment.

The impact of liberalization on the pattern of trade and income distribution is unambiguous in a two-country world. Liberalization is 'global' by definition and the least developed country of the pair is bound to increase its exports of labour-intensive goods and its imports of capital-intensive goods. The existence of only two partners is a critical – and hence implausible – assumption. So long as all other countries liberalize in a multi-country world, the factor intensity of a small country's exports will continue to mirror its endowment ratio even after trade liberalization. Thus, the trade position of a single country after liberalization within a given set of world prices is theoretically indeterminate, the consequences for employment and wages cannot be predicted and may well be perverse.

These shortcomings aside, the standard model purports to show that trade reform, stylized as a tariff reduction, causes a permanent change of the structure of production of the country that benefits sectoral employment and real wages. The crucial mechanism at work is the prompt response of factor owners to the reward differentials created indirectly by the tariff cut. So long as governments do not distort factor markets, the creation of these differentials is a necessary and sufficient condition for the desired outcome.

5.2.3 Short-term vs. Long-term Effects

However, the evident existence of factor immobility renders this instantaneous response mechanism highly implausible. To incorporate factor immobility into the HOS model, the Ricardo-Viner model (RV) developed by Samuelson (1971) and Jones (1971) assumes each sector employs an immobile specific factor (capital or land) and a generic factor (labour), which can freely move from one sector to the other. The intersectoral reward differential created by liberalization creates strong incentives toward sectoral relocation, so that capital becomes mobile in the long term and the economy adjusts as predicted by the HOS model. Mussa (1974) and Neary (1978) have reinterpreted the RV model to simulate the response of the economy in the short run by assuming the specific factors are not physically distinct. The results of liberalization in the short run differ greatly from those in the long run. For instance, the equilibrium real wage can fall in the short run. As labour is mobile, nominal wages fall by the same amount in both sectors. However, wages in the exportables sector fall and rise in the importables sector in the long run. Wages fall in the exportables sector because the productivity of labour declines as workers move into the sector, while the capital stock remains the same. In the importables sector, the effect on labour productivity is the opposite, as fewer workers use the same stock of capital and become more productive, although this gain is more than offset by the fall in output prices.

Except for their smaller magnitude, the changes in output and employment in the short run are similar to those in the long run. If labour and capital are immobile, then the two sectors would be completely independent and the reduction in prices of importables would have no effect on the exportables sector. Rather, it would reduce wages and rentals in the importables sector, but as the internal terms of trade improved, average real wages and real rentals would, in fact, increase. This could be interpreted as being equivalent to the short-run scenario, but the outcome is particularly important when skills are specific to a particular sectoral technology (Mussa 1978).

The results do not change substantially if the dimensions of Ricardo-Viner economy are increased. Following Jones (1971), Edwards (1988) analyses the behaviour of a three-goods (importables, exportables, nontradables) economy in the (short) medium and long term. Under the heroic assumption that nontradables are less labour-intensive than exportables but more labour-intensive than importables, his model predicts that: (i) the exportables sector expands in the medium run and even more in the long run; (ii) the importables sector contracts in the medium run possibly by as much as in the long run; (iii) the nontradables sector expands in the medium run but may contract in the long run; and (v) equilibrium real wages increase in the long run but may decrease in the medium run because nominal wages only rise relatively to the price of importables.

5.3   EXTENSIONS OF THE STANDARD MODEL

5.3.1   Labour Market Distortions

In both the HOS and the RV models, unemployment is ruled out *ex hypothesi*. One of the fundamental assumptions underlying the standard model is that labour markets clear if wages are flexible, and that the level of aggregate employment cannot change because the supply of labour is given. Unemployment in the short or medium run can occur, but only if nominal (or real) wages are rigid. If equilibrium real wages fall but actual real wages do not, then the labour market cannot clear. Furthermore, employment in the importables sector falls more than necessary and does not increase sufficiently in the rest of the economy. It is important to point out that in labour-intensive countries, downward wage rigidity is not a sufficient condition for unemployment because equilibrium wages are supposed to increase following liberalization, although it would be a sufficient condition in capital-intensive countries. Similarly, factor immobility alone does not generate unemployment. The root cause of unemployment in these models is the combination of factor immobility, which causes equilibrium wages to fall in the exportable sector, and downward wage rigidity, which prevents wages in the exportables sector from falling enough to reach equilibrium – an equilibrium that could of course be below the subsistence level.

In the absence of rigidities, the only relevant factor would be the capital-labour ratios of the small country and of the world. In the presence of rigidities, the sector effect can be determined easily in a two-country HOS world, but with difficulty in a multi-country world. In this case, the effect of wage rigidity depends on the countries' positions in the 'trade ladder', particularly for semi-industrialized countries trading with both more and less developed partners. Wage rigidity and factor immobility could cause trade liberalization to lead to unemployment in the short run in both capital-intensive and labour-intensive sectors. However, the standard model continues to determine unemployment in the longer run because the equilibrium real wage will eventually increase to reach the previous level.

Standard theory has traditionally attributed nominal wage rigidity to state regulation of minimum wages and job security or to trade unions' power to impose above-equilibrium wages and regulate new entrants. More recently, efficiency-wage theory has attributed wage rigidity to the rational behaviour of employers. The incentive effect on productivity, efforts to reduce turnover and implicit transactions costs in training, hiring and firing may inhibit firms from cutting wages despite excess labour supply. Implicit contracts with the workforce may also account for firms' efforts to maintain wages (and employment) above the equilibrium level during the downswings and below the equilibrium level during the upswing.

Edwards & Cox-Edwards (1994) analyze the effects of a tariff reduction under various labour market configurations in the framework of the two-factor three-sector RV model. In this model, economy-wide and sector-specific minimum real wages are combined with an initial unemployment that is caused by rural-urban migration and unionization. They conclude that in the presence of labour market distortions, liberalization 'may cause non-trivial unemployment', and sectoral employment and income distribution outcomes may be quite open. The alternative models examined above suggest that employment always falls in the importables sector but usually expands in the exportables sector, but that the impact on employment in the nontradables sector (and consequently on aggregate employment) is ambiguous. Furthermore, if real wages are not flexible in the importables (import-competing) sector, then intersectoral wage differentials will tend to rise.

In the case of import-competing sector-specific wage rigidity, all unemployment other than the active job search type is still ruled out. Employment falls substantially in the import-competing sector but is completely absorbed by the rest of the economy that is characterized by flexible wages. In these sectors, wages fall by more than in the case of economy-wide flexible wages because the number of workers released by the import-competing sector is larger. Finally, unemployment is theoretically possible in the dynamic interpretation of the RV model; it essentially remains a temporary phenomenon. As capital shifts between sectors and labour productivity increases in the exportables sector, unemployed workers are reabsorbed over time. The tendency of the labour market to become more flexible as non-trivial unemployment weakens the trade unions and forces the government to remove restrictive regulations reinforces this process.

5.3.2 Growth and Adjustment

According to the static neoclassical trade model, liberalization yields static gains in terms of allocative efficiency. Strictly, this means a once-and-for-all increase in real income, but trade reform is also supposed to have lasting effects on the rate of growth (Edwards 1993). In the neoclassical framework, the theoretical link between trade and growth operates through the change in the relative return of capital and hence on the rate of capital accumulation, but the effect can be ambiguous. On one hand, trade liberalization in the HOS model reduces the reward differential to human and physical capital and should therefore lower the rate of investment. If consumption is import-intensive, savings should also fall. On the other, trade liberalization reduces the cost of imported investment goods. Therefore, it should cause a reallocation of income from consumption to investment. If it removes the bias against exports, then liberalization will also release the foreign exchange constraint on imports of capital goods. Hence, the net effect is theoretically indeterminate.

In a neoclassical world, the rate of output growth is a weighted average of capital and labour growth rates and trade liberalization changes these weights. If exports are labour-intensive and the labour supply grows faster than capital, then liberalization may raise the rate of output growth by raising the weight of labour in the equation. However, if capital stock grows faster, then the opposite holds (see Corden 1971: 134).

Nevertheless, trade liberalization is always potentially beneficial. Factor-owners respond to price signals, resources are reallocated, and the economy achieves a superior equilibrium point. The standard theory does not ignore the problem of adjustment and indeed recognizes that rigidities do affect the market. The economy does not adjust instantaneously and costlessly because factors have to move from one location to another, they are often sector-specific, and face considerable start-up costs. Since adjustment costs are a positive function of the transition speed and the incentive (the intersectoral factor reward differential) falls as equilibrium is approached, the optimal velocity of adjustment is less than infinite (Mussa 1974). However, the existence of this lag in the adjustment process does not yet justify the adoption of gradual trade reforms *per se*.

In the wake of the unsatisfactory results of many trade reforms introduced in the 1980s by LDCs on the basis of the standard model, more recent literature has emphasized governments' limited capacity to resist pressure from interest groups and provide correct and consistent price signals to investors (Thomas 1991).[3] These policy and credibility constraints are seen as sufficient reasons to prefer gradual to 'shock' liberalization. The current debate focuses on how the reforms should be implemented, addressing problems of timing, speed and sequencing.[4]

Despite these advances, the literature generally retains complete confidence regarding the perceived benefits of liberalization and its sustainability in economic (as opposed to political) terms. In other words, the long-run benefits of liberalization always offset the short- and medium-term costs. In addition, the adjustment process continues to be seen as reasonably swift and occurring mainly due to market forces. Resources are employed more productively simply by changes in relative prices, while the removal of labour market imperfections ensures that full employment can be maintained through the transition process (Michaely et al. 1990, Michaely et al. 1991). Not surprisingly, there is little emphasis placed on the role of the government in facilitating the adjustment process through specific micropolicy interventions, such as retraining and investment promotion.

5.4   PROBLEMS WITH THE STANDARD MODEL

Under very specific conditions, the HOS and RV models offer precise predictions as to the employment and wage effects of trade liberalization. As we have seen, these results are very sensitive to the assumptions made regarding the endowment base and thus the 'inherited' comparative advantage of the country in question, the sectoral factor-intensities and thus the existing technology, the existence of labour market rigidities and thus the prevailing institutions and skills, the homogeneity of the production function and thus access to new technology, and the speed of adjustment and thus response to incentives. Not only are these assumptions implausible in a general theoretical sense, but in contrast to justifiable analytical simplifications (such as similar information and demand patterns, given commodity prices, or absence of trade in intermediate goods), these assumptions also exclude the very 'development problem' that trade policy is designed to address.

First, the standard model concludes that the demand for (particularly unskilled) labour increases in the aftermath of trade liberalization. This conclusion is based on the assumption that developing countries trade with more developed countries and that exportables from developing countries are relatively more (unskilled) labour-intensive than their importables. Although this assumption may be realistic in the case of the poorer agricultural exporters, it cannot be taken for granted in either semi-industrialized or even modern agricultural exporters, let alone mineral economies.

The basic HOS model considers two trading countries: one that is capital-rich and the other that is labour-rich. Countries are positioned within an 'industrial ladder' and trade with both less and more developed partners. Thus according to the standard model, trading countries should export relatively capital-intensive goods to the former group, and relatively labour-intensive goods to the latter one, and generate a corresponding import pattern. However, if liberalization expands trade with less developed countries more than with developed countries, then the net effect on factor demand will be the opposite of that predicted by the standard model. This outcome is more likely among middle-income countries engaged in South–South trade, especially if liberalization occurs on a more regional than global scale due to the creation of free-trade areas or customs unions. The corresponding outcome of liberalization in the multi-country model would be that employment declines in both the most and the least capital-intensive sectors as these are both competing with foreign products, albeit from different classes of trading partner.

Second, many LDCs enjoy a relative abundance of natural resources such as minerals as well as unskilled labour. Trade liberalization would stimulate the export of these primary products relatively more than the export of labour-intensive light manufactures. As the extraction and export of these products are usually more capital-intensive than the production of importables, liberalization would logically reduce rather than increase (unskilled) labour demand and real wages.

In addition, the differential is generally exaggerated where exportables and nontradables are more unskilled labour-intensive than importables. For instance, the actual skill content of garments (the archetypal 'cheap-labour' manufacture) may differ considerably depending on whether they are exported or sold locally. If garments are produced for the local market, then the skill content tends to be lower and the main competitive factor is labour cost. If garments are produced for the export market, then the skill content is often significantly higher because production must not only aim to lower costs, but also comply with foreign customers' specifications and international quality standards, as well as quick adjustment to delivery schedules and sudden demand fluctuations. Moreover, specialized support services (such as export credit, management of exchange risk, insurance, shipping and marketing) are as important factors as cheap labour in transforming local firms into successful exporters. Most of these services are skilled labour-intensive and are often provided by foreign firms as part of sub-contracting and buy-back arrangements. Thus, the expansion of exports is likely to increase the demand of skilled workers substantially, although not necessarily in the exporting LDC itself.

Third, the literature often assumes that the most regulated and unionized labour markets are those of import-competing sectors (see Edwards & Cox-Edwards 1994). In effect, the substantial employment losses caused by trade liberalization occur only in these sectors, and aggregate employment may not fall if there are other sectors with flexible labour markets that can absorb displaced workers. In reality, however, the most rigid labour markets are often found in exportables and nontradables activities such as plantations, mining and public administration. Further, there is widespread empirical evidence that real wages have fallen substantially in manufacturing sectors because of liberalization (Horton et al. 1994). Moreover, the entry of unemployed workers into the informal sector may only involve the sharing of existing demand between more traders or casual labourers because of the sector's limited capacity to increase output, resulting in falling average incomes in the informal sector (FitzGerald 1993).

Fourth, the standard model assumes that the production function is continuous and that firms can substitute swiftly between factors of production by choosing from a continuum of technically optimal techniques based on factor prices alone. Implicitly, the standard model also assumes that the choice of technique is unconstrained by quality considerations. The general implications of these assumptions are significant for the impact of liberalization on unemployment. Given flexible wages and countries' ability to produce and export any good regardless of their factor endowment, these assumptions automatically exclude unemployment. Excess supply of (unskilled) labour can always be eliminated by lowering wages and shifting production technique, since normally capital-intensive techniques can be replaced by a sufficiently large number of unskilled workers at sufficiently low wages. Moreover, the absence of technical and quality constraints ensures that import-competing sectors can regain their competitiveness by reducing wages. It also implies that workers released from these declining sectors may be promptly employed in expanding ones, while guaranteeing that the increase in the relative price of exportables is a sufficient condition for export expansion.

However, these assumptions are hardly realistic and the implications of this are so important that they undermine the standard theory entirely (Wood 1994). Most factors of production are not substitutable: regardless of their wages, illiterate workers make poor substitutes indeed for mechanical engineers, and even mechanical engineers are poor substitutes for electrical engineers. Further, quality is a critical competitive factor on export markets. Local products must satisfy minimum international quality standards if they are to be exported: certainly, manual assembly of microchips may be less costly than automatic assembly, but the loss in quality more than offsets the cost gain. Finally, the technical coefficient of the production function can only take a restricted number of discrete values: under conditions of a non-continuous and non-concave production functions, the Stolper-Samuelson theorem no longer holds.

The reformulation of the relevant behavioural functions has important consequences for the impact of liberalization on employment and wages. On one hand, import-competing industries can only cope with liberalization by adopting specific quality-improving labour-saving techniques, so that even if wages are flexible, these industries may be forced to lay off workers and phase out certain capital stock. Once laid off, these skilled workers lose their established skills as they move to new industries (although presumably gaining new skills), while existing plant and equipment cannot be used to manufacture different products. On the other hand, even if released unskilled and ex-skilled workers were willing to accept lower wages, competitive industries are unlikely to be able to hire all of them, particularly if expansion is limited by industry-specific skills, credit or infrastructure, among other factors. Although the RV model explicitly takes into account the existence of technical constraints by assuming capital is sector-specific, it still supposes that labour and capital are good substitutes and that quality is irrelevant. Unemployment occurs only if wages are rigid. Replacing these unrealistic assumptions by more plausible ones means that trade liberalization can cause aggregate unemployment even if labour markets clear.

Fifth, the standard model implicitly assumes that the adjustment process takes place within a reasonable period of time. The inevitable lags and costs are mainly due to frictional problems arising from poor information, moving costs, and so on, and from the need to appease pressure groups or rent-seekers opposed to change. Obviously, the economy is bound to adjust in the long run through the generational turnover of the labour force and the scrapping of capital. However, there is no reason to assume that adjustment will be rapid once government regulations are lifted, particularly since wage rigidity can be a rational market response. By assuming investors respond instantaneously, the focus on factor reward differentials as the main mechanism for resource reallocation ignores the technical constraints discussed above. It fails to give sufficient importance to the aggregate rate of new investment and investment in the exportables sector and neglects the importance of the rate of adaptation and accumulation of technological capabilities by firms. Both of these rates inevitably proceed relatively slowly and depend upon a wide range of policies other than relative factor prices.

5.5 NEW TRADE THEORY AND THE MICRO-ECONOMICS OF TRADE LIBERALIZATION

It is logical to expect that an alternative approach to trade liberalization could be found in the 'new trade theory' (NTT), which is much more explicit about the time and the cost of adjustment (Grubel & Lloyd 1975, Stewart 1984, Helpman & Krugman 1989, Grossman & Helpman 1991, Alam 1994). The NTT states that countries can gain from trade even if they have the same technology and the same factor endowment. Indeed, trade allows countries to consume a larger variety of products without incurring the higher costs that characterize small-scale production. In contrast to standard theory, NTT assumes that increasing returns to scale and non-homogeneous products characterize production, with considerable consequences for industrial and trade policy. Originally developed to explain inter-industry trade between developed countries, NTT appears to be relevant to most middle-income LDCs although the relative weight of HOS and NTT mechanisms in any one country will differ according to its production structure.

Unfortunately, NTT does not make any explicit predictions regarding the consequences of liberalization on employment and income distribution. Because nothing can be said *a priori* about the pattern of specialization of each country, the direction of the intersectoral reallocation of resources and the change in the relative demand of factors of production remains indeterminate (Helpman & Krugman 1989). Nevertheless, it is still possible to derive meaningful hypotheses about the adjustment process from the assumptions upon which the theory is constructed.

By increasing the relative productivity of capital and thus encouraging the substitution of capital for labour, trade may reduce the employment elasticity of output. By shifting the pattern of demand towards scarce and non-substitutable inputs such as specialized skills, information, infrastructure or credit, trade may reduce the level of output and therefore the level of employment. According to NTT, the unit cost of production decreases with the size of both the firm and the industry due to technical economies of scale and the learning process itself. The existence of technical economies of scale is determined by the fact that the cost of investment goods increases less than proportionally to their production capacity. The learning process depends on the knowledge accumulated by the company as the result of specific investments in R&D and training as well as 'learning by doing'. The peculiar characteristic of knowledge is that it is costly to produce but can be used at zero additional cost. Moreover, some of the knowledge autonomously accumulated by each firm becomes available to all other firms so that the expansion of an industry benefits each firm by increasing the stock of knowledge to which it has access.

Their effect on wages and employment derives from the fact that economies of scale and the learning process are not factor-neutral. The productivity of physical and human capital tends to increase faster than that of unskilled labour. In order to become more competitive, firms adopt more capital-intensive techniques and expand output: their investment in R&D (or equivalent) increases demand for skilled workers. Moreover, the return on investment in training is higher for educated workers because they learn more quickly and learning opportunities are better in their occupations. Thus, the increased competition and international standards imposed by trade liberalization will change factor productivity, and hence their relative demand and price. This will reduce the employment elasticity of output and widen wage differentials, in sharp contrast to the predictions of the standard model.

The central long-term issue for NTT is whether trade liberalization stimulates economies of scale and innovation (Grossman & Helpman 1991). The case for this is made by four main positive effects. First, trade expands the output market of exporting industries and allows them to exploit economies of scale in production and knowledge accumulation. Second, trade fosters technological spillover as it provides access (at a cost) to the world stock of knowledge. Third, foreign competition reduces the duplication of R&D efforts and makes them more effective.

Fourth, the contraction of import-competing sectors can release skilled workers for exports. However, there are also negative effects associated with liberalization. First, it increases foreign competition and imitation, which can outweigh the enlargement of output market and reduce the return of investments in R&D. Second, latecomers may be forced to relocate to stagnating industries, and thirdly, unskilled labour-intensive countries are obliged to specialize in traditional industries with few technological spillovers. In this way, liberalization may not only interrupt the process of accumulation of new knowledge, but also instigate the loss of that which had already been accumulated.

Therefore, trade has, at least in theory, ambiguous effects on innovation and hence on growth. The strong empirical evidence that openness is associated with higher growth rates (Edwards 1993) would suggest that the positive effects prevail for 'successful' economies in the long run. However, the direction of causality is not yet properly understood and the performance of many LDCs, particularly the more industrially backward ones that opened their economies in the recent years is still unclear. The microeconomic theory discussed above would indicate that the effects of trade liberalization depend on the stage of industrialization. Firms must have the capacity to exploit the opportunities offered by exposure to world markets, and this capacity depends on both new investment and the existing stock of knowledge and infrastructure, which also attracts foreign investors. Because of the time required to plan and carry out investments, considerable lags will occur before trade liberalization leads to endogenous growth. Consequently, incentives must be sustained throughout the resource shift: in other words, trade policies must entail more than just 'credible' tariff reductions. Unemployment may turn out to be transitory if exports grow fast enough and permanent wage dispersion is to be expected in the case of both manufactures and natural resource exporters.

Thus, there are three different stories to liberalization. The first story is that of a semi-industrialized country that has achieved a critical, albeit undefined, level of industrial development, where trade liberalization has a positive effect on innovation. In the short run, import-competing industries shed unskilled labour, which becomes unemployed, while the expansion of exporting industries is constrained by a shortage of skilled workers. However, this constraint is overcome by state investment in human capital and infrastructure that firms alone would not find profitable. Through the pre-existing stock of knowledge and infrastructure, the country would be able to attract foreign capital and skills to complement its own resources.

The second story is that of a semi-industrialized country that has not achieved the critical level of development, where trade liberalization has a negative effect on innovation. Import-competing industries release un-skilled workers but because they cannot reach international quality standards, exporting industries are unable to expand. Excess demand and an increasing trade deficit force the state to cut back on investment in infra-structure, and eventually the country becomes locked into a vicious circle of endogenous stagnation. The country cannot attract productive foreign investment, and the effect of trade liberalization is to shift the country back towards natural resource exports and effective deindustrialization.

The third story is that of a non-industrialized country that exports natural resources. In this case, NTT does not appear to be very appropriate for the analysis of trade liberalization, but the HOS framework is more relevant. The effect on wages and employment follows Stolper-Samuelson lines and depends crucially on whether the export sector is labour-intensive. Nonetheless, even in this case the accumulation of knowledge and economies of scale would be important factors in the development of nontraded support services necessary for the expansion and diversification of production. These would lead to wage differentiation and a gradual reduction in the demand for unskilled workers. Thus, as in the previous two cases, for trade liberalization to be successful it would have to be accompanied by a considerably increased rate of public and private investment.

5.6   NEW KEYNESIAN THEORY AND THE MACROECONOMICS OF TRADE LIBERALIZATION

The standard theory of trade liberalization sees the distributive problem as essentially microeconomic in nature: a relative price shift induces a beneficial resource reallocation, and any effect on employment and wages derives from the distortions in local labour markets. However, the shift in relative prices arising from the removal of import tariffs, export subsidies and trade quotas (to bring domestic prices into line with world prices) inevitably produces balance of payments problems. These balance of payments arise because of the implicit revaluation of the domestic currency. Indeed, New Keynesian theory widely agrees (Dornbusch 1980, Dornbusch 1993) that even in theory at least two complementary measures are needed for balance of payments adjustment. First, the domestic currency must undergo a real devaluation in order to shift traded and non-traded prices for the economy as a whole in favour of the former. Second, fiscal and monetary measures must be implemented with a view toward restraining demand while exports recover, particularly through reductions of import demand and real wages. Moreover, these macroeconomic measures designed to force balance of payments adjustment are likely to form part of parallel stabilization policies to reduce domestic inflation and a structural adjustment programme to promote privatization. These not only affect the trade reform process itself but also rely on import liberalization for their own effectiveness (Greenaway 1993). Consequently, trade liberalization theory must take into account the macroeconomic implications of its own support policies.

Clearly, the new trade theories discussed above offer additional macroeconomic implications. For instance, the initial shock of import liberalization will change the structure of industry and the behaviour of various actors, and hence affect sectoral performance. This effect extends far beyond the increased price elasticities assumed by standard theory to reflect a permanent shift (i) in the income elasticity of import demand as tastes change or can be realized and (ii) in the import coefficients for producer goods as technologies advance, as well as (iii) in improvements in quality and marketing systems with increased export penetration. However, the process of adjustment of the human and physical capital stock will take a number of years and require sustained public and private investment. This view of adjustment lags broadens the preoccupation of the standard model with the credibility of government trade policy to embrace wider issues of investment determination.

The dynamics of the capital account of the balance of payments also have a profound effect on trade liberalization in practice. A rapid increase in capital inflows, for example, will not only lead to currency overvaluation and hence discourage the production of traded goods production, but also leads to changes in investment behaviour, particularly in non-traded sectors. These capital 'surges' appear to be systematically linked to trade liberalization, albeit for different reasons in lower- and middle-income countries. In the case of the least developed countries, official development assistance is frequently conditional on particular economic reforms, particularly when co-ordinated by the Bretton Woods institutions, which means that trade liberalization may be followed by an increased aid inflow. Indeed, this incentive is designed explicitly to sustain imports in the short term and avoid the consequences of sharp demand contraction for employment and wages that would otherwise be necessary. Aid-induced real exchange rate overvaluation accelerates the rundown of uncompetitive import-substituting industries but fails to stimulate export investment, although non-traded sectors such as construction will expand to meet rising demand (Bevan et al. 1990).

A further point of critique of the standard model of trade liberalization is its failure to consider three important points. One is the constraint imposed by protectionism in world markets on LDC export growth, particularly for primary products and certain 'sensitive' manufactures as well. The other is the implication of domestic ownership structures for price determination and technology transfer (Taylor 1983). Finally, the standard model also neglects to consider the depressive effects of external debt overhang on private investment. External debt overhang diverts foreign exchange from producer goods imports towards debt service, while debt service has a significant impact on the fiscal balance (Bacha 1990).

Despite these important considerations, the lifting of controls on capital movements, financial liberalization and the privatization of state-owned enterprises often accompany trade reform. In many cases, these changes have led to massive inflows of short-term capital, since trade reform itself has a tremendous signaling effect. This is particularly true if trade openness forms a part of binding regional or multilateral trade agreements, which indicates that this (and other economic reforms) will be reversed. However, capital surges have also resulted in an overvalued exchange rate, thereby preventing the relative price shift required by the standard model of structural adjustment (IMF 1991). Moreover, financial liberalization often involves rapid expansion of household credit, leading to (non-traded) construction booms and accelerating imports of consumer durables. As in the case of aid flows, the negative impact of liberalization on import-substituting industries will be greater than that stipulated by standard theory, while the positive impact on export sectors will be less and non-traded sectors continue to flourish. Policies to peg the nominal exchange rate in order to provide an 'anchor' for domestic inflation exacerbate this effect. At best, large modern firms are able to sustain exports mainly by laying off labour; at worst, the current account deficit becomes unsustainable and a financial crisis ensues.

Ironically, 'orthodox' macroeconomic policies accompanying trade liberalization tend to sustain the real exchange rate at a level higher than that level implied by the standard model. Further, they hold employment at a lower level quite independently of the functioning of the labour market. Computable General Equilibrium (CGE) models of structural adjustment (Bourguinon et al. 1989), inspired by Stolper-Samuelson, exemplify this contradiction. In these models, the positive effect of structural adjustment on income distribution derives almost entirely from the effect of real devaluation on sectoral labour demand and from the transfer of production from nontraded industrial sectors towards traded primary goods sectors in response to the consequent relative wage shift.

Further, the standard macroeconomic policy model holds that public expenditure depresses private investment *ex hypothesi* due to its crowding-out effect on the use of limited household savings (Khan et al. 1990) and fears of future fiscal insolvency (IMF 1995). However, there are good theoretical reasons and ample empirical evidence to suggest that public investment in infrastructure and current expenditure on health and education have positive effects on growth through the 'crowding in' of private investment. In addition, domestic savings are able to adjust to the resulting aggregate investment level through portfolio adjustments, albeit only through the real balance effect of inflation (Taylor 1991).

As will be seen in Chapter 3, the implications of endogenous growth theory undermine the critical assumptions of the standard model as to longer-term growth (Baumol et al. 1994). Similarly, we saw in Chapter 2 that uncertainty and access to funds comprise effective constraints on private investment decisions (Dixit & Pindyck 1994), intersectoral capital reallocation (Dixit 1989), and on the relative rates of expansion of large and small firms (Fazzari et al. 1988) than does the interest rate. Macroeconomic variables are even more important to private investment behaviour than the relative price effects of the real exchange rate and the interest rate alone. In particular, the rate of GDP growth itself (reflecting aggregate demand) and public investment rates (infrastructure provision) have positive effects on private investment, while the size of the external debt overhang (reflecting exchange rate risk) and the *variance* in the real exchange rate (policy instability) have negative effects (Serven & Solimano 1993, FitzGerald et al. 1994). Similarly, the existence of imperfect markets requires a macroeconomic theory disaggregated by different types of representative firms, ranging from transnational corporations to peasant households, as shall be see in Chapter 7. Despite this, standard views of LDC macroeconomics fail to consider systemic market failure more seriously.

An extension of the familiar HOS model from trade to factor flows (whereby capital shifts to take advantage of natural resources and cheaper labour skills) asserts that greater access to international capital markets (in the form of foreign direct investment, bank loans, portfolio flows or official aid) enhances poor countries' growth. However, there is no reason to believe that this will lead to optimal resource allocation once externalities are taken into account (Lucas 1990), and there is overwhelming evidence that direct foreign investment (DFI) is attracted to those LDCs with relatively large endowments of human and public capital (UNCTC 1992). Similarly, we saw in Chapter 3 that financial liberalization has had perverse consequences in many developing countries that have lead to exchange rate overvaluation and balance of payments fragility.

5.7   A PARTIAL EQUILIBRIUM MODEL:
Real Exchange Rates, Investment, Wages and Employment under Trade Liberalization

So far, we have raised a number of substantial objections to the standard model of the effect of trade liberalization on wages and employment, ranging from its assumptions regarding factor substitutability and technological change to the exclusion of capital flows and macroeconomic support policies. Ideally, we would construct a complete general equilibrium model based on alternative assumptions that are more plausible and make a rigorous comparison between the two. However, this is an almost impossible task, if only because the implausible assumptions are precisely what make the standard model tractable and make an unambiguous analytical solution achievable, as an elegant survey of modern general equilibrium models applied to the current account makes clear (Sen 1994). As soon as we introduce discontinuous production functions, factor immobility, scale economies or asymmetric investment response, the models become difficult to solve, except under specific conditions.

Therefore, we will attempt to lay out an eclectic analytical framework where real exchange rate, real wages, employment levels, private capital formation and public investment are all determined endogenously. This framework will be used to see how trade liberalization affects the interrelationships between these variables over three time periods under the more plausible behavioural assumptions discussed earlier. This partial-equilibrium model will allow us to draw some very interesting conclusions.

Consider an economy with two sectors: an exportables (or traded) sector and a home goods (import-competing and non-traded) sector with distinct technical coefficients but facing a common wage rate and interest rate. Open unemployment ensures that firms can obtain the labour they need at the going rate. The two sectors have different and non-substitutable capital stocks (X, Q) expressed in terms of annual production capacity, and (x) and (m) are the export and import coefficients, respectively. Firms use these capital stocks fully in the short run in order to maximize profits, but stocks can be increased by investment, or run down by annual depreciation at a common rate (d). We employ simple linear functions for ease of exposition and assume no scale economies in production. However, the response of imports (M) and exports (N) to changes in the real exchange rate (e) given by (n) and (z), respectively, imply that capacity can be used more intensively in the short run if necessary. The balance of payments (5.1) is closed by external capital flows (F), which depend on the difference between domestic (r) and international (r^*) interest rates.

We will examine three periods (t): first, the pre-liberalization period $(t=0)$, when an unemployment equilibrium exists constrained by the balance of payments but the liberalization of trade for the next period is announced; second, the shock period of liberalization itself $(t=1)$ after the tariff (T) is removed and the trade coefficients instantaneously shift after the lifting of controls; and third $(t=2)$, the period when the capital stocks can be increased by investment in the previous period. For each period (t) then:

$$N_t + F_t = M_t \qquad (5.1)$$

$$N_t = x_t X_t + z_t e_t \qquad (5.2)$$

$$M_t = m_t Q_t - n_t e_t (1 + T_t) \qquad (5.3)$$

$$F_t = f_t (r_t - r^*) \qquad (5.4)$$

The real exchange rate (e) is thus endogenously determined by the coefficients $(x, z, m, n$ and $f)$, the policy-set tariff rate (T) and domestic interest rate (r):

$$e_t = \frac{m_t Q_t - x_t X_t - f_t(r_t - r^*)}{z_t + n_t(1 + T_t)} \tag{5.5}$$

The standard model essentially eliminates the tariffs ($T_1=0$) but leaves all other parameters unchanged so the real exchange rate depreciates unambiguously ($e_1<e_0$) with the familiar consequences for intersectoral resource allocation. In contrast, our analysis would suggest that trade liberalization has a substantial impact on *all* the parameters, which undergo a once-and-for-all structural shift.

From the arguments presented in Sections 5.3–5.5 above, we can expect that the major change will be in the import coefficient for the home goods sector ($m_1>>m_0$) due to the lifting of non-trade barriers against competitive products, but that the export sector will take some time to respond as it must penetrate new markets ($x_1=x_0$, $x_2>x_1$). However, the 'price elasticities' of demand for both exportables and home goods sectors should rise as firms are exposed to international market conditions ($n_1>n_0$, $z_1>z_0$). Further, firms adopt a passive policy for capital stocks during the shock period, so while export sector capacity is maintained ($X_1=X_0$) by replacing depreciation, capital stock in the home goods sector is allowed to depreciate at the given rate (d) in order to adjust to import liberalization. Finally, trade liberalization attracts foreign investment ($f_1>f_0$) and the authorities raise domestic interest rates simultaneously ($r_1>r_0$) in order to protect the balance of payments in compensation for lifting the import tariff. This yields:

$$e_1 - e_0 = \frac{m_1 Q_0(1-d) - f_1(r_1 - r^*)}{z_1 + n_1} -$$

$$\frac{m_0 Q_0(1-T_0) - f_0(r_0 - r^*)}{z_0 + n_0} \tag{5.6}$$

The result is technically ambiguous in the sense that e_1-e_0 can be positive or negative on the numerical values of the parameter. For reasonable parameter values we would expect a real devaluation ($e_1<e_0$) to result from trade liberalization. However, a significant increase in the import price elasticity (z) due to the decontrolling of imports or a large foreign investment response (f) could force a real revaluation, as indeed has occurred in many cases in practice.

The effect of this first period shock on labour, apart from the employment loss in the home goods sector, is determined by the relationship between real wages and the real exchange rate. As there is no short-term substitution between capital and labour (see Section 5.4), this relationship is determined by the resulting macroeconomic equilibrium. For any level of the nominal wage rate (W), the real wage (w) will depend on the equilibrium level of home goods prices (P_q). Although the domestic price level can be expressed in terms of a 'basket' of goods from the two sectors (Dornbusch 1980), this only complicates the algebra without changing the analytical results. For this purpose, we can define the real exchange rate (e) in the usual way as the ratio between the nominal exchange rate (E) and home goods prices, setting world prices as unity.

$$w = \frac{W}{P_q} \qquad (5.7)$$

$$e = \frac{E}{P_q} \qquad (5.8)$$

Prices in the home goods sector are determined by the markup (g) on average costs derived from unit inputs of labour (l), imports (m) and capital charges (rk). The markup in turn depends on the degree of firm concentration, which presumably falls with trade liberalization:

$$P_q = (l + g)(Wl_q + mE + rk_q P_q) \qquad (5.9)$$

Substituting (5.7) and (5.8) into (5.9) and re-arranging yields

$$w = \frac{[(1+g)^{-1} - (me + rk_q)]}{l_q} \qquad (5.10)$$

Even if the real interest rate (r) remains unchanged during trade liberalization, we would expect the real wage rate (w) to fall because of both real devaluation ($e_1 < e_0$) and the shift in import coefficients ($m_1 > m_0$), which are positively correlated as seen in (5.5):

$$w_1 - w_0 = \frac{(m_0 e_0 - m_1 e_1)}{l_q} \qquad (5.11)$$

If the capital account reacts positively to trade liberalization, then the real exchange rate appreciates in which case the real wage rate can rise. However, this can occur only if real exchange rate appreciation is sufficient to counteract the shift in the import coefficients, and this may not happen in practice. In addition, if the accompanying stabilization policy raises the real interest rate, then real wages will fall even further due to the increase of home goods prices in (5.10).

New investment to increase capacity in period 1 does not take place in period 0 due to the pre-announced trade shock, but capital can be depreciated at a common rate (d) if real profits fall. The real profits (R) in the two sectors are given by:

$$R_x = \frac{[EX - (WXl_x + rXP_q)]}{P_q} \tag{5.12}$$

$$R_q = \frac{[P_qQ - (WQl_q + EmQ + rQP_q)]}{P_q} \tag{5.13}$$

Substituting (5.7) and (5.8) into (5.12) and (5.13) yields real profits in terms of the real wage and real exchange rates:

$$R_x = [e - (wl_x + r)]X \tag{5.14}$$

$$R_q = [1 - (wl_q + em + r)]Q \tag{5.15}$$

In fact, by further substituting (5.10), these real profit equations can be reduced to expressions in terms of the real exchange rate alone. By inspection, it is clear that real devaluation will increase profits (and profitability for a given capital stock) in the exportables sector and reduce it in the home goods sector:

$$X_1 = X_0$$
$$Q_1 = Q_0(1 - d) \tag{5.16}$$

Without factor substitutability, the level of employment is determined by the capital stock in the two sectors and unit labour requirements:

$$L_t = l_x X_t + l_q Q_t \tag{5.17}$$

Thus, the fall in employment between periods 0 and 1 is determined only by the scrapping (or routine depreciation without replacement) of home goods capacity:

$$L_1 - L_0 = -dl_q Q_0 \qquad (5.18)$$

Unemployment will rise by more, however, because of the natural growth of the labour force; output will also fall.

We can now turn to the post-shock period (2) when firms' expectations have stabilized around the new trade situation and investment during the previous period has taken place. Now there is implicit intersectoral resource allocation in the sense that the composition of the capital stock $X/(X + Q)$ can change, subject to depreciation or investment.

The two-period problem for the firm, which can easily be extended to an infinite-horizon generalization for the steady state, is to choose an investment path in period 1 such that discounted profits (V) are maximized. We shall focus on the exportables sector here, as home goods capacity (Q) will continue to decline until it begins to behave in a similar fashion. The representative firm must thus maximize:

$$V = R(X_1) + \frac{R(X_2)}{(1+r)} - H(I_1) \qquad (5.19)$$

where (H) is the investment cost function and is determined by the level of investment (I) and where

$$X_2 = X_1(1-d) + I_1 \qquad (5.20)$$

The investment cost function (H) increases with the level of investment (I) due to greater uncertainty and limited management capacity (Matsuyama 1987) and rising difficulties of obtaining funds (Fazzari et al. 1988). For algebraic convenience, the investment cost function is expressed as a quadratic function and contains the real exchange rate due to the import content of investment and the unit cost of adjustment (h):

$$H(I_1) = ehI_1^2 \qquad (5.21)$$

Substituting (5.14), (5.20) and (5.21) into (5.19), suppressing unnecessary subscripts and differentiating with respect to the level of investment chosen by firms yields the equilibrium condition:

$$\frac{dV}{di_1} = \frac{(e - wl)}{(1 + r)} - 2ehi_1 = 0 \tag{5.22}$$

so that:

$$I_1 = \frac{[1 - lw/e]}{[2h(1 + r)]} \tag{5.23}$$

In this case, real devaluation will have a positive effect on exportables investment, reinforced by its negative effect on real wages, but higher interest rates will of course reduce such investment. Thus, exportables employment can rise in period 2 and should exceed the continued loss of employment from depreciation in home goods. However, new capacity in the exportables sector will involve improved technology that is competitive in the international market, a technology whose labour intensity (l') is less that of existing capacity (l). Hence, there is a potential (but not inevitable) net increase of employment in period 2:

$$L_2 - L_1 = l'_x I_1 - d(l_x X_1 + l_q Q_1) \tag{5.24}$$

In other words, in our model real devaluation *forces* a tradeoff between real wages and employment growth. In contrast to the standard model, the tradeoff arises from *macroeconomic* processes in which the real exchange rate and trade liberalization determine both the real wage and the gradual scrapping of old plants and installation of new capital; whether unemployment will fall depends on the new technology implemented, the level of investment and the growth of labour supply.

The process of incorporation of new technology through new investment does not fully reflect the discussion in Section 5.4. To do so, the model would have to be expanded to include a public capital stock (J) that includes both economic infrastructure and economy-wide workforce skills. For convenience, we assume that firms have adjusted two private capital stocks (X, Q) to the desired proportions that reflect the post-liberalization parameter values and the new real exchange rate, and that the private capital stock can be expressed as a single variable (K). While there are no scale economies in private capital, there are positive externalities and scale effects in public capital. Thus, composite output (Y) is given by the familiar form from endogenous growth theory:

$$Y_t = AK_t J_t^a, \text{ where } a > 1 \tag{5.25}$$

Public capital provision is financed by a single tax rate (T) while the private investment function (5.23) is simplified so that the laws of motion are:

$$J_2 - J_1 = TY_1 \tag{5.26}$$

$$K_2 - K_1 = sY_1(1-T) \tag{5.27}$$

This yields a Barro-type growth model that incorporates the crowding-in and crowding-out effects discussed in Section 5.6 above. Output in Period 2 is given by substituting (5.26) and (5.27) into (5.25):

$$Y_2 = A\,[sY_1(1-T) + K_1][TY_1 + J_1]^a \tag{5.28}$$

Tax and expenditure policy is endogenized by assuming the government chooses a tax level (T^*) such that output (Y) is maximized. By differentiating (5.28) with respect to (T), the optimal tax level can be shown to be:

$$T^* = \frac{a}{1+a} \tag{5.29}$$

The resulting optimal composition of the capital stock is stable so long as the overall rate of private saving (s) is also stable:

$$\frac{K}{J} = \frac{s}{a} \tag{5.30}$$

The need to support trade liberalization through public investment in order to improve the competitiveness of exportables in world markets would imply $a_2 > a_0$ and thus $T_2 > T_1$. In other words, to stimulate private investment and employment in the long run, tax pressure should be increased rather than reduced as suggested by the standard model.

5.8 CONCLUSIONS

This chapter has contrasted the extended form of the standard model of trade liberalization as applied to the 'rest of the world' outside the OECD by drawing on new trade theories and New Keynesian macroeconomics. Although the extended standard model yields somewhat ambiguous results regarding the effects of trade liberalization, this ambiguity is mainly attributed to distortions in the labour market or to the credibility of policy, bolstering assertions that further deregulation and privatization would ensure that employment and wages both rise. The policy implications of the standard model are clear: trade liberalization is unambiguously good for employment and wages in the medium term, and the main criterion for policy evaluation is speedy and effective implementation, which is more of a matter of political tactics than of economic strategy.

In contrast, new trade theories and their antecedent in modern endogenous growth theory imply that the market itself will produce inefficient results where economies of scale and knowledge externalities are involved. This is particularly true of semi-industrialized countries engaged in manufactured exports. To support export growth, and make subsequent net employment and average real wage gains, high levels of public and private investment should precede and accompany the process of trade liberalization, although wage dispersion will tend to increase.

New Keynesian macroeconomics also has considerable implications for the effect of trade liberalization given that the adjustment of production to world markets requires high levels of private investment in the traded sectors. Private investment may be impaired by accompanying trends in public investment, real exchange rates and interest rates because their levels affect the desired capital stock, while their variance affects the speed of adjustment and thus the speed of export growth and employment creation.

The trade–employment linkage is clearly more complex and fragile than the standard theory allows, and our model shows that positive medium-term consequences of trade liberalization for employment and wages depend not only upon the maintenance of a competitive real exchange rate but also on the scale of the initial trade shock, which tends to depress investment as well as eliminate jobs, on the maintenance of public investment levels to 'crowd in' private investment, on the provision of credit at low real interest rates for reduction of the investment implementation lag, and the avoidance of excessive capital inflows.

Above all, this chapter has shown that there are convincing theoretical reasons rooted in modern micro- and macroeconomics to suppose that for many of the more vulnerable developing countries, unilateral trade liberalization will lead to stagnation and deteriorating income distribution.[5] Furthermore, for trade liberalization to be successful in both productive and distributive terms, developing countries must be capable of sustaining an explicit investment strategy over a long period.

6 Investment and Distribution under Capital Account Liberalization[1]

6.1 INTRODUCTION

The benefits of recent integration to international capital markets to developing economies, particularly the 'middle-income' or 'industrializing' countries are substantial. Access to international savings raises the rate of investment (thereby prompting industrial progress and income growth), dampens the effects of exogenous shocks, and permits efficiency gains from the transfer of competitive technology and financial skills (IMF 1997). Despite these benefits, however, short-term capital flows following financial liberalization are cause for concern, as they can bring about sudden shifts in real exchange rates, domestic interest rates, asset values and domestic credit levels (IADB 1996). National authorities are often forced to shift fiscal and monetary policy suddenly in order to offset such shocks, and the international institutions they appeal to become even further involved in policy conditionality and last-resort lending. Correspondingly, interest in the feasibility of short-term capital flow controls, from specific taxes and restrictions on overseas borrowing by firms to counterpart deposits and active sterilization policy, has grown (D'Arista & Griffith-Jones 2001).

The concern over the impact of short-term capital movements extends beyond immediate concerns over systemic risk in the financial system that arises from the differing maturity of assets and liabilities over the transmission of uncertain expectations from one institution or market to others ('contagion'). Although these flows have a negative effect on the 'real economy' (production, investment, wages, social services and so on), the transmission mechanisms are not fully specified.

One suggested transmission mechanism is that inflows (and subsequent outflows of capital) shift relative prices. In other words, capital flows distort resource allocation decisions (such as the acquisition and subsequent sale of domestic financial assets by non-residents), particularly through fluctuations in the exchange rate and the domestic interest rate.

Abrupt fluctuation in aggregate demand constitutes another transmission mechanism. This fluctuation may be due to changes in the money supply that reflect shifts in the foreign exchange reserves held by public and private financial institutions as capital flows in or out. It may also be due to monetary interventions by the authorities as they attempt to manage the balance of payments. Yet another mechanism suggests that the fluctuations themselves raise the level of country risk, depressing foreign investment and making government borrowing abroad more difficult, with long-term consequences for growth and employment.

However, rather than focus on the economic consequences of the instability itself, debate has focused on the appropriate combination of institutional reform and macroeconomic policy required to reduce capital market instability. Surely, this is unwise. Such fluctuations might very well have few or no negative consequences and hence would not be a matter for policy concern. More importantly, unless the consequences of capital market instability for the real economy are clear, it is difficult to see how an appropriate policy would be designed. In fact, beyond the flows generated routinely by the monetary authorities (or private banks) to maintain operational liquidity (such as short-term borrowing to balance the annual foreign exchange cycle for a primary agricultural exporting economy), the consequences of short-term capital flows for the real economy are not yet clear.

One negative consequence of short-term flows is the distorting effects on salient macroeconomic variables (such as the real exchange rate) during the inflow. Although these would reverse in a subsequent outflow, the cumulative inflow could have negative effects on real investment or growth. Another might be the asymmetric effect on real variables such as production, investment, employment, wages and tax revenue or government expenditure. Structural adjustment, which in the case of long-term capital inflows would be efficient, might become inefficient when policy reversal on the capital outflow is difficult or creates further distortions in the economy. Lastly, the fluctuations in asset value, credit levels, interest and exchange rates, and even the rate of growth itself, might have a negative effect on business expectations. Increased uncertainty might depress private investment levels, reduce the efficiency of public expenditure and force economic agents to adopt liquid positions and hedge their wealth through capital flight.

This chapter explores these 'real effects' in some depth. Although financial liberalization and integration to international capital markets have important longer-term implications for sustainable growth and income distribution (see Dutt 1995, and also Chapter 7), the analysis here focuses on the short and medium term.

Section 6.2 examines the consequences of short-term capital flow instability arising from the desire of investors to hold liquid assets in the face of uncertainty. The transmission mechanism towards the real economy consists of two elements. The first is an indirect effect though price variables such as the interest rate and the real exchange rate. The second is a direct effect through changes in the demand for bank deposits and government bonds. Section 6.3 examines the impact of short-term capital inflows and outflows on fiscal behaviour. It demonstrates that the shifts in the primary budget deficit that are consistent with solvency can shift dramatically with investor sentiment and force large fluctuations in public investment expenditure. Section 6.4 considers the impact of short-term capital flows on firms. Their effect on the availability of bank credit for firms is found to have a considerable and asymmetric impact on output and investment. Short-term capital instability creates financial vulnerability in domestic firms and has grave consequences not only for employment but also for long-term private investment, which is particularly sensitive to uncertainty. Section 6.5 examines the effect of capital flows on employment and the real wage rate through fluctuations in the real exchange rate and aggregate output, although the relative adjustment of employment and wages depends on the government's macroeconomic stance. Section 6.6 concludes with some tentative implications for national and international policymakers who are concerned with mitigating the negative effects of short-term capital flows.

6.2   CAPITAL MARKET STABILITY IN OPEN DEVELOPING ECONOMIES

'Short-term capital flows' take a variety of forms. For our purposes, they are limited to purchases (or sales) by non-residents of corporate equities and government bonds on local capital markets, and to the deposit (or withdrawal) of funds with maturities of less than one year by non-residents from domestic banks. This working definition could be extended to include changes in the net position of residents in foreign assets ('capital flight') without analytical difficulty, but the reduced definition makes the exposition clearer. The respective portfolio composition of resident and non-resident financial investors explains a large part of the difference in their behaviour. Resident investors have a much greater weighting of local assets ('home bias') that leads to a different response to sovereign risk (Hallwood & MacDonald 1994). Access to information and control over investment outcomes seems to differ between residents and non-residents, although here the distinction may well lie in the size of investors rather than in their location. Moreover, decades of overseas asset acquisition by domestic wealth-holders ('capital flight') have led to portfolios with a large foreign exchange-denominated component. Furthermore, much of what appears to be 'foreign' portfolio investment inflows is often in fact the reduction of external asset positions by domestic investors ('repatriation of flight capital'). Finally, annual fluctuations in flows that are conventionally regarded as 'long term' such as international bank loans, global bond issues and foreign direct investment may also reflect short-term liquidity considerations. However, these long-term flows are not considered here because non-residents cannot sell the *stock* of such capital through the domestic capital market to residents in the short-run. Hence the same destabilizing consequences for the domestic economy do not occur.

Nonetheless, fluctuations in short-term portfolio flows cannot sensibly be considered 'perverse'. Indeed the very attraction of the three short-term 'portfolio' assets identified here (equities, bonds and deposits) to non-resident investors lies precisely in their *liquidity*. Consequently, uncertainty as to future asset values can be controlled to some extent by the ability to dispose of these assets quickly to a local market maker such as a commercial bank or the government treasury itself. Because their debt is not traded locally, international banks involved in

long-term government loans attempt to reduce uncertainty by interbank syndication, better information through their local branches and –
in the last resort – by obtaining support from international financial
institutions. Similarly, a foreign corporation can reduce uncertainty
about the future value of its assets in the local economy by direct participation in management and – again in the last resort – by appeals to
international legal arrangements. In the absence of efficient insurance
markets, liquidity thus becomes the best means of hedging against uncertainty. High-risk emerging market assets with high returns are attractive for global portfolio investors because the riskiness of their
overall portfolio is considerably reduced by the low covariance between regional markets. However, this does not prevent fund managers
from switching frequently between markets as they attempt to maximize short-term profitability.

Consequently the volatility of portfolio flows cannot be attributed to
investor irrationality or even to 'speculation' other than in the technical
sense of international or intertemporal arbitrage (Hirschliefer & Riley
1992). One factor is the scale of portfolio flows in relation to the size of
the domestic capital market (in terms of the proportion of the domestic
capital stock effectively 'on the market' and the size of the local market
relative to the international market in which non-resident investors operate). Another factor is the high covariance between asset prices within a given developing economy or region. So while capital movements
towards 'emerging markets' should depend ideally upon international
portfolio managers assessing future income streams on the basis of
'fundamental valuation efficiency', in practice misallocation is widespread and sudden corrections are frequent (Tobin 1989). In practice,
assessing future income streams is a difficult endeavour that relies
largely on observing the behaviour of other investors.

The direction of causality also posits a complex question. For ease
of exposition, the *changes* in the short-term asset holdings of non-residents are assumed to be exogenous to fluctuations in the real economy
(output, investment, employment and wages). In this case, the styliza-
tion is justified for three reasons. First, we are interested in the determination of real economy and income distribution variables, rather than
of capital flows as such. Second, it is widely agreed that the larger part
of the fluctuations in short-term capital flows to any one developing
country is caused by changes in global capital markets (IMF 1994).
Third, financial markets (particularly in developing countries) are sup-

ply-constrained (Stiglitz & Weiss 1992) so that they are in stable disequilibrium, with adjustments determined by creditors rather than debtors, because demand is in effect infinitely elastic at the equilibrium
interest rate. Consequently, changes in the asset demand pattern that
reflect the international portfolio composition of non-resident investors,
rather than the supply of liabilities by residents, are taken, in this case,
as the immediate cause of short-term capital flows.

The conventional view of the effect of capital flows in the policy
literature derives from the presumed mechanics of the 'debt cycle'.
External savings (the acquisition of domestic financial assets by non-
residents) raise domestic fixed capital formation and provide foreign
exchange, and thus potential output expands. Subsequently, domestic
saving rises too, which eventually permits the debt to be repaid through
an increased domestic surplus available to the debtor (whether public or
private) through increased tax yields or company profits. Simultaneously, the excess of new saving over new investment should be reflected in
an increased surplus (or reduced deficit) on the current account of the
balance of payments, which provides the foreign exchange required to
complete the cycle.

These relationships are reflected in the 'accumulation balance' – the
national accounting identity which relates the savings of the public sector (S_g) and the private sector (S_p) and investment in the two sectors (I_g,
I_p) to the changes in the short-term asset position of non-residents (A),
long-term external debt and foreign investment stocks (D) and the level
of reserves (R) – which must hold *ex post* at all time:

$$\left(I_g - S_g\right) + \left(I_p - S_p\right) \equiv \Delta D - \Delta A - \Delta R \qquad (6.1)$$

Public saving depends on fiscal revenue (T) and current expenditure
(G) and private savings are disposable income ($Y - T$) less consumption
(C):

$$S_g = G - T \qquad (6.2)$$

$$S_p = C - Y + T \qquad (6.3)$$

Substituting (6.2) and (6.3) into (6.1) yields:

$$\left(I_g + G - T\right) + \left(I_p + C - Y + T\right) \equiv M - X \equiv \Delta D - \Delta A - \Delta R \qquad (6.4)$$

If short-term liabilities (A) rise *ex ante* and the other capital account items (D, R) are given, then one of the left-hand side variables must adjust *ex post*. The crucial issue in evaluating the effect of short-term capital flows is to determine which variable or variables adjust, and what the consequences of this adjustment are.

If the debt cycle is to end virtuously, then this adjustment must involve increased rates of investment (Devlin et al. 1995). Specifically (i) short-term capital inflows should increase investment rather than consumption ($dI/dA > dC/dA$); (ii) the resulting investment should be efficient in the sense that it leads to factor productivity growth ($dY/dA >1$); (iii) investment must be in tradables in order to create the required trade surplus ($dX/dA > dM/dA$); and (iv) marginal savings rates must exceed the average ($dS/dY > S/Y$).

This essentially optimistic picture has been modified by recent experience since private capital flows returned to developing countries in the early 1990s. The initial belief was that the virtuous circle could be guaranteed by eliminating the fiscal deficit (or at least the 'primary' deficit before interest payments) so as to prevent excess pressure on capital markets and the balance of payments. Subsequently attention has been drawn to strengthen the domestic financial system in order to prevent bank insolvency from poor asset management in the face of liquid liabilities. Finally, there is a perceived danger of capital flows being skewed towards non-traded sectors (not only through the so-called 'Dutch Disease' effect of exchange rate overvaluation but also due to speculative investment in sectors such as real estate), so that the foreign exchange required to service debt and repatriate dividends is not in fact available.

Apart from the longer-term effects on saving and investment, capital inflows are generally regarded as being expansive in the sense that they increase domestic absorption (Y), unless they are fully sterilized by an increase in reserves (R). Thus, the orthodox policy response to short-term capital flows is based on the need to maintain an external account target reflected in the maintenance of a minimum and maximum level of reserves. For instance, in the IMF 'monetary programming model' (Khan & Huq 1990), an autonomous inflow of capital will permit the government to relax monetary policy and increase growth and a subsequent outflow would result in the opposite policy. However, this expansive process is not the same as an autonomous rise in government expenditure (or even an export-led boom) because a financial asset has been acquired from a domestic agent. Much depends upon that domestic agent's consequent response: to consume, invest or acquire external assets in the case of private agents, or to spend, invest or reduce debt in the case of government. The different maturity of the assets and liabilities created in this process may also be crucial: a short-term deposit in a banking system is converted into a medium-term loan to a firm that acquires fixed capital. By the same token, a broad notion of the 'lifting of a foreign exchange constraint' as in the World Bank 'standard macroeconomic model' does not seem very helpful unless we are considering an administered economy where the central bank assigns foreign exchange directly to producers. It is necessary to define more clearly how more or cheaper imports affect the behaviour for governments, firms and households.

However, the financial liberalization that makes short-term flows possible pose an obstacle to achieving the necessary conditions for a 'virtuous debt cycle' based on short-time flows. Unsterilized short-term capital inflows often lead to an unsustainable appreciation of the exchange rate. This prevents export promotion and generates an import boom, while the expansion of domestic credit tends to result in unsafe loans being made by banks at low rates of interest in the expectation of rapid growth in income as well as asset prices. The subsequent outflow usually forces cutbacks in domestic absorption to restore the external balance, which – to the extent that rigidities prevent resource reallocation – lead to a fall in current output levels. In this way, the contractionary malabsorption effects on non-traded sectors outweigh any expansionary substitution effects in traded sectors, and the fragile banking system may very well collapse under the pressure of bad debts and the fall of asset prices as interest rates rise and domestic activity declines (Rojas-Suárez & Weisbrod 1995). In the Chilean crisis in the early 1980s and the Mexican crisis in the mid-1990s, banks played a critical role in the euphoric period before currency collapse. Banks in both countries intermediated very large capital inflows, which besides being unsustainable also financed the consumption boom. When exogenous shocks brought about a slowdown of capital inflows and a significant decline in the demand for deposits, these banks found themselves in a precarious financial situation. By the time the crisis had erupted, levels of output and employment in both countries experienced significant decline (see Edwards 1996).

To be sure, financial deregulation itself can be regarded effectively as a permanent shock to the banking sector that alters the environment in which the intermediation is carried out (Bacchetta 1992). The lifting of regulations on asset portfolios and reserve ratios and greater privatization are designed to encourage better risk management and narrower risk margins, but may actually encourage excessive risk acquisition in the search for market share. Monetary policy becomes more difficult to implement as the behaviour of monetary variables becomes more volatile with the reduction in market segmentation and the subsequent increase in elasticities of substitution between assets (Melitz & Bordes 1991). Indeed, the high real interest rates associated with financial liberalization actually *increase* banking fragility. A recession generally causes a deterioration in the asset quality of financial intermediaries due to bankruptcies in the real sector, although these problems are often seen as transitory by regulators who are themselves reluctant to intervene in major institutions due to the risk of contagion (Minsky 1982).

Inflation and exchange rate instability have usually provided banks with large windfall profits before liberalization, but lending skills (such as risk appraisal) are generally weak because of previous experience of oligopolized credit markets. With poor information on borrowers, banks cannot become efficient overnight, and depositors may believe banks to be more solvent than they actually are. Real interest rates rise not because of an increase in real capital productivity but because of tight monetary policy and competition with issuance of domestic government bonds. Regulators underestimate the problems faced by an underdeveloped banking system with a weak domestic savings base. This occurs because high interest rates and rising asset prices attract foreign portfolio investors and generate large short-term profits so that there are strong domestic pressures on regulators to permit the boom in asset values to continue. It takes a number of years for distress lending to build up to the point where bad loans can no longer be rolled over, during which time things appear to be going well and the reforms continue. However, the subsequent collapse of asset values becomes contagious, spreading from individual firms to entire sectors, and eventually affecting country risk evaluations.

This experience underlines the fact that local capital markets do not clear according to textbook principles. The local interest rate does not perform the expected role of resource allocation for two fundamental reasons. First, capital market equilibrium is determined by quantity ad-

justment due to the prevalence of asymmetric information and agency
problems that force lenders to ration credit, and much the same is true
of equity investors (Stiglitz & Weiss 1992). Second, financial intermediation involves the conversion of liquid into illiquid assets and thus
the assumption of risk, which cannot be expressed in interest rates due
to the adverse selection effect. In the face of incomplete financial markets (particularly for long-term assets), any large imbalance tends to be
thrown onto the most liquid markets where securities are quoted in foreign exchange. Third, interest rates in small open economies that are
exposed to the international capital market are not determined by the
marginal productivity of capital or by the intersection of the investment
and savings schedules, but by three other components:

the international interest rate (i_s),

the expected depreciation of the exchange rate $\left(\dfrac{E_e - E}{E} \right)$ and

the country risk proper (ρ). Thus:

$$i = i_s + \frac{\left(E_e - E \right)}{E} + \rho \qquad\qquad (6.5)$$

The first term is clearly exogenous and fluctuates considerably in
the short term. The second term depends not only on the current macroeconomic policy of the government but also on expected policy in the
future and on fluctuations in *other* currencies. Above all, the third term
depends on foreign investors' perceptions of the country in the context
of changing circumstances in the region and the world as a whole.
Thus, rather than being a market-clearing mechanism as such, the domestic interest rate is determined by many of the same domestic and
external factors that determine short-term capital flows.

This chapter adopts an approach which characterizes market economies in general and semi-industrialized countries in particular as 'credit
constrained': firms require working capital in order to undertake production but this capital is limited by banks' behaviour. Blinder (1987)
sets out a complete exposition of a credit-constrained economy where
supply is constrained by an asymmetric information type of bank lending behaviour. This bank behaviour creates a category of 'effective
supply' upon which our approach is based. Another approach to asymmetric shocks transmitted through the credit system that is based on

interest rate spreads rather than credit rationing also produces similar results (Edwards & Végh Gramont 1997). Interest rate changes are also regarded as essentially exogenous, with the exchange rate as the main instrument of government macroeconomic policy. Portfolio flows are considered to affect the real economy through their effect on bank credit. For instance, the purchase of an existing security by a non-resident from a bank will make credit more available; its purchase from an individual will have much the same effect when she deposits the proceeds in her bank account. Finally, if a *new* security is issued by a firm and purchased by a non-resident, this can be seen as reducing the firm's use of bank credit and thus releasing this resource for other uses. Again, purchases of new government securities by non-residents increases the resources available to the public sector.

6.3 THE IMPACT OF SHORT-TERM CAPITAL FLOWS ON THE REAL ECONOMY I: Government, Borrowing and Public Investment

The principal direct impact of short-term capital flows on the fiscal balance is through conditions on the government bond market, particularly the government's ability to maintain or increase the planned public sector borrowing requirement at reasonable rates of interest. The essential policy issue is whether short-term capital inflows affect budgetary behaviour asymmetrically, causing capital expenditure to fluctuate more than other fiscal variables.

In addition to the direct impact on the fiscal balance, short-term capital flows can affect the budgetary balance in three indirect ways.

One way is through variations in the exchange rate, which have an effect on the budget, although the direction and the scale depend upon the currency composition of income and expenditure. Normally the primary effect is through the cost of external debt service, so that capital inflows causing the appreciation will improve the budget balance. However, in the case of primary exporters where revenues are dollar-based, such appreciation may very well cause a deterioration of the budgetary balance.

Another way is through fluctuations in the domestic interest rate that accompany capital inflows and affect the cost of debt service. In theory, inflows should cause interest rates to fall (and should thus reduce the budget deficit), but in practice, the reverse may be the case, as these inflows are closely associated with financial liberalization involving high real interest rates. To the extent that these inflows are sterilized by the monetary authorities, the reverse may turn out to be the case, but outflows will generally be accompanied by further increases in interest rates.

Finally, to the extent that monetary policy becomes less effective due to the integration of capital markets, or is confined to a single target such as price stability, fiscal policy will have an increased role in the maintenance of macroeconomic stability and countering external shocks. In the face of revenue inflexibility and large fixed commitments to wage bills, transfers and debt service, capital expenditure may become the only macroeconomic instrument available to accomplish this.

Though the indirect impact is significant, the impact of short-term capital inflows and outflows on fiscal behaviour is felt mainly through the local bond market whose creation and expansion has been one of the most salient features of financial liberalization. The impact is felt not so much through the interest rate itself as through market perception of fiscal solvency, which is in effect a form of credit rationing.

Formally, fiscal solvency can be said to exist when the discounted sum of future fiscal revenue (T) and expenditure (G) at some discount rate (i) is greater than or equal to the present debt:

$$\sum_{t=0}^{\infty} \frac{T_t - G_t}{\left(1 + i_t\right)^t} \geq D_0 \qquad (6.6)$$

In other words, the debt can be paid off eventually, rather than rising exponentially in what is known as a 'Ponzi game'.

Conventionally, fiscal solvency models assume that fiscal revenue and expenditure are constant ratios of GNP (given by r, g respectively), that there is a fiscal surplus ($r > g$) and that the growth of output (y) and interest rate (i) are fixed to an infinite time horizon where ($i > y$), so that the solvency condition is simply reduced to a critical debt-output ratio (z):

$$z_0 = \frac{D_0}{Y_0} \leq \frac{r - g}{i - y} \qquad (6.7)$$

In practice, such parameter stability does not occur and fiscal consolidation tends to lie in an uncertain future. It is more realistic to regard governments (and bond purchasers) as targeting a particular debt to GNP ratio (z^*) that reflects their assessment of the prospects of fiscal consolidation (r, g), output growth (y) and capital market conditions (i) without perfect foresight. At best, this ratio will fall over time; at worst, it will not rise. IMF-inspired stabilization programmes may be viewed in a similar manner that produces the familiar rule for the level of the primary (or pre-interest payments) fiscal deficit as a proportion of GNP (c), through the *accounting* definitions that link the level of debt (D) and GNP (Y), the rate of amortization of the debt (d) and the gross borrowing requirement (B):

$$D_t = D_{t-1}(1-d) + B_t \tag{6.8}$$

$$B_t = i_t D_{t-1} + d D_{t-1} - c_t Y_t \tag{6.9}$$

$$Y_t = Y_{t-1}(1 + y_t) \tag{6.10}$$

$$z_t = \frac{D_t}{Y_t} = \frac{D_{t-1}}{Y_{t-1}} \cdot \frac{1 + i_t}{1 + y_t} - c_t \tag{6.11}$$

Substituting into (6.11),

$$z_t \approx z_{t-1}(1 + i_t - y_t) - c_t \tag{6.12}$$

The minimum level of the primary fiscal balance consistent with fiscal solvency is derived from this accounting balance and is based on the requirement that the debt ratio (z) does not rise over time beyond its target level. In other words, it reaches an equilibrium solution:

$$z_1 = z_0 = z^* \tag{6.13}$$

$$c_1 = z^*(i_1 - y_1) \tag{6.14}$$

The corresponding fiscal deficit (f^*) consistent with debt solvency is thus:

$$f^* = c^* + iz^* \tag{6.15}$$

$$f^* = z^* y \qquad\qquad (6.16)$$

This 'rule of thumb' is parallel to that for the acceptable current account deficit consistent with the ratio of external debt to GDP, where the current account deficit net of factor payments replaces the primary budget deficit.

However, for large short-term capital flows into (and out of) a developing country we consider *disequilibrium* situations by definition. In general, the debt ratio desired by the government is larger than that which international investors regard as sustainable (due perhaps to asymmetric information, but probably more to do with distinct incentives) so that the government is in effect rationed by not being able to place sufficient bonds on the local capital market under acceptable conditions to fund the programmes it desires to undertake. The circumstances of the inflow of short-term capital are almost always characterized by a marked change in market perceptions as to the sustainable public debt ratio (z^*) due to improved expectations for economic growth, exchange rates and country risk in the future. The effects of public enterprise privatization often reinforce these expectations, although the revenue is rarely used to write off debt. In addition, aggregate output will rise as aggregate liquidity expands.

Consider the situation where as a result of these changes, the (apparently) sustainable level of the debt ratio (z^*) rises sharply between the initial level in one period (0) and the next period (1) with this rate being maintained in the following period (2). Not only does the permitted fiscal deficit (f) rise, but in the 'transition' period (1) this deficit can be very large indeed in order to absorb the sudden change in the debt ratio (from z_a to z_b) and the increased growth rate (y_a to y_b) arising from the demand expansion:

$$
\begin{aligned}
f_0 &= z_a y_a \\
f_1 &= \left(z_b - z_a \right) + z_a y_b \\
f_2 &= z_b y_b \\
f_1 &\ll f_2 > f_0
\end{aligned}
\qquad (6.17)
$$

In practical terms, the effect is large (Table 6.1). For modest but realistic changes in the parameters (z^*, y), the acceptable or 'apparently compatible with public debt solvency' fiscal deficit shifts suddenly from 0.8 per cent to 6.2 per cent of GNP in the period of transition.

Thereafter, with the debt ratio stabilized at its new value, the fiscal deficit settles at 1.2 per cent of GNP. The corresponding primary fiscal balance (before interest payments) moves from zero (the target of orthodox monetary policy) through a relatively large yet apparently sustainable deficit of nearly five per cent of GNP before returning to a modest surplus in order to meet increased interest charges.

Table 6.1   *Changes in primary fiscal balance*

	Per cent of GDP		
	Before inflow (Period 0)	During inflow (Period 1)	After inflow (Period 2)
Debt ratio target (z^*)	25.00	30.0	30.0
Growth rate (y)	3.00	4.0	4.0
Target fiscal deficit (f)	0.75	6.2	1.2
Real interest rate (l)	3.00	5.0	5.0
Primary fiscal balance (c)	0.00	-4.9	0.3

The subsequent result is familiar. Once foreign investors see the macroeconomic result of their individual decisions, sentiment shifts back suddenly to a solvency ratio (z^*) that is probably even lower than before the shock. In consequence, the market demands that the government achieve a large fiscal *surplus*, in a reversal of the previous exercise in order to finance the repayment of enough of the *existing* stock of debt to sharply reduce the debt ratio. This would be followed by a new equilibrium in the medium term, but meanwhile panic-induced selling of government bonds sets in when the foreign exchange reserves are insufficient to permit them to be cashed in *and* the proceeds repatriated.

The government is obliged to adjust the remaining fiscal variables in order to allow for the exogenous fluctuations in its borrowing capacity. Developing countries have difficulties adjusting in the short run, and in practice, it appears that public investment bears the main brunt of the shock. This can occur for two reasons. The first is the traditional rule that budgetary borrowing should only be used for capital expenditure (Heller 1975) so that the current expenditure and revenue budget may be kept in balance. In consequence, any fluctuation in the primary deficit would be fully reflected in public investment expenditure. The second is the practical fact that when borrowing capacity rises, it is always politically attractive for governments to initiate new projects to gather political support. By contrast, when there is a need to reduce the deficit, it is always politically easier to postpone promised investment programmes rather than to lay off public sector employees such as teachers and nurses. In view of the fact that current expenditure is of the order of 20–30 per cent of GNP in emerging market economies and public investment is only 5–10 per cent, a shift of the order of five per cent of GNP in the fiscal balance hypothesized above can clearly have a disproportionate effect on capital expenditure.

The consequences of these sharp fluctuations in public investment (even if the mean is stable over the longer term) are clearly negative, as public services such as transport, health, and education are unable to maintain an effective development programme. This leads to losses in efficiency when new projects are implemented without proper planning in order to take advantage of unanticipated resources while these are available, or when ongoing projects are delayed or frozen during construction. Furthermore, reductions in public investment due to lack of access to capital markets have negative multiplier effect on private investment and thus on employment levels in the economy as a whole (FitzGerald & Mavrotas 1997).

6.4   THE IMPACT OF SHORT-TERM CAPITAL FLOWS ON THE REAL ECONOMY II: Firms, Output and Private Investment

Short-term capital flows have a marked effect on credit availability. These inflows affect the deposit base of the banking system directly in a number of ways: (i) through direct deposits of funds or purchases of bank paper; (ii) through the deposit of the proceeds of equity sales to non-residents; (iii) through the reduction of government credit requirements due to bond sales to non-residents, and (iv) through the general relaxation of monetary policy which tends to accompany them. The reverse occurs with capital outflows, and bad debt accumulating in asset portfolios of banks exacerbates the situation.

In developing economies (and indeed in most developed ones too) firms do not rely directly on securities markets for their long-term funding requirements. Rather, firms rely on retained profits for the bulk of their investment funds and on bank finance for much of their working capital. In addition, company control in developing countries is usually retained by family groups or by foreign corporations so that securities markets do not really act as a medium for 'disciplining' management since a controlling shareholding cannot be obtained through the open market. Of course, the control of domestic corporations or even the receipt of dividends is not the objective of non-resident portfolio investors. Instead, they focus on capital gains on the resale of the securities as the aggregate market index rises. Therefore the long-run effect of portfolio capital inflows on private sector fixed capital formation in LDCs has been found to be insignificant (FitzGerald et al. 1994, FitzGerald & Mavrotas 1997). This also explains why equity markets in developing countries are so narrow and shallow, and why they oscillate widely in response to changes in foreign investor interest.

Given that equity markets in developing countries do not represent a significant source of fresh investment capital of a way of improving firms' efficiency, then perhaps equity market fluctuations would not have a great effect on firms' behaviour. Thus, equity market fluctuations could act as an efficient 'buffer' for volatile capital flows by absorbing any consequent risk element. Unfortunately, this is not the case as the aggregate effect of stock market fluctuations on expected variations in external reserves and monetary policy is considerable.

Firms' response to changes in short-term capital flows can be conveniently analyzed through the effect of changes in bank credit. In principle, the effects of variations in international credit extended directly to large domestic firms would be similar. Consider a representative firm with a capital structure (C) made up of variable capital (V) for wages, inputs, inventories and so on, fixed capital (K) as assets, and bank credit (D) and own equity capital (S) as liabilities. The balance sheet is then:

$$V + K = C = D + S \qquad (6.18)$$

The level of output (Q) at a given level of prices is directly related to the amount of variable capital (V) committed to production and is constrained by the level of fixed capital:

$$Q = aV \leq bK \qquad (6.19)$$

The firm has a desired ratio (α) of variable and fixed capital when at full capacity utilization ($Q = bK$) so that

$$\frac{K}{V} = \alpha = \frac{a}{b} \tag{6.20}$$

This ratio is assumed to correspond to the point of maximum efficiency where the net present value of the firm to its owners is maximized (Sen 1994), so the firm will attempt to adjust towards this capital structure in the long run. The firm also has a desired balance (β) between loan capital (D) and its 'own' capital (S) made up of equity and reserves. 'Own' capital can only be increased out of retained profits (ignoring dividend payments and new equity issues for the sake of convenience), which are a constant proportion (s) of net output (Q) less debt service (D) at a given interest rate (i).

$$S = S_{-1} + sQ - iD \tag{6.21}$$

The firm has a *demand* for bank credit that is expressed a gearing ratio between debt and equity and based on its optimal exposure to creditors. In principle this optimal exposure depends on interest rates and tax patterns. Since the level of debt desired by the firm is not met in a credit-constrained economy, loan capital (D) is exogenously set by the banks on the basis of collateral available (n) in the form of assets which can be resold by the creditor. Thus:

$$D \le nK < \beta S \tag{6.22}$$

Thus at the credit-constrained equilibrium, the firm has a liability structure that is determined by its own past saving and its exogenously determined borrowing capacity:

$$C = S + D = S_{-1} + sQ + (1 - i)D \tag{6.23}$$

Banks will set the credit level (D) according to the deposits they receive. We assume that banks renew credit to firms annually, so that they can reduce as well as raise firms' debt levels at will. The maximum lending level will be determined by the firm's own fixed assets (K), beyond which the bank will not lend further even if it has sufficient resources:

$$C = S + D \le S_{-1} + sQ + (1 - i)nK \tag{6.24}$$

To maximize profits, the firm will adjust its output and thus its asset structure, so that capacity is fully used:

$$C = V + K = \frac{Q}{a} + \frac{Q}{b} \tag{6.25}$$

The firm's continual adjustment of the balance between assets and liabilities yields the level of output (Q) as a function of the level of credit (D):

$$Q\left(\frac{1}{a} + \frac{1}{b}\right) = S_{-1} + sQ + (1 - i)D \tag{6.26}$$

$$Q = \frac{S_{-1} + (1 - i)D}{a^{-1} + b^{-1} - s} \tag{6.27}$$

Thus the level of output (Q) depends not only positively on the level of bank credit (D) – or the collateral ratio (n) if the banks have enough liquidity – but also negatively on the interest rate (i) as this affects retained profits and thus the ability to finance production from the firm's own resources. These credit restrictions will in turn constrain the fixed assets that a firm can hold (K) and thus the level of investment ($I = \partial K$), assuming that the level of desired investment is always greater than the level of credit the bank will permit.

The level of working (V) and fixed (K) capital can be directly derived from the equation above. Note that the level of credit (D) has a positive effect on the level of output (Q) but the interest rate (i) has a negative effect on the level of output because it affects retained profits and thus the firm's ability to finance production from the its own resources.

Short-term capital flows produce similar fluctuations in bank credit levels (D). If we assume that banks are lending less to firms than they would wish (otherwise greater foreign deposits will not lead to further lending to firms but rather to the accumulation of liquidity in banks), then an increase in the allowed credit level ($\partial D > 0$) allows output to rise proportionately by providing resources for working capital. If the firm is already operating at full capacity in its credit-constrained equilibrium point, then fixed assets will also rise. Specifically,

$$D < nK \tag{6.28}$$

$$\partial Q = \frac{(1-i)}{\theta} \partial D \tag{6.29}$$

where $\theta = a^{-1} + b^{-1} - s$.

Employment will increase proportionately to production, and new fixed investment (I) is determined by

$$I = \partial K = \frac{(1-i)}{b\theta} \partial D \tag{6.30}$$

Finally, if (for simplicity of exposition) it is assumed that increased short-term deposits of foreign capital (∂A) are all passed on to firms in the form of bank credit (net of the reserve requirement of banks, n) then when $\partial A > 0$,

$$\partial Q = \frac{(1-i)}{(1-n)} \frac{\partial A}{\theta} \tag{6.31}$$

$$I = \frac{(1-i)}{(1-n)} \frac{\partial A}{b\theta} \tag{6.32}$$

Now, if bank credit *falls* ($\partial D < 0$) by the same amount, the effect is not 'equal but opposite', because investment decisions are irreversible (Dixit & Pindyck 1994). In other words, once installed, fixed assets cannot easily be sold, especially on a declining market, so it is not possible to adjust the fixed capital stock downwards to achieve the new (credit-constrained) desired capital structure. Because K is fixed, *all* the downward adjustment must be undertaken by reducing working capital (V) and thus output (Q), so that:

$$\partial Q = \frac{(1-i)}{\Phi} \partial D \tag{6.33}$$

where $\Phi = a^{-1} - s < \theta$.

In other words, the downward movement of firms' output following a given outflow of short-term capital will be much larger than the upward movement in output following an inflow of the same size. Where fixed investment is zero ($I = 0$) and $\partial A < 0$,

$$\partial Q = \frac{(1-i)}{(1-n)} \frac{\partial A}{\Phi} \qquad\qquad (6.34)$$

This asymmetry means that the greater variability of capital flows and bank credit around the mean, the lower the average output level. In other words, volatile capital flows reduce output and investment.

Unless short-term capital flows are fully sterilized, there is presumably a close correlation between capital flows and the domestic rate of interest. This occurs because perceived risk declines (rises) and stimulates greater inflows (outflows) at a given international interest rate or because the international interest rate falls (rises) and there are greater inflows (outflows) for a given level of risk. This correlation reinforces the asymmetric effect on output and investment. The capital inflow will drive down the interest rate (i) and thus stimulate output (Q) and investment (I) even more due to the increase in resources available to the firm, and vice-versa for the capital outflows. The fluctuations in domestic output and investment will thus be even larger than in our simple model. In other words, local capital markets will have a pro-cyclical effect rather than buffering external shocks.

The scale of these shocks can be considerable. The consequences of a unit inflow of short-term capital (of say one million dollars) supposing a plausible parameter set ($a=0.5$, $b=0.3$, $s=0.1$, $i=0.05$, and $n=0.2$) are illustrated in Table 6.2. The output decline on the downswing ($0.59 million) is nearly three times greater than the increase on the upswing ($0.22 million). Although on the downswing, investment is zero by construction, on the upswing, the increase in fixed investment ($0.70 million) on the upswing is less than the capital inflow. This result is well known from the empirical literature: as domestic investment has risen by less than foreign savings, domestic savings must have fallen (by $0.30 million in this case). Further, if for simplicity all the working capital (V) is assumed to be used for wages and the wage (w) is assumed to be fixed, then employment (L) is simply given by the change in working capital. For a wage rate of a plausible order of magnitude ($w=0.004$, or roughly $2 an hour) then while a $1 million capital inflow would generate 110 jobs, the same outflow would lose 295 jobs.

Table 6.2   Estimated impact of a $1 million capital inflow and outflow

	Capital inflow $(\partial A > 0)$	Capital outflow $(\partial A < 0)$
Θ	5.23	
Φ		1.90
Output (∂Q)	0.22	- 0.59
Investment $(I = dK)$	0.70	0.00
Employment $(\partial L = \partial V/w)$	110	- 295

In sum, it is clear that: (i) capital flows have a considerable effect on levels of output but the effect is asymmetric, with outflows depressing output more than if it is raised by an equal inflow; (ii) these effects are exacerbated by the response of interest rates; (iii) the investment effect is also asymmetric even though capital inflows are only partially translated into fixed investment; and (iv) domestic savings fall with capital inflows and rise with outflows.

6.5   THE IMPACT OF SHORT-TERM CAPITAL FLOWS ON THE REAL ECONOMY III: Households, Employment and Wages

Households are affected by real macroeconomic shocks through the level of employment and wages and through the availability of government services and bank credit (particularly for residential construction and consumer durables purchases). There, the impact of short-term capital flows on households will largely reflect the response of the fiscal and firms sectors to external shock as described in Sections 6.3 and 6.4. With respect to households, three responses are of particular importance.

First, capital flows have a negative effect on public investment stability, and thus on the effective provision of social infrastructure. This leads to a reduced supply of and effectiveness in health and education services, public transport systems and urban services.

Second, capital flows have an asymmetric effect on the volatility of corporate output, and thus on the level of current 'formal sector' employment and, through the level of investment, on longer-term employment.

Third, capital flows have a negative effect on capital market and exchange rate volatility, and thus on the level of private investment with long-term consequences for the level of sustainable employment and thus for income distribution.

However, as in the case of trade liberalization, the most significant negative consequence of short-term capital flow instability on welfare is probably the long-term consequences for because private investment (more than low wage rates or even labour skilling) is the main source of sustainable long-term employment, as we saw in Chapter 5. Nonetheless, the broader effect of capital flows on the real exchange rate is of considerable interest because through relative prices it affects the level of aggregate employment in the economy as a whole (including the small-scale sector) and the level of real wages.

Consider an economy with a current account deficit (CAB) composed of exports (X), imports (M), interest (i) on external debt (D) and short-term assets (A) that is balanced by the change in short term assets held by non-residents, the change in external debt and the change in reserves (R):

$$M + i(D + A) - X = CAB = \Delta D + \Delta A - \Delta R \qquad (6.35)$$

As in the case of fiscal solvency, external debt solvency relates to the long-term ability to repay external debt from which a sustainable debt-to-GNP or debt-to-exports ratio can be derived (World Bank 1997a). On exactly the same basis as the analysis of fiscal debt solvency outlined in Section 6.3 above, the level of current account deficit (b) as a proportion of GNP consistent with a stable external debt to GNP ratio (π) and a given GNP growth rate (y) is given by:

$$b = \pi y \qquad (6.36)$$

As in the case of the fiscal deficit, when asset demand constrains the international capital market, a small change in the perceived creditworthiness of a particular country will permit a large increase in current account deficit. This deficit will be financed by foreign investors but remains a transitory feature:

$$
\begin{aligned}
b_0 &= \pi_a y_a \\
b_1 &= (\pi_b - \pi_a) + \pi_a y_b \\
b_2 &= \pi_b y_b
\end{aligned}
\qquad (6.37)
$$

A relatively small shift in non-resident investors' view of credit-worthiness (π) generates a large current account deficit during the transition period of five per cent of GNP that is financed from short-term inflows (Table 6.3). This shift permits an 'import boom' of 25 per cent of GNP (although GNP growth rates have only risen slightly) if the authorities take no compensatory action. The mechanics of this boom often take the form of banks extending consumer credit backed by the short-term capital inflows, rather than banks extending it to companies as in the model in Section 6.4. This boom is not sustainable, however, and to remain consistent with market expectations of solvency, the current account should be closed again in the subsequent period and imports should fall sharply again *even if the capital inflow is not reversed.*

Table 6.3   Estimated macroeconomic impact of short-term capital inflow

	Per cent of GNP		
	Before inflow (Period 0)	**During inflow (Period 1)**	**After inflow (Period 2)**
External debt ratio target (π^*)	50.0	55.0	55.0
World interest rate (I)	4.0	3.5	3.5
GNP growth rate (y)	3.0	4.0	4.0
Target current account deficit (b^*)	1.5	7.0	2.2
Exports (X)	20.0	20.0	20.0
Imports (M)	20.5	25.2	20.3
Resource balance ($X - M$)	0.5	- 5.2	- 0.3
Factor payments ($i\,\pi^*$)	2.0	1.8	1.9
Actual current account deficit (b)	1.5	7.0	2.2

In practice, halting an import-and-credit boom generated by short-term capital inflows is very difficult. This is the case for the technical reason that reducing credit levels to consumers implies rapid repayment of debt that cannot be achieved by selling the corresponding household assets (such as houses or consumer durables), and for the political reason that the euphoric sense of economic success is difficult to abandon. In consequence, it is not surprising that the authorities seek to sustain the boom in the hope that *further* short-term capital inflows can be attracted. However, the reverse process ensues when foreign investors reach the conclusion that the deficit is unsustainable. Capital outflows require that the domestic economy generate a large *surplus* on the current account of the balance of payments of five per cent of GNP in this case, and when drastic reductions in domestic demand have caused widespread bankruptcy and household distress, capital outflows force the domestic economy to borrow heavily from international financial institutions in order to acquire the domestic assets of non-resident investors.

The macroeconomic consequences of short-term capital inflows depend upon the policy response of the authorities: whether they adjust the real exchange rate or they adjust the level of activity. Consider the situation where external trade is a function of the real exchange rate (e) and the demand effects of world income (H) for exports and of domestic income (Y) for imports, respectively. So:

$$M = m_1Y + m_2e \qquad\qquad (6.38)$$

$$X = x_1H + x_2e \qquad\qquad (6.39)$$

At least in principle policymakers can achieve any current account balance (CAB) in response to an external capital flow and thus determine how much the reserves change (or how much of the inflow is sterilized) if long-term debt is taken as given:

$$\Delta R = \Delta D + \Delta A - CAB \qquad\qquad (6.40)$$

Adjustment of either the real exchange rate (e) or the level of domestic output (Y) (or both) by an appropriate monetary and fiscal stance in the familiar way can yield the desired current account deficit. The employment and wage effect of short-term capital flows depends crucially on which stance is adopted.

Consider two scenarios. In the first scenario, if output is held stable (conventionally by fiscal means), then:

$$\frac{\partial e}{\partial A} = \frac{1}{-x_2 + m_2} < 0$$
$$\frac{\partial Y}{\partial A} = 0 \qquad\qquad (6.41)$$

In the second scenario, if the real exchange rate is held stable (conventionally by monetary means), then:

$$\frac{\partial Y}{\partial A} = \frac{1}{m_1} \tag{6.42}$$

$$\frac{\partial e}{\partial A} = 0 \tag{6.43}$$

The implicit assumption is that short-term capital flows do not affect the other balance of payments parameters (x, m). This reflects the fact that their positive effect on efficiency or export capacity is much less than that of FDI.

In the case of a capital inflow, an active monetary policy would involve some domestic inflation in order to force up (or devalue) the real exchange rate and allow output to rise, which may well be politically unattractive. This may be the reason why in Latin America there has been a tendency to allow exchange rates to appreciate during periods of short-term capital inflow, given the recent experience of high inflation. In Asia, by contrast, less inflationary experience has resulted in more willingness to allow domestic prices (and thus the real exchange rate) to adjust. Upon outflow of short capital, the exact reverse situation should hold, but as nominal prices are more or less rigid downwards in practice, it is much more difficult to devalue the real exchange rate than to revalue it, so that a forced reduction in output (Y) is much more likely. In sum, an inflow followed by an equal outflow is likely to have asymmetric effects characterized by the fall (or appreciation) of the real exchange rate with the inflow, and by the fall of output on the outflow.

What are the employment and wage effects of this cycle? In LDCs, there is widespread unemployment and surplus labour is held in the informal sector, so that employment can rise without inflationary consequences if output rises unconstrained by the balance of payments. The employment effect can thus be regarded as the effect of the increase (or decrease) in aggregate demand if the real exchange rate (and thus real wages, as shall be seen) is held steady. Consider an aggregate production function has the familiar form:

$$Y = K^\alpha L^\beta \tag{6.44}$$

Under these circumstances we can simply derive:

$$\frac{\partial L}{\partial A} = \frac{\partial L}{\partial Y} \cdot \frac{\partial Y}{\partial A} = \frac{\beta}{m_1} \cdot \frac{L}{Y} > 0 \tag{6.45}$$

The impact on real wages is slightly more complicated but may be derived using the approach set out in Dornbusch (1980). The real exchange rate is defined in terms of the relationship between the nominal exchange rate (E) and the ratio of world prices (P^*) to domestic prices (P); and the real wage rate (w) as the ratio between the nominal wage rate (W) and domestic prices (P):

$$e = E\frac{P^*}{P} \qquad (6.46)$$

$$w = \frac{W}{P} \qquad (6.47)$$

World prices are of course exogenous, but domestic prices are formed by a markup (r) on costs composed of labour inputs (l) at an institutionally negotiated nominal wage (W) and imported inputs (m) so that

$$P = (1+r)(lW + mP^*e) \qquad (6.48)$$

The relationships in equations (6.46), (6.47), and (6.48) yield a simple expression of the real wage (w) in terms of the real exchange rate, where the higher (or the more depreciated) is the real exchange rate, the lower will be the real wage:

$$w = \frac{1}{l}\left(\frac{1}{1+r} - me\right) \qquad (6.49)$$

In the case where output (Y) does not vary, we can derive a relationship between short-term capital flows and the real wage rate, where an inflow causes the real wage to rise and vice versa:

$$\frac{\partial w}{\partial A} = \frac{\partial w}{\partial e^*} \cdot \frac{\partial e^*}{\partial A} = (m_2 + x_2)\frac{m}{l} > 0 \qquad (6.50)$$

This analysis of the response of the real exchange rate and aggregate demand to short-term capital inflows and outflows also reveals a-symmetric implications for wages and employment. The real exchange rate rises on the inflow, but does not fall proportionately on an equal outflow, so that aggregate demand falls more on the outflow than it had risen on the inflow. Real wages will rise with the inflow but employment will remain the same. With the outflow, real wages would not fall but employment would decline. As an essential problem of income distribution is the balance between the incomes of the employed and the incomes of the un-(or under-)employed, fluctuations in external capital flows can be expected to have a negative effect on income distribution.

6.6   CONCLUSIONS: VOLATILE CAPITAL FLOWS, PRIVATE INVESTMENT AND PUBLIC POLICY

To summarize, this chapter has established the following general propositions regarding the impact of exogenous changes in short-term capital flows.

First, the principal direct transmission effects on the real economy are through variations in the credit available to firms and in the demand for government bonds; the principal indirect effects are through variations in the real exchange rate and in the level of economic activity.

Second, the impact of short-term capital flow instability on the fiscal sector is seen mainly through sudden shifts in the perceived solvency of the public sector, and hence in the perceived sustainability of the debt level by foreign investors; the effect of these fluctuations is felt in volatile levels of public investment, which reduce the efficiency of public provision of infrastructure and social services.

Third, the impact of short-term capital flow instability on the firms sector is mainly through the supply of working capital, which generates asymmetric responses in investment and output due to the impact on firms' balance sheets; the volatility of expected profits has a strong depressive effect on private investment.

Fourth, the impact of short-term capital flow instability on the household sector is mainly through employment and wage effects; these effects arise directly through firms' response to short-term capital flows and as a consequence of fiscal instability and indirectly through the impact of real exchange rate variations on real wages and aggregate employment levels.

However, there is a potentially greater consequence of volatile short-term capital flows for private investment, and hence for the growth of employment and productivity in the longer run. Volatility affects firms' expectations about the profitability of investment through the impact of macroeconomic variables such as the real exchange rate as well as the credit conditions for the firm itself.

Most investment expenditures are largely irreversible and sunk costs cannot be recovered if market conditions turn out to be worse than expected. In an open developing economy these conditions are as much a consequence of macroeconomic conditions as they are of the circumstances of a particular sector. Since firms can delay investments until amassing more information, there is an opportunity cost associated with investing now rather than waiting. The value of a unit of investment must therefore *exceed* the cost of purchase and installation by an amount equal to the value of keeping the investment option alive, which increases with the level of uncertainty (Dixit & Pindyck 1994). Hence, increased uncertainty will reduce the level of private investment. For reasonable parameter values, a standard deviation in annual profit expectations as low as 20 per cent can generate an option value of twice the original investment cost, requiring a far higher expected rate of return in order to justify investment. The literature on irreversible investment postulates that if the goal of macroeconomic policy is to stimulate investment (and hence growth), then stability and credibility may be more salient than particular levels of taxes or interest rates (Pindyck & Solimano 1993). Moreover, policy reforms such as tax incentives designed to stimulate investment may themselves have very little effect if there is a probability that the policy will be reversed (Rodrik 1989). These findings would apply *a fortiori* to short-term capital flows.

Drawing from data for 43 LDCs over 1970–92, Aizenman and Marion (1996) find a significant negative correlation between various volatility measures that are standard deviations of fiscal, monetary and external (effective real exchange rate) variables and private investment. Though they test short-term capital flow volatility directly, their volatility measures clearly respond to changes in the determinants of these flows and hence may provide empirical support for the findings of this chapter. Their results hold even when standard control variables such as initial school enrolment rate, initial population growth rate and the average trade share in GDP are included.

To be sure, firms in LDCs are not a homogeneous group, and in practice they do react quite differently to similar macroeconomic shocks, as we saw in Chapter 4. The affiliates of multinational corporations, for instance, will not face the same liquidity constraints as local firms. Unlike local firms, affiliates can always rely on their headquarters as 'lender of last resort' or raise credit from international banks with the international assets of the corporation as implicit collateral. However, even large domestic firms (often organized as 'groups') enjoy preferential access to bank credit at any one time (often because there is a bank within the group). Hence, they should suffer less from capital market fluctuations, and indeed, it is often the case that banks are vulnerable to the non-financial firms in the group rather than the other way around. By contrast, independent domestic firms are the most vulnerable to shifts in bank credit because they lack access to alternative sources of liquidity. Small enterprises outside the formal credit system are also vulnerable to the business cycle because they rely on subcontracts from larger firms or on the expenditure of wages by their employees.

The policy implications of the argument set out in this chapter are of great interest. Logically, the identification of the causes of the original fluctuation in short-term capital flows – and indeed a judgement as to whether this represents a temporary or a permanent shock – should precede the design of an appropriate macroeconomic policy. Flows that may be reversed would presumably be handled through compensatory reserve management, but permanent flows would require some form of macroeconomic adjustment. In the absence of any clear basis for a judgement on shock permanency, the proverbial admonition to 'treat all positive shocks as temporary and all negative shocks as permanent' remains a good guide.

Certainly the source of fluctuations in short-term capital flows varies widely to include alterations in local conditions (such as structural conditions like banking liberalization and privatization, and policy shifts such as in interest rates), in international capital markets (for instance, variations in prudential regulation or in domestic asset yields), and most importantly, in the perceived risk associated with a particular market. A distinct policy response is associated with each source of volatility. A change in domestic demand for money, for instance, can be countered by monetary accommodation, while a change in international perceptions of risk may best be handled by the sterilization of capital flows, particularly if the policy objective is to maintain a stable real exchange rate in order to promote exports. In all cases, however, the overriding goal should be to maintain high rates of private investment in traded sectors through macroeconomic stability and low real interest rates.

Clearly, such 'fine tuning' is a difficult task, particularly because much of its effect depends upon the reputation of the economic authorities. Indeed, with the international integration of capital markets, the only way to reduce the shocks arising from external capital flows would be a completely clean float or an irrevocable currency union (Obstfeld 1995). For most developing countries, however, a pure float is probably unworkable because monetary aggregates do not provide a reliable policy anchor (particularly during periods of financial liberalization). In any event, fluctuations in real exchange rates would spark negative real economy effects as discussed above. Monetary union is also not a feasible option for most developing countries, and where it has real prospects (such as in Mexico), the fiscal implications for the central economy of the region (in this case, the USA) are probably unacceptable. Consequently, in practice the options open to developing countries comprise: (i) fiscal policy design to reduce pressure on domestic debt markets, (ii) sterilized intervention combined with a strong reserve level and low real interest rates as the basis of monetary policy, (iii) high but flexible marginal reserve requirements on banks to mitigate the effects of capital flows on credit provision, and (iv) active management of the nominal exchange rate to maintain a stable, competitive real exchange rate.

However, '...with heavy capital flows, no single policy will do to simultaneously target money and exchange rates and to aim for external as well as internal balance' (Reisen 1996: 93). Clearly, meso-policies are also required, and these stabilizing measures may be summarized as follows:

First, to sustain public investment programmes, LDC governments should avoid the use of short-term debt as a source of funds, undertake a tax reform sufficiently extensive to generate a structural fiscal balance, and avoid the refinancing of long-term external debt with short-term internal debt.

Second, to shield aggregate savings, LDC governments should avoid high real rates of interest as these not only do little to stimulate aggregate savings but also depress private investment and attract volatile capital flows while increasing the budgetary cost and the vulnerability of domestic firms.

Third, to sustain private investment through the cycles caused by short-term capital flows, LDC governments should ensure that long-term credit is available to firms possibly by the provision of rediscount facilities at the central bank and tax incentives for long-term profit retention.

Fourth, to protect small firms and home-building from the effect of credit restrictions, LDC governments should introduce dedicated loan schemes and restrict the capacity of larger firms and banks to borrow abroad if this makes their capital structures vulnerable to exchange rate fluctuations.

Fifth, to avoid excessive fluctuations in real wages and employment resulting from capital inflows and outflows, LDC governments should maintain a stable real exchange rate by sterilizing capital flows and imposing variable reserve requirements on banks.

Insofar as domestic capital markets form part of the global capital market, the stabilizing measures outlined above would be greatly strengthened by appropriate action at the international level. International taxation and regulatory arrangements in particular would provide the incentives to foreign investors necessary to support longer-term investment in tradable production and human capital formation in developing countries (see FitzGerald forthcoming). As we will see in Chapter 7, international financial institutions' insistence on financial deregulation and capital account liberalization alone as ends in themselves (World Bank 1997b) does not include a more comprehensive view of the implications of capital instability for the 'real economy', and as such, these recommendations are not generally consistent with sustainable economic development. Clearly, domestic policy response to capital instability in small open developing countries must counter the detrimental effects of short-term capital flows on the 'real economy' if it is to stabilize the economy and remain on target for sustainable economic development.

7 The Institutional Integration of Developing Countries into Global Markets

7.1 INTRODUCTION[1]

The end of the 1980s proved eventful for LDCs: the Cold War was ending, the debt crisis was ebbing at last, and economic policy appeared to converge toward a general consensus. The global expansion of free trade and the integration of capital markets heralded the arrival of a dynamic 'global economy' in which LDCs were expected to be the primary beneficiaries. In this context, policymakers were confident that the implementation of sound economic policies in poor countries would raise export growth and encourage massive foreign investment inflows, leading to efficient production structures and the elimination of poverty. Nevertheless, the difficulties surrounding World Trade Organization (WTO) negotiations in Seattle in 1999, culminating in violent street demonstrations by anti-globalization groups, bitter altercations between rich and poor countries, and increasing evidence of chronically unstable global financial markets – as evidenced by a series of financial crises in East Asia, Mexico and Russia – have exposed the limitations of international regulatory institutions and the risks to developing countries of rapid integration to global markets.

Increasingly volatile exchange rates have spurred greater economic disruption, thereby reducing the volume of international trade and productive investment. At the same time, major exchange rate misalignments (particularly between the dollar, mark and yen) have resulted in the misallocation of resources and major adjustment problem. Combined, these two phenomena render LDCs particularly vulnerable to the inconsistencies in which private capital markets make funds available to them (Mussa 1994). These vulnerabilities have repercussions for the rest of the world, for although LDCs account for only 18 per cent of world trade, its share is growing rapidly; LDCs already generate nearly 37 per cent of world production and absorb 40 per cent of global investment (Table A.5 in the Statistical Appendix).

The first Article of Agreement of the International Monetary Fund (IMF) states that its primary aim is:

> To facilitate the expansion of balanced growth in international trade, and to contribute thereby to the promotion and maintenance of high levels of employment and real income and to the development of the productive resources of all members as primary objectives of economic policy.

This chapter evaluates the different roles of the IMF under the central criterion of the need to provide adequate institutional support for an orderly global capital market that can promote worldwide trade and investment.

Section 7.2 briefly reviews the experience of the Bretton Woods System (BWS) and its *de facto* successor practice: on this basis, Section 7.3 identifies the subsequent systemic problems caused by the rapid expansion of global capital markets over the last two decades. Sections 7.4 and 7.5 then examine the two implicit approaches to 'global central banking' contained in current trends in last-resort lending by the IMF and prudential supervision by the BIS, respectively. Section 7.6 draws the policy implications for the powers and procedures of the IMF, and its place within the emerging system of global financial management and regulation. This leads to the conclusion in Section 7.7 that the political basis of the IMF (or any other potential global central bank) will have to be reconstructed if it is to be effective in ensuring an orderly international capital market.

7.2   THE BRETTON WOODS SYSTEM

7.2.1   The Original Design

The wartime US–UK negotiations, which led up to the Bretton Woods conference in July 1944, had begun as early as 1941 and were conducted by technical experts who enjoyed relative freedom from normal domestic pressures. Their principal aim was to prevent a return to the inter-war experience of post-bellum recession and unstable world trade and financial flows. As such, the creation of reliable mechanisms to ensure an adequate provision of liquidity and a stable payments system – in other words, global central banking functions – were central to their proposals (Tew 1988). Keynes' proposal for an international clearing union between economies (through their central banks) aimed to overcome this problem while permitting autonomous domestic macroeconomic policy. However, in the absence of an automatic mechanism (such as a clearing union) or international policy co-ordination to offset the deflationary tendency of asymmetric adjustment, the implementation of conventional Keynesian policy for full employment would not be viable in one country (Kregel 1994).

Nevertheless, the position of the US during and post-BWS ensured that it did not directly encounter the destabilizing impact on global demand of asymmetric adjustments by creditor and debtor nations to disequilibrium under a fixed exchange rate system. Indeed, some critics would suggest that during the post-war period it has fallen to the IMF to ensure that any country that attempts an independent expenditure policy will be forced to reverse it in the interests of stability.

The institutional design at Bretton Woods clearly aimed to help non-industrial countries, though it should be borne in mind that these were viewed as what are now termed middle-income countries (for example Central and Southern Europe, the 'Dominions' and Latin America), rather than as proper LDCs, with the possible exception of India. Although Keynes' original plans for a global central bank, an international investment fund and a commodity stabilization system were not implemented; the central intent of the BWS was clearly to stabilize the world economy, improve expectations, raise investment and increase employment levels – issues that are even more urgent today, although world economic leadership at the end of the Cold War seems to have fallen far short of its counterpart in 1944.

7.2.2 A Limited Life

Although the BWS was technically in place from 1945 until 1973, its period of operation was, in fact, much shorter. The failure of US to force the UK to accept Bretton Woods rules as a condition for post-war reconstruction loan to Britain was compounded by the bilateral administration of Marshall Aid, the reconstruction of European trade and payments on a regional basis, and the replacement of the International Trade Organization (ITO) by the General Agreement on Tariffs and

Trade (GATT). Only when the European currencies became convertible in 1958 did the BWS become operational, although by then the deterioration of the US gold position began to reveal its inherent weaknesses.

During this early period, the role of the IMF was confined mainly to providing technical support for the re-establishment of payments systems. The world's major creditor nation, the US, also compensated deficits in its current account balances through foreign and military aid, meeting Keynes' original requirement for expansive surplus rather than recessive deficit reductions. After 1958, a *de facto* gold–dollar standard emerged as the US opposed an increase in gold prices, but it lasted for little more than a decade due to its inherent instability. Continued US deficits would have undermined dollar convertibility, while their elimination would have caused a global liquidity crisis that the modest issuance of Special Drawing Rights (SDRs) would been unable to resolve. Flotation of the private price of gold in 1968 saw the effective demise of the gold–dollar standard, while under the 1971 Smithsonian Agreement, the US successfully persuaded other countries to revalue their currencies against the dollar while maintaining the dollar's gold inconvertibility. The Deutschmark was floated in 1973, which permanently marked the end of the dollar standard and the shift towards a system of floating exchange rates and liberalized capital flows that has persisted to the present day. As the US lost its hegemonic security leadership, it also ceased to act as the world's central banker (Walter 1993).

The need for a more rational system akin to that envisaged by Keynes at Bretton Woods was understood quite early on (Triffin 1960), and became the basis for the subsequent creation of Special Drawing Rights (SDRs) to be administered by the IMF as a source of liquidity. However, the two major crises faced by the international financial system in the 1970s and 1980s, caused by the recycling of petrodollar surpluses and the sovereign debt problem, were of quite a different nature. Meanwhile, the provision of trade finance became the task of rapidly expanding private capital markets rather than central bankers as such. Coincidentally, the first OPEC oil shock occurred just after the Bretton Woods System broke down in 1973, generating a severe deflationary shock to the world economy and the first major post-war recession which the newly-created SDRs were ill-equipped to resolve.

The massive recycling of petrodollars during the 1970s occurred largely through the commercial banking system: OPEC trade surpluses were initially matched by OECD deficits, but a shortage of investment opportunities in OPEC economies shifted funds into US and European banks, which lent them on to their own governments and to a number of middle-income countries that sought to finance their trade gaps and public investment through sovereign debt. Whereas the OECD countries managed to find new energy sources, economize on energy use, and adjust their own export prices, the non-industrial countries adjusted less efficiently to the oil shock and tended to accumulate debt instead. Neither the IMF nor the central banks played a central role in petrodollar recycling, a role that had been anticipated under the BWS. Although the IMF (and the World Bank) managed to channel some funds (with considerable welfare benefits) towards poorer countries acutely affected by the new oil price regime, they were nonetheless unable to affect world financial markets significantly. More seriously, neither the IMF, the BIS nor the respective national authorities appear to have attempted to exercise *ex ante* control over the larger borrowing governments nor, as importantly, over the lending banks to prevent the accumulation of bad debt. Indeed, the petrodollar recycling was widely regarded as a considerable success at the time, and the problem of world financial management was thought to have shifted from one of avoiding liquidity shortage to one of coping with excess liquidity.

7.2.3 Two Decades of the 'Non-system'

The ensuing 'debt crisis' arose from overlending to both oil importers such as Brazil as well as oil exporters such as Mexico. Both commercial bank loan officers and borrowing governments appeared confident that real commodity prices would remain high and that real interest rates would remain low, but the reversal of US monetary policy, its continued fiscal deficit, and declining terms of trade for natural resource exporters rendered the resulting sovereign debt service unsustainable. The IMF proved unable to halt banks from overlending and governments from overborrowing. Capital markets were not capable of writing off deteriorating asset values, particularly since the leading international banks feared the consequences of a write-off for their own capital structure and solvency. Restructuring the debt of major borrowers who found themselves at or close to default (which might have sparked a systemic crisis in world financial markets, as insolvency was transmitted from one large institution to another as was the case with

Mexico in 1982) once again called upon the US Treasury as lender of last resort.

Despite the fact that the LDC debt crisis may no longer pose a threat to world banking, the matter is still far from resolved. Although most middle-income countries have enjoyed sufficient export growth to reduce the debt service burden, the issue of debt relief remains, and is of particular concern to the poorest countries. Poorer countries have benefited from some debt cancellation by donor governments under the so-called 'Naples Terms' at the Paris Club negotiations. However, bilateral debt cancellation for poorer countries is constrained by declining aid budgets against which debt cancellations must be charged as current expenditure. Furthermore, successive attempts at debt relief over the past 15 years have favoured lengthening repayment schedules and debt maturity through longer-term loans from the World Bank and the IMF (in the hope that LDC exports will recover sufficiently in the future to pay them back) over orderly workouts, since both the Fund and the Bank are precluded from multilateral debt cancellation. Consequently, the debt has neither been repaid nor written off.

The IMF's key role in this world financial crisis was not, in fact, to overcome capital market failure. Rather, the IMF focused on ensuring the fiscal and foreign exchange resources needed to maintain (restructured) payments obligations by reducing domestic absorption. Debt restructuring through the Paris and London 'Clubs' was not chaired by the IMF. The World Bank became responsible for the restoration of solvency through longer-term structural adjustment programmes designed to restore export and sustain economic growth through domestic market reform. These stabilization policies were quite effective in their own terms, although the notion that acceptance of IMF conditionality would restore governments' creditworthiness with commercial banks was not borne out by events: the commercial banks effectively abandoned the LDC sovereign loan market.

Just as a number of OECD countries expressed doubt as to the value of the IMF to international economic management toward the end of the 1980s, the end of the Cold War gave a new role to the IMF as administrator of radical liberalization of the Eastern European economies. After its experience in Latin America, it was clearly the only institution with the staff and the model capable of undertaking this task.

However, the relative success of this transitional role in Eastern Europe, now replaced by the longer-term tasks of industrial modernization, had little to do with the regulation of global capital markets. In addition, since the late 1980s, the process of privatization and financial liberalization has attracted a new type of foreign investor to 'emerging markets': the institutional fund manager. These new capital flows of the 1990s were not regulated by the IMF either, whose inability to overcome asymmetric information and agency problems culminated in another Mexican collapse in 1994–95. Once more, the US Treasury was called upon to intervene and bail out US investors. This rescue operation constituted the largest loan in IMF history, which was arranged in record time and without rigorous conditionality.

7.2.4 The Pressure for Reform

Though floating rates have not been quite the disaster that the Bretton Woods fathers envisioned on the basis of their inter-war experience, the macroeconomic policy autonomy expected by its proponents also failed to materialize (Obstfeld 1995), except in the case of the G3:

> The authorities in the three largest industrial economies appear to have reached the judgement that, in the light of their limited trade linkages with each other and relatively asymmetric underlying disturbances, the benefits provided by stabilizing exchange rates between these three currencies are outweighed by the potential losses that would result from less flexible domestic policies. (Mussa 1994: 22)

The interests of the rest of the world were, of course, another matter.

The twenty-year experience of floating rates and continued instability in foreign exchange markets – particularly the strains within the European Monetary System (EMS) and the decline of the dollar during the 1990s – has renewed interest in the possible role of the IMF in preventing and managing crises in international financial markets. With the decline in capacity (and willingness) of US authorities to act as the world's central banker, and growing inability of German and Japanese authorities to share the burden effectively, this development should not be too surprising. Indeed, the degree of volatility experienced since 1971 under floating exchange rates associated with lower growth rates, led the BWC to strongly recommend a return to an administered, or flexible, fixed-rate system that is co-ordinated by the IMF as representative of the G7 (BWC 1994).

Certainly, the Bretton Woods Systems institutions are also facing increasing pressure from the US Congress to drastically scale back its operations. The Meltzer Commission (sponsored by the US Congress and headed by Allan Meltzer, economist at Carnegie Mellon University) has called for the IMF to concentrate solely on short-term crises in emerging markets and to provide funds only to solvent governments that meet pre-set conditions.

7.3   THE PRESENT PROBLEM: ORDERLY CAPITAL MARKETS IN A GLOBAL ECONOMY

7.3.1   Interest Rates and Market Clearing

The experience of steady growth and price stability under the BWS is often cited in support of a return to a managed fixed-rate system similar to that in 1958–71 (BWC 1994), or even to the gold standard system operated by leading central banks between 1873 and 1914 (McKinnon 1988). Although econometric research broadly supports the former view (Eichengreen 1994), the positive effects are essentially confined to the 1960s, the periods of fixed exchange rates are not necessarily associated with greater output stability, and the international transmission of business cycles may not be necessarily avoided by flexible rates.

What is more, exchange rate instability has been closely associated with successive cases of major financial distress in the past two decades, including the persistence of US deficits, the global stock market collapses of 1987 and 1989, property market slumps in the UK and Japan after overlending, frequent secondary banking failures, and major sovereign debt insolvencies in non-OECD countries. Nevertheless, exchange rate instability is not the sole cause of financial distress. Rather, the integration of capital markets, the securitization of persistent fiscal deficits, the dissolution of financial boundaries between institutions and countries, and the emergence of new and heterogeneous financial instruments have also created new sources of instability in world capital markets.

In this context, exchange rates are as subject to capital movements and asset prices, as they are to trade flows (Dornbusch 1980). Current account deficits and surpluses balances are viewed increasingly as deriving from domestic imbalances between the savings and investment patterns of public and private sectors, and less as deriving from trade flows (IMF 1991). Indeed, in many cases trade flows react to capital account movements rather than the other way around, as illustrated by the current dollar/yen problems.

Further, interest rates do not necessarily clear these disequilibria. Interest rates are, in effect, related to the desire to hold the stock of bonds, but the adjustment process involves changes in asset balances rather than asset priceS (Goldstein & Mussa 1993). In principle, of course, the level of investment in an open economy need not be constrained by savings; international capital flows could be relied upon to finance the resultant current account balance. Such flows were relatively small under the BWS of fixed exchange rates, so that savings and investment moved together in most large economies. As discussed in Chapter 2, capital has become much more mobile from the late 1970s onwards. Moreover, the acquisition of financial assets reflects a 'home bias' that probably arises from issues such as currency risk, agency problems and asymmetric information that are endemic to market structures themselves (IMF 1991).

As seen in Chapter 2, world interest rates do not bring savings and investment into equilibrium on a global scale so as to clear the international market, and exchange rates do not affect trade flows sufficiently or rapidly enough to adjust current account deficits and avoid asset adjustment. These imbalances lead to successive asset bubbles based on subjective expectations and market sentiment and thus introduce a systemic capital rationing system. Market perceptions are also based on assessments of the 'quality' of that country's bonds, and hence on variable assessments of a country's longer-term growth potential and fiscal solvency.

7.3.2 The Standard Model of International Capital Markets

Standard analytical models of international capital markets between industrial countries still rely on an implicit model of independently and identically distributed random shocks and a homogeneous population of consumer-investors who differ (at most) by their risk-aversions and endowments. These standard models are thus unable to readily explain the origins of global financial instability, speculative currency crises, systemic problems of international fiscal co-ordination, or the rationing out of risky sovereign borrowers (van der Ploeg 1994). More seriously, while industrial organization theory has been applied to model the impact of decisions of multinational corporations on foreign investment (Dunning 1992), it has yet to be applied to banks and mutual funds.

On the other hand, leading international macroeconomic policy models in academia (McKibbin & Sachs 1991) and the MULTIMOD-II used by the IMF (Masson et al. 1990) are still demand-driven. In these models, output of industrial countries is assumed to rise until it reaches a capacity constraint or an employment/inflation corner. Savings are essentially the inverse of the household consumption function, and investment behaviour is a simple accelerator model. Monetary policy stances determine interest rates, which in turn are crucial in exchange rate determination. Though interest rates have income effects through the debt service burden, trade (with capital flow adjustment) is the basic macroeconomic transmission mechanism from one economy to another. In this way, trade generates a potential 'locomotive effect' from G7 (or even G3) economies to the rest of the global economy. By extension, effective co-ordination between economies (for example in policy stances) can increase the aggregate level of world GDP reached at equilibrium. This approach still informs most views of the benefits of global macroeconomic co-ordination.

Moreover, the standard paradigm for the structural adjustment of developing economies still identifies the world market as an efficient allocator of global resources. Openness as a development strategy is a self-evident proposition where any difficulties are *ex hypothesi* due to misguided domestic policy:

> [It] constitutes perhaps the most important opportunity for raising the welfare of both developing and industrial countries in the long term. ... Globalization comes with liberalization, deregulation, and more mobile and potentially volatile cross-border flows, which means that sound macroeconomic management commands an increasingly high premium. Penalties for policy errors rise. Globalization thus requires closer monitoring and quicker policy responses at the country, regional and global levels.
>
> The process of integration will affect countries unevenly and could increase international disparities ... The global outlook is in general bright, but masks wide differences across regions and countries – for many, global optimism coexists with local pessimism. Accelerating outward-oriented growth in the poorest countries will be a special challenge. (World Bank 1995a: v)

Despite this optimism and the evident success with which some newly-industrialized countries have approached globalization, it is widely agreed that in practice: (i) not all poor countries have been able

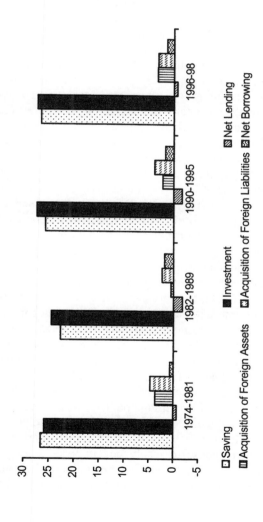

Figure 7.1 Sources and uses of funds in developing countries, 1994–99 (% of GDP)

Source: Table A.8 in the Statistical Appendix.

to take advantage of trade liberalization, particularly those whose trade is heavily dependent on primary commodities, or whose industrial capacity lacks competitiveness; and (ii) international financial instability has slowed growth in the industrial economies, while excluding developing countries from participating in global capital markets.[2]

7.3.3 Segmented Markets in Practice

In practice, capital flows between the industrial economies and the rest of the world (ROW) are clearly divided by portfolio acquisition, foreign direct investment (FDI), bank credits and official development assistance (World Bank 1994). Each form of asset acquisition appears to be driven by a different institutional behaviour, but in all cases, the country's perceived 'quality' appears to be a determinant factor. As Chapter 2 pointed out, this is true even in the case of FDI, when the investment and savings decisions are taken by the same agent, but where externalities prevent profitability from reflecting factor scarcity, and infrastructure and skills are central to the choice of location.

As explored in Chapter 2, there is also a clear segmentation of capital flows by country grouping, with very serious repercussions for the equilibrating mechanisms of investment and savings. Bank credit flows from industrial economies (IEs) to the ROW have declined since the 1980s debt crisis, while portfolio and FDI flows have been confined to a few upper middle-income countries and relatively few NICs. Only aid flows, which in any event are determined by non-economic factors, have tended toward the poorest countries.

As developing countries increasingly rely on capital flows to sustain investment (see Figure 7.1), they are even more acutely and disproportionately affected by international financial volatility. For instance, exchange rate instability, high interest rates and low rates of investment that slow down growth in OECD countries ultimately depress OECD demand for ROW exports. Similarly, high interest rates raise the cost of debt service and cause fiscal strain in LDCs, sparking macroeconomic instability and reducing private investment. Likewise, global market uncertainty excludes many developing countries from access to private capital flows, while subjecting others to destabilizing volatility in private capital flows. Moreover, the inability of capital markets to work out debt burdens in response to insolvency imposes a long-term resource burden on poor countries, and further reduces their attractiveness to foreign investors. Furthermore, the more vulnerable LDCs become subject to policy conditionality that goes beyond ensuring that international obligations are met, and breaches issues of sovereignty.

7.3.4   The Implications for Global Central Banking

The founding fathers of the IMF at Bretton Woods were concerned about the consequences of volatile capital flows. These concerns sprang from the immediate post-war circumstances as well as from real fear of a return to unfettered private capital movements that had caused such instability in the inter-war period (Kindleberger 1988). The solutions they proposed, however, are no longer relevant: the implicit assumption that capital flows would be channeled through central banks no longer holds, while integrated international capital markets constrains the implementation of expansionary policies by leading surplus governments. Nevertheless, Keynes' keen perception of uncertainty as a driving force in market sentiment, and his subsequent recommendation for the creation of institutional structures to reduce uncertainty and promote productive investment, seem more relevant than ever. More than a decade before Bretton Woods, Keynes had already identified the discrepancy caused by divergence between of rate of interest required to attract foreign capital and cover the current account deficit, and the rate of interest required to support the recovery of full-employment investment (Kregel 1994). This issue not only remains highly relevant to Latin America and Southern Europe; any hope that the UK might escape this trap by leaving the exchange rate mechanism (ERM) swiftly proved illusory. Clearly, bond markets are the one component of the global capital market that is efficiently integrated.

In sum, the most salient issues in global financial regulation today are quite distinct from those during the Bretton Woods negotiations in 1944 and from those during IMF and BWS negotiations in the 1970s. These new global issues share two dimensions with central banking in a closed economy: (i) the provision of liquidity as the 'lender of last resort' to smooth temporary fluctuations in market sentiment; and (ii) the establishment of an orderly financial market through prudential self-regulation by financial intermediaries. In effect, when the discrepancy between asset demand and liability supply becomes unmanageable by the market, the central bank must step in to undertake 'public action': firstly to provide the required assets (liquidity) and to restructure liabilities in the short run, and secondly to regulate asset acquisition in a rationed credit market (where the demand for funds exceeds supply) to re-occurrence in the longer run.

At the opening of the 21st century, in an increasingly integrated international economy where capital markets impose fiscal discipline on governments and investor confidence is increasingly fragile, central banks have become the guarantors of global prosperity.

The impact of the US economic slowdown on the ROW economy, and the continuing instability of the dollar/euro/yen ('triad') exchange rates has underlined lack of a global monetary authority. The establishment of a 'Global Central Bank' is not politically feasible; while a return to the post-war Bretton Woods System, even if politically acceptable, would imply a degree of control over capital movements incompatible with modern markets. Global monetary stability depends, therefore, on the G3 central banks.

The industrial economies have all liberalized their financial markets and set budgetary objectives based on short-term balance and long-term fiscal solvency. This means that the only instrument of domestic (and, by extension, international) demand management is monetary policy. The opening of capital accounts and the creating of a global capital market means that real long-term interest rates are converging on a global mean. Therefore the only remaining instrument is the short-run interest rate set by central banks and supported by open-market operations in government bonds.

Central banks have two constitutional functions. The first is to maintain the integrity of the domestic monetary system itself by monitoring the state of the banking system, regulating the payments system, and supervising financial intermediation where not devolved on a separate bodies. Central banks also act as 'last-resort lender' to banks with liquidity shortages, or if insolvent, ensure their orderly liquidation or merger. The second function is that of maintaining the integrity of the domestic currency. Central banks conduct monetary policy under a set of rules set in a 'constitution', which can be interpreted by the executive and legislative branches as keeping inflation below a defined level, as maintaining the exchange rate within a defined band, or as ensuring macroeconomic stability.

Both these functions are necessary to ensure that domestic financial markets can work in an orderly manner. Logically they are also necessary at the global level, although the ability and willingness of the G3 central banks to perform this role are far from evident.

The US Federal Reserve is constitutionally obliged to ensure economic stability as well as keep inflation in check. During the Greenspan era, with inflation at historically low rates, the Fed has been mainly concerned with managing the business cycle so as to prevent both overheating and recession. This has been achieved with considerable success so far, but has had the consequence that the balance of payments deficit has steadily widened and dollar exchange rate has fluctuated widely. In consequence, the impact of the Fed's policies on the ROW economy has not been positive.

Since its foundation, the European Central Bank (ECB) has focused on its constitutional target of inflation reduction through the setting of short-term interest rates, and takes a passive stance on the exchange rate. The stubborn refusal to undertake interest rate reductions in order to stimulate growth has been a response to the persistent tendency for European prices to edge above the two percent target growth rate. Nonetheless, pressure continues to strengthen for the ECB to give greater priority to growth and eventually for an active position on the Euro exchange rate itself. This in turn will require a reformulation of the constitution of the ECB.

Meanwhile, the Bank of Japan has maintained an expansionary monetary policy in the short run for the past ten years in order to stimulate domestic demand, while attempting to return to a positive interest rate (and thus some degree of monetary control) in the medium term. To these difficult tasks have been added the need to cope with the insolvent state of the Japanese banking system. In consequence, the yen exchange rate has been allowed to drift and depends largely on short-term capital flows towards the US – generated both by Japanese investors seeking to protect asset value and international investors engaged in interest rate arbitrage (the 'carry trade').

There does exist a "central bankers' central banker" at Basle in the form of the Bank for International Settlements. The BIS brings together the leading central banks as shareholders, and as its name implies, exists mainly to ensure the integrity of global interbank payments and to collect data on international bank exposure. However, the 'Basle Accords' under the aegis of the Bank set the capital adequacy requirements for banks worldwide. Recently the net has widened to coordinate securities regulators and support for the G7's Financial Stability Forum, which in turn is establishing a set of international 'codes and standards' for supervision and reporting of fiscal accounts, domestic banks and highly leveraged institutions.

In a broad sense, therefore, the emerging set of Basle-based arrangements do provide the potential basis for a multilateral system to ensure global capital market integrity, thus fulfilling the first of the two central banking functions defined above. Nonetheless, the BIS is hardly in a position to suggest to central banks what strategies they should pursue, let alone how they might co-ordinate their policies.

The finance ministers of the US, EU and Japan (the G3) do meet regularly under the G7 mantle to discuss global economic issues, and to in effect have the International Monetary Fund at hand as their potential executive arm. Under the post-war Bretton Woods System, the Fund was in fact the intergovernmental banker for the OECD countries. The interventions in the second half of the 1990s to resolve emerging market crises indicate a growing recognition of the need for a 'lender of last resort' when system stability is threatened.

However, there is no domestic political support within the G3 to change the constitutional rules under which the three central banks work, a necessary pre-condition for co-ordination and global liquidity management. The US is moving away from multilateral co-operation under the current republican administration. The EU has both the ECB and the Bank of England, but the European Commission has not acquired fiscal, financial or monetary powers. Japan is trapped in domestic banking crisis that appears to preclude an active part in global monetary affairs.

In sum, the G3 central banks are not able to resolve the problem of global recession due to their own constitutional limitations on the one hand and a combination of US unwillingness to pool sovereignty, European Union diffusion of monetary authority and Japanese procrastination on the other.

7.4   GLOBAL CENTRAL BANKING I: LENDER OF LAST RESORT

7.4.1 Short-term Financing Facility (STFF)

The potential role of a global central bank as lender of last resort is evident in IMF proposals to create a new 'short-term financing facility' (STFF). This STFF could be disbursed very rapidly to counter swings in market sentiment and speculative pressures that do not reflect economic fundamentals. Furthermore, the STFF would complement the IMF's existing facilities for the management of perverse capital movements, particularly in cases involving critical discontinuities, where support must be immediate if it is to be effective. The cases include (i) the defense of an exchange rate peg, and (ii) illiquidity causing default risk. To be sure, the BWC considered this role central to the IMF's future (BWC 1994).

Certainly, the IMF is the most plausible candidate for the provision of 'backstop finance' on a regular basis. Though G7 central banks (and particularly G3 central banks) have assumed responsibility for the major rescue operations in post-war history, they lack an institutional apparatus. In the case of the European Union, the existing co-ordination mechanism (which was based on the Bundesbank) evolved into the European Central Bank, but it is unlikely to extend further afield in the foreseeable future. In the past, the BIS has only provided bridging finance, and has no developing country participation nor operating experience in stabilization programmes.

As illiquidity was foreseen as a current account problem when the IMF was conceived as a potential lender of last resort, Article VI specifically precluded lending to finance capital outflows and implied that it should be handled by administrative controls. In practice, however, Article VI is not applied and the IMF now argues against capital controls, although it appears to support various sterilization measures. Although this preclusion should not prove a real obstacle, the need for open-market operations – and thus capacity to significantly affect the market for G7 government bonds – would certainly remain problematic.

7.4.2 Scope and Scale of the STFF

Coverage under the STFF scheme would presumably be limited to non-industrial countries, and would depend on whether fixed exchange rates are felt to be a desirable policy. Assuming flexible parities remain the rule (if only as a measure to maintain a stable real exchange rate), then the STFF would be justified mainly in those cases where indebted countries find themselves at the margin of the private capital market. However, this country category could be further reduced if argued that last-resort lending should be restricted to cases where default would pose a systemic threat, spilling over into a withdrawal of funds from neighbouring or similar countries.

Clearly, some such market intervention is crucial for a return to flexible rate bands, as the European ERM (Exchange Rate Management) system has demonstrated (Williamson & Miller 1987). Market intervention could only be avoided if there were automatic mechanisms to force surplus countries to adjust their asset positions themselves. This, however, would require a high degree of intervention in the fiscal and monetary affairs of these countries and a complete change in IMF competency.

Coverage under the Camdessus proposal ('Short-Term Financing Facility' paper presented to the IMF Executive Board, 26 September 1994) would be limited to some fifty (mainly upper middle-income) countries with a high degree of involvement in the international capital market. The terms of access would be based on specific 'drawing right' provisions made under the regular Article IV consultation, where the Fund determined that the country has a sound policy record and no fundamental balance of payments problem. Coverage could be made automatic and thus very rapid, but only at some risk to the IMF, particularly if it ended up effectively funding (and thus enabling) capital flight. The level of access (which could be arranged in trenches) would need to be commensurate with potential reserve losses, although without financing capital flight fully, but rather relying on positive signaling effects on markets, and could reach 300 per cent of quota. However, the maturity of the loans would be short (three months), and if the problem persisted, the STFF could be replaced by a normal standby or extended arrangement.

The IMF proposes that such a facility could be financed from the IMF's normal resources, perhaps by activating General Arrangements to Borrow (GAB), although this would imply confining access to the established rules for standby, and extended arrangements.

Ideally, the funds required for the STFF should be provided by new sources of liquidity, by issuing special drawing rights (SDRs) or by the expenditure of excess reserves of surplus economies such as Japan, as proposed by the IMF Managing Director at the Copenhagen Social Summit in March 1995. To be sure, the use of SDRs for this purpose has been a standing proposal since the original Bretton Woods conference, once the automatic use of reserves of surplus countries proposed in the Keynes Plan were reformulated to allow for open market operations by the Fund (Triffin 1960). The use of SDRs would also require modification of Article XVIII requiring SDRs to be allocated *pro rata* to existing quotas. This restriction is already under strain due to current G7 proposals for the allocation of the first SDR increase since 1981 exclusively to the transition economies, to the detriment of developing countries as a whole.

In any event, if the conversion of SDRs into a true fiduciary reserve asset is deemed unacceptable by the more conservative members of the G7, then the STFF could involve the IMF borrowing on financial markets, effectively creating liquidity by converting long-term liabilities into short-term assets. As in the case of the World Bank, the willingness to subscribe would not arise from the quality of IMF assets (for instance, the STFF loans) but rather from their underwriting by the G3. If forthcoming, the relevant criterion becomes the likely effectiveness of such a scheme. On the one hand, like all last-resort lending, it could delay rather than facilitate adjustment. Thus, it requires fine judgement as to future government behaviour, even if the 'moral hazard' dilemma is more applicable to creditors than to debtors in such circumstances. On the other hand, the speed of intervention is crucial, and automatic access on country request (or at most, on approval by IMF executives), while necessary, would also effectively disenfranchise the Executive Board. Thus the quality of the Fund's assessment is crucial in determining whether the effects will be positive, and in giving the right signals to international capital markets, particularly where, by definition, it is necessary to intervene *against* prevailing market sentiment.

However, the scale of intervention in two recent crises give some idea of the funding problem involved in global central banking, regardless of country size. In one day alone in early June 1995, the G3 central banks spent $20bn to support the dollar, an effect that lasted for little more than a week. During the 1992 ERM crisis, some $130bn were mobilized (mainly by the Bundesbank) in defense of the currencies of Denmark, Ireland, Italy, Portugal, Spain and the UK – countries whose combined IMF quotas reached only $23bn, and which, under the proposed 300 per cent rule, would have been able to draw only $70bn.

At first sight, the recent Mexican crisis is perhaps a good example of the potential use of such a STFF. At $7.8bn, the initial IMF access offered to Mexico was three times the quota, and rose rapidly to $17.8 bn, or seven times the quota. Although it comprised only a third of the $50bn required for the rescue plan, it was widely regarded at the time as an impressive display of flexibility by the Fund at a time when world capital markets (or at least emerging markets) faced a systemic threat.

In retrospect, however, the episode is clearly evidence of the continued power of the US Treasury to change unwritten rules and regulations to support US investors. Furthermore, the scope of the operation (refinancing Mexican treasury bills) was such that medium-term rather than short-term resources were clearly needed.

The STFF was later re-invented by the IMF in an effort to focus on crisis prevention and re-introduced in 1998 as the Contingent Credit Lines (CCL) facility. The CCL is hoped to help countries take *ex ante* measures in a crisis by arranging commercial CCL and taking steps to extend maturities. The CCL is offered as a precautionary line of defense to countries with sound economic policies that may face balance of payments problems arising from international financial contagion. The cost of borrowing under the CCL was lowered and access to a large amount of resources in case of a crisis made more automatic. Although credits extended under the CCL are subject to the same repayment expectations and obligations as those extended under the SRF (Supplemental Reserve Facility), the initial surcharge is lower. To combat the risk of moral hazard (countries may neglect to implement sound economic policies and investors may be encouraged to lend to them) that might arise if the IMF is perceived to be too ready to provide an extra financial cushion, the CCL is available only to countries with a strong record of sound policies with well-managed external debt and whose relations with private creditors are likely to enable continued access to private credit during a crisis. The CCL also aims to ensure more effective use of IMF resources by encouraging countries to repay loans early if the financial troubles are resolved.

7.4.3 Wider Implications of the STFF

In this context, the Mexican experience did not seem very promising, as the Fund failed to warn either side adequately before the event, although leading private sector ratings agencies also failed to do so. Even after the event, the Fund was unable to pinpoint the origins of the problem, offering instead three alternative explanations for the excessive current account deficit generated by the private sector, which it had not previously considered significant (see IMF 1995: Annex I).

Several potential externalities arise from intervention on this scale. First, the potential 'crowding in' of foreign investment (due to increased confidence arising from an IMF support operation) might be accompanied by a 'crowding out' of other lending activities of the IMF.

Clearly, this is more likely to occur if the support operation were financed from the Fund's regular resources or gold sales, than if financed from another source (for instance the GAB) by special arrangement, or financed directly from the market. The problem would also be more serious if medium-term resources were tied up in this way, or if nonparticipating developing countries were expected to contribute, as they would do if, under present rules, an SDR issue were to be reallocated by G7 decision to fund the STFF.

Second, there would be a general gain if the creation of the new facility reinvigorated the IMF as part of a stronger system of global economic management, particularly if this involved active participation of industrial economies as potential beneficiaries and greater co-ordination of their macroeconomic (and hence exchange rate) policies. Co-operative handling of debt overhang, transition to market systems, and access to capital markets would benefit the country directly involved and LDCs in similar situations, through both the learning process and the enhanced investor confidence.

Third, financing of the STFF involving the provision of liquidity rather than insistence on recessionary stabilization programmes would help sustain steady global demand growth. This is distinct from the notion that large amounts of aid transferred from North to South would somehow stimulate world trade and recovery, whose expansionary effect depends entirely on how the aid is financed. Further, if private investment response in the North is perverse, it may even lead to reduced world growth and terms of trade deterioration (Vos 1994).

A logical complement to discretionary intervention for the compensation of market failure *ex post* is the reorganization of markets themselves to reduce the likelihood of such failure *ex ante*. This problem of creating 'orderly markets' is the subject of the following section.

7.5   GLOBAL CENTRAL BANKING II: PRUDENTIAL SUPERVISION

7.5.1   Capital Market Volatility and the Developing Countries

International public institutions range from securities market regulators to the Bretton Woods bodies themselves. Among other indicators, their effectiveness can be judged by their ability to maintain an orderly market and stimulate real investment, growth and employment on a global scale.

The rapid development of international financial markets in recent years has paradoxical consequences. The increased marketability of assets has led to increased liquidity, which has reduced the need for access to official borrowing in the case of most middle-income countries and many large low-income countries such as India and China. Indeed, the World Bank has experienced a *negative* net resource flow towards these countries in recent years (World Bank 1995a). Paradoxically, this liquidity has also increased systemic risk. Collapse or insolvency may be more rapidly transmitted from one market or institution to another (OECD 1991). It has been apparent for some time that this problem is particularly acute where regulatory systems have incomplete coverage or where they overlap inconsistently, creating opportunities for speculative profits. To be sure, 'there is a growing tendency to build financial links along regulatory fault lines where the responsibility for supervisory oversight is weak, divided or clouded' (Federal Reserve Bank of New York 1985).

With the exception of the European Union, the process of financial deregulation – lifting restrictions on lines of business, location, credit restrictions, capital movements and so on – has been essentially national in nature, but with pressure from Washington, financial deregulation has spread worldwide. Facilitated by technological advances, the process of financial deregulation has dramatically reduced the transactions costs involved in acquiring and managing diversified international portfolios, permitting pension funds, insurance companies and other large institutional investors to dominate cross-border capital flows.

Financial deregulation should improve the efficiency of international capital markets in two ways. First, greater competition between financial intermediaries should reduce interest rate margins and improve information flows. Second, resource allocation, whether by arbitrage or diversification, should create a wide range of assets that carry the same risk-adjusted rate of return, with all countries having access to the pool of world savings.

However, financial deregulation has also reduced the participation of banks in the financial intermediation between savers and investors, sparking a 'disintermediation' process (Dale 1992). 'Disintermediation' is associated with new threats of default by small or undercapitalized market participants due to the large and often leveraged flows involved.

Thus, there appears to be a greater need than ever for an organized settlement system that will reduce systemic risk, and for clearer rules to ensure that international banks will be able to withstand sudden demands on their resources (BIS 1994).

From the point of view of non-industrial countries, there are particular problems arising from this process. First, LDCs require greater investor protection and incentives to encourage longer-term investment. Second, LDCs face the threat of contagion from default in neighbouring regions. Third, LDCs confront additional macroeconomic instability caused by fluctuations in the narrow and shallow domestic security markets favoured by foreign capital inflows.

Stable access to international capital markets is crucial if high levels of investment are to lead to sustainable growth of output, productivity and employment, particularly under conditions of exogenous shocks. It is now well established that private investment is particularly sensitive to uncertainty about future profitability and capital costs (Dixit & Pindyck 1994). Consequently, market access stability will be as important for firms' decision-making as for governments' decision-making. For one thing, macroeconomic policy and welfare provision hinge upon external shocks (FitzGerald 1993). Certainly, the level of employment and wages appear to be highly sensitive to the size and composition of capital flows (FitzGerald & Mavrotas 1994). This point, however, is conspicuously absent from the Fund's rather simplistic model for financial programming in the construction of conditionality for IMF stabilization programmes (IMF 1987).

In principle, international capital markets can reconcile inconsistent national saving and investment plans through a system of international financial markets cleared by flexible interest rates and by asset prices that reflect risk and maturity. In practice, of course, the institutions of asset-acquiring countries use 'rules' to reflect the perceived 'quality' of assets specific to their country of origin that runs the multi-stage portfolio acquisition process (Brainard & Tobin 1992). Furthermore, this perceived asset quality is determined by expectations that vary by the type of asset in question. Foreign direct investment flows are associated with 'endogenous growth' fundamentals, bonds are associated with fiscal stances, and equities are associated with other investors' expectations. Under these conditions of asymmetric information and agency problems, this 'herd behaviour' by investors is to be expected, particularly if the investors in question are institutional managers who are re-warded according to their performance relative to other managers.

7.5.2 The BIS and a Rules-based System

The operations of the BIS – a pre-Bretton Woods institution founded in 1930 to prevent payments crisis – are in stark contrast to those of the Fund. The BIS favours the co-ordination of increasingly autonomous OECD central banks over the representation of various ministries of finance, and focuses on the maintenance of payments systems rather than on the provision of liquidity. In other words, the BIS represents the other aspect of global central banking: that of prudential regulation, which is becoming evermore important as international capital flows increasingly shift from public to private sectors.

The main objective of the BIS is to curb excessive risk-taking be-haviour by lenders *ex ante* rather than stepping in to bail out borrowers *ex post*, which appears to be the Fund's preferred course of action. To-ward this end, the BIS regulates the asset portfolios of financial inter-mediaries and co-ordinates leading central banks in crisis situations (the 1995 Mexican crisis is one instance), but refrains from making loans, save for bridging finance. In addition to important work on the regulatory system, the BIS is also an agent and trustee in international settlement systems. Nonetheless, the BIS believes there is still much scope for improvement in market transparency and market structure re-silience through disclosure and the strengthening of settlement systems (BIS 1994).

Though present Basle rules on capital adequacy apply to banks only, the BIS sees a clear need to extend these rules to securities firms, to clearly define the jurisdictions of national regulators, and to define the role of internal risk management systems. Deposit insurance and lender-of-last-resort facilities are normally only available to banks, while other intermediaries are more liable to collapse. Moreover, tradi-tional capital adequacy rules – which are based on the nature of the counterparty and the credit risk involved on individual asset classes – are unable to manage derivative trading and complex portfolios. Super-visory recognition of an institution's internal market risk management model would permit the BIS to cope with this.

The European Commission's Capital Adequacy Directive of 1993 applies to both credit institutions and securities firms, while taking cer-tain unsettled obligations into account explicitly. Certainly, the creation of a Single European Market in financial services has been a slow and difficult process. Unlike traded goods, financial services involve a series of future obligations whose eventual value is difficult for the purchaser to directly assess. Consequently, the purchaser's interests must be safeguarded legally. By accepting firms or products authorized in one member country, into another, the so-called 'passport' has helped facilitate the modification of the legal system, but nonetheless, cross-border financial services must rest upon a transnational European legal system (Lasok 1994).

The similarities between the concerns and functions of overseeing payment and settlement systems, and those of prudential regulation and supervision, have subsumed both functions (directly or indirectly) under central bank authority through a financial superintendence. Historically, both functions originate from the central bank as the ultimate supplier of a risk-free medium to the financial system. Certainly, the provision of liquidity is the last line of defense in the containment of systemic crises:

> Distinguishing solvency from mere liquidity problems is a difficult task; it becomes practically impossible without the necessary advance knowledge of the financial condition of participants ... The information needs of the central bank are an important dimension of the problem of the organisation of the lines of defence to deal with systemic risk ... [as] ... the progressive expansion in the sphere of markets and hence in trading can be expected to further heighten the risks involved in the execution of financial transactions, whether these are incurred by the counterparties to the trades or by the intermediaries facilitating their completion. (BIS 1994: 191–2).

Though both the US and the European Union are currently integrating their financial supervision systems, only the latter can provide a model for eventual global arrangements. To be sure, the model of international co-ordination between domestic security regulators, through the International Organization of Securities Commissions (IOSCO) for instance, has been unsuccessful in paralleling for securities firms what the Basle Accord has accomplished for banking, mainly because of disagreement between the US and other fifty member countries. In contrast, OECD countries have achieved considerable progress towards integrating regulations on direct foreign investment. Nonetheless, the integration of financial supervisory systems is unlikely to be extended under the WTO umbrella due to the unwillingness of LDCs to keep up the pace of liberalization set by the industrialized nations.

7.5.3 Creating an Orderly Market

The creation of an orderly market would ideally influence the three essentially subjective factors that generate considerable capital market instability: (i) national propensities for net financial saving; (ii) long-term expectations regarding the yields on assets; and (iii) attitudes toward liquidity. The creation of an orderly market would require appropriate institutional design in terms of both operational rules and discretionary intervention. Of these three factors, the first might be the proper subject of international tax regulation, while the latter two relate more to the prudential regulation of capital markets discussed in Section 7.5.2. By extension, global market stabilization would presumably relate to two crucial money values: money wages and the quantity of money. At the global level, the former would presumably relate not only to eventual nominal exchange rate stability (adjusted for productivity) but also to labour standards enacted through the WTO. Only the latter would relate to the proposed role of the IMF as provider of global liquidity in the form of bancor or SDRs.

There is a strong argument for establishing a system of 'orderly workouts' for sovereign debtors (so that creditworthiness may be restored quickly after restructuring) that is based on 'Chapter 11' US bankruptcy provisions. This system might involve the creation of a representative council for bondholders and an independent arbitral tribunal to help co-ordinate the activities of the Paris and London 'Clubs', the introduction of corresponding changes to future bond covenants, and statutory monitoring by the IMF under Article V.2.b, which empowers the IMF to perform financial and technical services if authorized to do so (Eichengreen & Portes 1995). However, this system will only be enforceable for sovereign debtors and *a fortiori* for other forms of cross-border liabilities if existing international public law is modified substantially (Greenwood & Mercer 1995).

However, the stark absence of a private international law system, despite the globalization of private trade and capital flows, severely cripples the establishment of such a system of rules. The rules that do exist (for instance, the GATT/WTO) draw from the treaty obligations of contracting states under international *public* law (Dixon 1993), whose domestic governments are responsible for regulating and representing their citizens. Indeed, the doctrine of private international law is known as the 'conflict of laws', and the principle of *lex loci delicti* generally prevails (Hill 1994). Private international law dispute settlement normally requires parties to international financial contracts to agree upon an appropriate jurisdiction, which customarily means New York. However, there appears to be a considerable lack of clarity and consistency even among New York courts regarding the appropriateness and applicability of legal principles in international commercial cases, particularly given the rapid change in market instruments, institutions and regulations (see Morris & North 1984: Chapter 30).

Furthermore, the system of 'orderly workouts' would also require a change in current Fund and World Bank practices. Currently, the Fund and the World Bank maintain that they cannot write off LDC debt, as this would damage their capital base. However, it is frequently suggested by their critics that the IMF and the World Bank can afford to write off LDC debt in its entirety through use of reserves, limited gold revaluation, and enhanced income from short-term lending to middle-income countries, without jeopardizing their credit rating. The IMF response is that total debt cancellation in the absence of full funding by bilateral donors would impair the Fund's financial integrity, credibility and ability to lend (Dawson 2001). As it is, thanks to successive restructuring during the past decade, the Fund and the World Bank are now the largest creditors for most of the poorest countries.

Without a doubt, LDCs stand to gain from a global commitment to improve the working of capital markets. Capital markets are clearly ill-equipped to clear investment and savings flows (and subsequently unable to correct current account imbalances) or properly revalue existing assets because of imperfect information and contract enforcement, which, in turn, lead to rationing behaviour by institutions. Consequently, any scheme for international monetary reform must include new provisions for *ex ante* monitoring and *ex post* workouts, for appropriate prudential regulations and information systems for such markets, and for discretionary intervention by an international central bank to provide asset-holders with liquidity when and where required.

7.6   POLICY IMPLICATIONS FOR THE IMF

7.6.1   The Requirements for Global Central Banking

Even in its most embryonic form, global central banking clearly requires a combination of crisis intervention and prudential regulation, not simply provision of liquidity as lender of last resort. In any case, liquidity in a complex global capital market is more a matter of asset preference than of money supply as such. Intervention and regulation are both relatively ineffective without each other, so that, at the very least, closer co-ordination between the IMF and the BIS is both desirable and necessary. Providing the basis for an orderly market is clearly a public good, but one which provides a strong incentive to participants in the form of the cost of exclusion.

Non-industrial countries probably have more to gain from a rule-based than from a discretionary system. Although the latter allows recognition of their special circumstances during a crisis, the former recognizes them as partners in the global system. As the experience of the Uruguay Round makes clear, establishing global rules is no easy task, and the operational benefits and lower costs of negotiation, transactions and collective action problems tend to favour regional and multicountry rule-making. In the case of capital markets, however, it is abundantly clear that in the absence of prohibitive exclusion costs, an incomplete system is an open invitation to speculation, evasion and resultant instability.

Indeed, the Bretton Woods Commission has felt that 'the time is now ripe to restore the original focus of the IMF on international monetary issues' and strongly recommended that 'the IMF should be given a central role in co-ordinating macroeconomic policies and in developing and implementing monetary reforms'. Before undertaking IMF reform, however:

> [F]irst, the major industrial countries should strengthen their fiscal and monetary policies and achieve greater overall macroeconomic convergence; and
> second, these countries should establish a more formal system of co-ordination, involving firm and credible commitments, to support these policy improvements and avoid excessive exchange rate misalignments and volatility. (BWC 1994: A-4)

While clearly desirable for member governments to pursue macro-economic stability and growth within a rule-based system that is supported and policed by global agencies such as the IMF and the OECD, it is not at all clear whether G7 government could actually implement strategic monetary and fiscal policies, even if they could agree on which policies to pursue in the first place. These difficulties arise from governments' inability to guarantee that their legislatures (which respond to domestic voter concerns) and their autonomous central banks (whose objectives are often restrictive) will implement the policies, and from growing private sector independence from domestic policy and responsiveness to international sentiment.

7.6.2 The Governance of the IMF

The current debate on the governance of the IMF rests on two related but distinct issues. One concern is that IMF directors are not sufficiently senior to take major decisions. Consequently, finance ministers must first convene before taking any major decision, which entails a high cost in terms of loss of speed and discretion that disrupts effective central banking (BWC 1994). A more regulatory stance might reduce the need for such delegates, but an enhanced international role (even as executive secretariat to some international body) would still require directors with some minimum degree of authority both among their peers and in their home government. The other is concerned with the longstanding observation that the IMF board reflects the opinions of industrial-country 'shareholders'. Even taking into account the non-industrial countries' share in world output, LDC representation should be greater, but it should not be obtained at the cost of reducing the IMF's potential power to regulate the G7 policies. Again, a more regulatory – rather than interventionist – approach would allay fears on all sides and make a balanced solution more likely. This might take the form an 'economic security' body similar to the UN Security Council with permanent G7 membership with rotating minority membership for the ROW (Stewart 1995).

The Mexican crisis is a very good example of the operational problems raised by international crisis management. To be sure, the US$50 bn underwriting of Mexico's short-term debt refinancing in early 1995 required an unprecedented degree of co-ordination between the US Treasury, the IMF, and the BIS. However, despite formal agreement on the support package at the Toronto G7 meeting, other members strongly resented what they considered to be inadequate prior consultation on an operation to acquire one-third of the Mexican debt (Griffith-Jones 2001).

Although most G7 members agreed that rapid action on this scale was required in order to stabilize international financial markets, Germany was particularly concerned by the moral hazard implicit in saving US investors from their poor judgement, while France was only mollified by retaining their control of the chair of the IMF. Britain and Germany (along with Denmark, The Netherlands, Belgium and Switzerland) abstained in the IMF vote to raise the IMF's contribution from US$7.8bn to US$17.8bn, and the scale and form of the contributions from Europe and Japan to the BIS' US$10bn commitment were never fully worked out. The EU was also extremely concerned that extra facilities for Mexico might make it more difficult for the IMF to provide large-scale loans for Russia and the Ukraine.

Monitoring the support operation remained a delicate issue. The IMF found it difficult to monitor its own US$17.8bn standby loan (indeed, the largest in its history), and would have faced further difficulties if the US Treasury and the BIS had imposed different conditions, unless they are willing to transfer these responsibilities to the IMF. The difficult issue of debt seniority also remained, with the European governments insisting that their potential 'involuntary' US$10bn contribution through BIS be given priority when Mexico began to repay.

Finally, the absence of adequate and timely information on international asset risk and the inability (or unwillingness) of markets to handle issues of long-term debt appears to have been at the very heart of the Mexican crisis, which, incidentally, the IMF neither foresaw nor forestalled. This is not an issue confined to emerging markets in the developing world with their unforeseeable political and economic shocks. The debt problem in other OECD economies, such as Korea and Turkey, required co-ordinated international action in subsequent years in order to prevent financial market instability from bringing the global economy to a standstill.

7.7   CONCLUSIONS: CAN THE IMF FULFIL ITS ORIGINAL MANDATE?

If the Fund is to fulfil its original mandate, it must set up a structure for surveillance and early warning in order to monitor and respond to emerging crises. However, it is not entirely obvious whether the IMF is the best institution for the job – the Fund's power are essentially confined to extending funding that is conditional on the fiscal and monetary policy stance of the borrowing government. It is not authorized to conduct nor impose the kind of open-market operations and temporary administrative regulation of capital flows that is required in international emergencies – powers which are normally conferred on central banks in order to cope with financial crises at the national level – nor can it conduct prudential regulation of lending institutions to control losses on unsafe asset portfolios that lead to systemic risks.

Indeed, without such powers or close co-operation with those national or international institutions which might have (or obtain) them, it is very difficult to see just how the IMF will fulfil the task with which it was entrusted at Bretton Woods: namely, that of regulating lenders and borrowers as national financial authorities do as a matter of course.

Whether the IMF is able to fulfil this role depends on whether the failure of international financial institutions to create an 'orderly market' is regarded as a public-action problem (Kapstein 1994) or as the re-establishment of hegemony in a new monetary order (Walter 1993). To the extent that existing nationally-based regulations become inadequate, and given the remote likelihood of the creation of a supranational authority and the limited capacities (and interests) of private actors, managing global capital markets will necessitate intergovernmental co-operation, but with much more far-reaching management of private actors. Intergovernmental co-operation could be achieved and enforced either through international institutions (such as the IMF or the BIS) along the lines of the WTO, or through greater willingness to enforce commonly agreed international norms within national legal jurisdictions, as is the practice in the European Community. However, in the measure in which particular national and sectoral interests press for deregulation, insist the only current problem is one of timely information and debtor discipline, and take threats posed by market disorder lightly, support for re-regulation becomes even more unlikely. Therefore, international financial regulation, and by extension a more effective role for the IMF in crisis management and prevention, might have to be constructed within a hierarchically organized world economy, similar to the structures of the trade areas within the GATT/WTO systems.

Reconstructing Global Capital
8 Markets to Support Economic
Development

8.1 INTRODUCTION

[The inter-war experience suggests that without controls on capital movements], '[l]oose funds may sweep round the world disorganising all steady business. (Keynes 1980: 25)

It is not too soon to start thinking how the system could be improved. Fresh ideas on the subject could even have a beneficial effect on how the current crisis is handled. However, that would require questioning some of the most cherished tenets of the business community. To argue that financial markets in general, and international lending in particular, need to be regulated is likely to outrage the financial community. Yet the evidence for just that is overwhelming. (Soros 1997a)

Capital markets are increasingly globalizing, even if opinions continue to differ widely regarding the origins of evident exchange rate and capital flow volatility and the proper measures to stabilize them. Without a doubt, integration to international capital markets offers considerable benefits in terms of increasing investment, growth and employment, but nevertheless there is growing concern about the deleterious impact of global capital market volatility on developing countries, and particularly the 'emerging market' economies. The second half of the 1990s saw asset deflation and currency collapse in Latin America and East Asia, raising public action issues that have also introduced broader questions of the social benefits of economic globalization in light of such extreme asymmetry between large states and firms on one hand, and small nations and the poor on the other; and, by extension, the type of institutions required for the smooth running of a truly global economy.

The expansion and rapid integration of developing countries into the global capital market is a matter of fact (World Bank 1997b), but this phenomenon is associated with the marginalization of those groups or nations that are unable to compete efficiently due to a stark lack of resources, skills or institutions (UNRISD 1995). Moreover, there are good reasons to believe that financial markets are inherently unstable, and have historically required strong institutions to control them (Kindleberger 1996). This argument is intrinsically stronger at the international level than at the national one, but international institutions for prudential financial regulation and emergency intervention are weak or non-existent in comparison with equivalent institutions at the national level, and often such regulatory mechanisms are strongest in the most advanced (and hence, more smooth-running) market economies (IMF 1998a). Even leading representatives of the 'market' caution that there is something wrong.[1]

This chapter focuses on some current policy debates on the construction of the international institutional 'architecture' from the point of view of developing countries. In Section 8.2, we address the global causes of emerging market volatility, its local consequences and the failure of international financial institutions (such as the IMF) to contain it. The current attempt to extend multilateral bank regulation towards emerging markets and its limitations are discussed in Section 8.3, while Section 8.4 examines the effectiveness of transborder mutual recognition agreements and the proposed international credit insurance scheme. Section 8.5 explores the prospects for establishing a binding set of rules for international investment with logical consequences for both global capital taxation and international debt write-offs as the basis for a long-term solution, and briefly discusses the institutional framework required to create an orderly capital market.

8.2   COPING WITH VOLATILITY IN INTERNATIONAL CAPITAL MARKETS

8.2.1   Systemic Characteristics of Flows towards Emerging Markets

Asymmetric and incomplete information characterize global capital markets. The increasing international exposure of equity funds in industrial countries and financial systems in emerging market economies has not been accompanied by a corresponding depth of information regarding the true value of assets and liabilities. The speed and scale of shock transmission between markets has increased enormously due to technological advances in trading and settlement, which forces traders to act without knowledge of wider price movements and exacerbates fluctuations. Bank lenders and portfolio investors also confront substantial agency problems. Unlike multinational corporations that are involved in direct foreign investment, bank lenders and portfolio investors can exercise little direct control over their acquired assets and thus cannot protect its market value. In the measure that banks and fund managers are unable to rely upon their own governments or on international finance institutions (IFIs) to ensure payment of their loans or maintenance of asset value, the logical response will be to avoid assets that cannot be rapidly sold if conditions take a downturn.

These information and agency problems underpin the two principal characteristics of short-term investment in emerging markets. First, international portfolio investors and bank lenders seek liquidity and use 'quick exit' to contain downside risk. In this respect, indicators such as the 'quick ratio' of a country's short-term foreign liabilities to central bank reserves become critical for market stability, as they can easily trigger self-fulfilling runs on a currency. Second, rather than controlling risk through better information or greater direct control, fund managers control risk through portfolio diversification that is determined by an assumed lack of covariance between emerging market indices. However, competition for clients between fund managers[2] drives them to seek high-yield, high-risk markets and leads them to make frequent marginal adjustments to their portfolios. However, while these adjustments to the aggregate portfolio of savers in developed countries tend to be marginal with few destabilizing effects, these adjustments may nonetheless be non-marginal with highly destabilizing effects for investment in developing countries.

The way in which financial markets clear at the aggregate levels exacerbates the effect of these behavioural characteristics, which are sometimes confusingly characterized as 'speculation'. It is now well established both in theory and in practice (UNCTAD 2000) that because of information and agency problems, financial markets are inherently 'credit-rationed': at the profit-maximizing market equilibrium, demand for funds always exceeds supply. Information and agency problems yield asset prices and interest prices that do not fully reflect risk, leading lenders to use portfolio allocation rules, and hence rationing, to reduce that risk. In the case of domestic banking, loan limits and small differentials in lending rates reflect this rationing. These loan limits, however, are based on collateral rather than on the return on the project, so that bank regulators prevent excessive portfolio bias towards individual borrowers, independent of the rate of return. Offers of high interest rates by dubious borrowers will constrain rather than expand supply of funds.

In consequence, shifts in portfolio composition (rationing rules) correspond to changes in perceptions of country solvency by international investors rather than to variations in underlying asset value. Borrowers and lenders, however, tend to be asymmetric. While emerging market assets form a relatively small part of savers' portfolios in developed countries, they represent a large part of firms' and banks' liabilities in developing countries. Therefore, marginal shifts in lenders' positions tend to destabilize borrowers' liquidity.[3] Further, herding behaviour tends to worsen these surges due to mean variance portfolio optimization as the market grows.

As the market grows and the opportunities for diversification increase, news on the allocation of funds relative to initial allocations in a single country may result in massive outflows that threaten financial stability further. Even if information on the return (or risk) on a particular asset could be acquired at a cost, the benefit arising from greater knowledge declines as the opportunities for diversification increase. This causes massive information problems as investors lack incentive to gather information, since they presume to be shielded from risk by portfolio diversification and by holding more liquid assets. Given these characteristics, prudential regulation may be required of global lenders rather than of global borrowers.

Clearly, the volatility of short-term capital flows (or 'capital surges') presents a major problem for macroeconomic management in developing countries. As we saw in Chapter 6, the precise consequences for the 'real' economy (how the behaviour of government, firms and households translates into investment, growth, employment and welfare) are not yet fully understood. Given that the implications of capital surges for longer-term growth and policy design in developing countries are considerable, international regulatory arrangements should not prevent appropriate national policies. As we have seen in Chapter 6, uncertainty affects investors' desire for liquid assets, propelling short-term capital flow instability which affects the real economy through the interest and exchange rates as well as bank credit and government bond availability, which affects output and investment, employment levels and real wages.

8.2.2 The Effectiveness of International Financial Institutions

The existing international institutional 'architecture' to cope with these problems in emerging markets is grounded in the Bretton Woods bodies and the IMF in particular. As intergovernmental institutions, the international finance institutions (IFIs) are essentially 'lenders of last resort' to developing country governments, against which facility they can impose conditionality in return for the restoration of liquidity, as we have seen in Chapter 7. Conditionality commonly involves specific monetary and fiscal policies for stabilization of the economy and structural reforms (financial reform, trade liberalization, privatization and so on) for restoration of long-term fiscal solvency. The effectiveness of this approach to the middle-income sovereign debt crises of the 1990s or to the chronic economic problems of poor economies with weak states in Africa is certainly debatable. Clearly, this approach is inappropriate for the emerging market crises of the 1990s, since the Mexican and East Asian crises were essentially related to private sector asset deflation and liquidity shortages. Large international liabilities were built up by the private sector in emerging markets to finance infrastructure and real estate, and the strong growth record and nominal exchange rate stability, which corresponded to capital inflows, led private lenders to perceive a low currency risk. At the same time, financial liberalization encouraged private borrowers to seek foreign finance. The lifting of restrictions on corporate borrowing abroad aimed to help control the balance of payments, while higher domestic interest rates made corporate borrowing abroad increasingly attractive.

Therefore, the root causes of the breakdown were not prevented (and possibly have been exacerbated) by Bretton Woods policies of accelerated financial liberalization, exchange rate anchoring and encouragement of private portfolio investment as a substitute for sovereign borrowing. The problem has been worsened by decreasing clarity and agreement as to what 'fundamentals' actually are. Once gross fiscal and monetary imbalances have been overcome, inflation is under control, growth is reasonably rapid, and market liberalization is underway; all the main indicators become positive signals for investors. Large current account deficits are seen as a sign of success in attracting foreign investment, while corporate foreign debt is seen to express financial diversification. The IFIs appear to have taken the position that as long as the external deficit reflects a private investment–savings gap rather than a fiscal deficit, it must reflect rational decisions about consumption smoothing over time and is thus sustainable. What is more, even if they had wished to prevent such inflows, their only instrument to control borrowers is last-resort lending to borrowing countries while their influence over lenders is limited to issuing negative macroeconomic evaluation with the consequent danger of market collapse.

Global surveillance is not only carried out by the IFIs. The failure of the leading private ratings agencies to predict collapse in Mexico and East Asia is notorious. There are various reasons for this, including the methodology used to construct ratings (which are largely backward- rather than forward-looking) and the natural desire not to destabilize markets.[4] In principle, if the issue were one of information as such, the ratings agency should be able to invest in better information on country risk than any one investor and then provide what is effectively a public good for a modest fee. However, in practice the problem appears to be different: on the one hand, the way in which information is used by ratings agencies seems to be deficient, being an issue of economic interpretation rather than economic statistics;[5] on the other hand, portfolio investors and banks engaged in securitizing loans to their clients rely on portfolio diversification rather than careful risk assessment to prevent losses.

To summarize, the financial collapse of emerging markets in the second half of the 1990s has three essential characteristics. First, financial instability in emerging markets is largely a 'private sector' problem

of excessive lending by private banks and non-bank financial intermediaries in developed countries to private banks and corporations in developing countries. It is not an issue of sovereign borrowing as such, as
was the case in the 1980s, and hence it is not suitable for fiscal reme-
dies or for intervention by the intergovernmental IMF. Second, given
that developing countries are credit-rationed in global capital markets –
that is to say, that their demand for funds exceeds supply at the going
rate – the level of flows are determined by the decisions of *lenders*.
Insofar as these lenders favour liquidity to reduce uncertainty, reactions
to news inevitably causes volatility. Third, the problem for lenders is
largely one of risk management: assessing the risk inherent in exchange
rates and the covariance between different elements of an emerging
market portfolio. By contrast, the problem for international authorities
is ensuring an orderly market. Of course, these disparities are also inherent in *national* financial markets, leading to strict domestic bank
supervision systems. By extension to international financial markets, a
logical alternative to the IFIs would appear to be global prudential regulation of banks engaged in cross-border operations. This issue is explored in the following section.

8.3   EXTENDING THE GLOBAL BANK REGULATION SYSTEM TO EMERGING MARKETS

8.3.1 Bank Failure outside the G10

High-profile failures of a number of financial institutions in the leading
industrialized countries[6] highlighted the need for effective international
supervisory standards. Poor supervision of financial institutions in
emerging markets also poses a serious risk to the international financial
system. The globalization of financial markets and the resulting linkages between national financial system have heightened the risk of contagion spreading from emerging market banking systems to the international financial system with unpredictable, but potentially serious,
results. Moreover, the costs of rectifying problems resulting from a
banking crisis present a significant obstacle to the economic progress of
developing economies. Pervasive lapses in sound banking practice in
developing countries have been highlighted not only by the Asian crisis
but also by banking sector fragility in Latin America.[7] Meanwhile, persistent doubts regarding the soundness of banking systems in Russia

due to limited availability of fiscal resources for the support of ailing banks were later confirmed with the 1998 crisis.

A growing number of industrial and industrializing countries outside the G10 employ the Basle Capital Accord standards. This trend[8] is likely to be reinforced by publication of the Basle Committee on Banking Supervision 'Core Principles for Effective Banking Supervision' (reproduced in IMF 1998a), which established best practice for bank regulators in all jurisdictions. Amid increasing concerns about the systemic risks posed by ineffective banking supervision in emerging markets, the Basle Committee itself is seeking to extend its reach beyond the G10 countries, reflecting continuing concerns about the quality and effectiveness of banking supervision. Given the characteristics of emerging markets, the extension of Basle standards – which were originally designed for the industrial economies – to these markets has proved problematic. Poorly developed accounting systems and inadequate information on the quality of bank assets hamper the adjustment of bank capital for non-performing loans in emerging markets. In East Asia, for instance, the parlous financial position of supposedly well-capitalized local banks during the crisis was disguised by a failure to recognize the poor quality of their loan portfolios (BIS 1998).

8.3.2 Cross-border Supervision

In October 1996, the Basle Committee issued a report on 'The Supervision of Cross-border Banking', which had been agreed upon with the Offshore Group of banking supervisors, representing 19 offshore financial centres, including Hong Kong, Singapore, the Cayman Islands and the Isle of Man. The report provided a checklist of principles for effective consolidated supervision to ensure that no internationally active banking group escaped the oversight of a regulator capable of effectively supervising its global operations, including a number of Core Principles by which to assess the quality of supervision in financial centers.[9] More importantly, the report emerged from the formal recognition by the Basle Committee that agreement among the leading industrialized countries alone was no longer sufficient to preserve the integrity of the international financial system in an increasingly integrated global economy. Significantly, banking supervisors from 140 countries endorsed the report at the biannual International Conference of Banking Supervisors in Stockholm.

The Core Principles develop the standards outlined in the report on cross-border banking supervision in greater and more prescriptive detail.[10] In addition, the Principles emphasize the freedom to share information between national banking supervisors and their overseas counterparts for more effective supervision of banking supervision on a global consolidated basis. However, even with greater information-sharing and consolidated supervision, it is likely that 'fault lines' between regulatory jurisdictions will remain, with considerable potential for both profit-making and bank failure.

To extend the reach of its standards to emerging markets, the Committee's Core Principles were drawn up in close co-operation with a group of non-G10 supervisory authorities.[11] One particularly sensitive area for developing countries concerns the supervisory arrangements for state-owned banks. When a bank is state-owned, the regulators may be reluctant to close it or take corrective action when the government is known to stand behind it; this problem is identifies as 'regulatory forbearance' by the Committee. Similarly, the management of state-owned institutions may take excessive risks knowing that taxpayer funds will be made available to rectify their mistakes. Implicitly, the same principles would logically extend to large domestic *private* banks with a privileged relationship to governments.

8.3.3 The Limitations of the Basle Approach

Recent developments have forced the Basle Committee to rethink its traditional approach. Traditionally, the Basle Committee relied on the willingness of non-G10 countries to voluntarily adopt its standards, but this approach is clearly woefully inadequate to cope with modern capital markets. First, national financial systems are becoming increasingly integrated. Second, the very structure of capital flows is changing over time. Now a larger proportion of private short-term capital flows (that is, excluding official flows and direct foreign investment by multinational corporations) take the form of negotiable securities rather than bank credits as such. Third, a great part of these securities are marketed by banks or by securities houses with links to these banks, so that the final purchaser may not be fully aware of the fact that the risk is not being borne by the bank at all. Consideration of these factors has led to a more prescriptive approach by the Basle Committee in the Core Principles.

These Core Principles form the basis of the 'Framework for Financial Stability' (IMF 1998a) supported by the Bretton Woods institutions. Increased surveillance of member countries' financial systems by the Fund and the Bank is intended to provide the kind of enforcement mechanism currently missing from the G10 framework. Nevertheless, the *international* dimension again limits itself mainly to *borrowing* banks that then lend domestically.

In 1996, Brazil, China, Hong Kong, India, South Korea, Mexico, Russia, Saudi Arabia and Singapore were invited to become members of the BIS. Although the BIS has no regulatory function as such, membership of the Basle Committee (which is comprised of member central banks and other supervisory agencies) does mean the acceptance of best practice as well as a minor part in the setting of global regulatory policy. However, it would seem appropriate for the BIS to take a more active position. Nonetheless, the political sensitivities implicit in supervisory standards assessment have meant that the BIS has been reluctant to undertake this role. This hesitation is doubtless reinforced by the unwillingness of the US Treasury to relinquish the power of cross-border intervention to a body that it does not control and to a body where agreement must be reached with Europe and Japan in particular, and in future with major powers such as China and Russia as well.

In consequence, under US leadership the IMF has expanded its regular Article IV consultations with member countries to examine the quality of domestic banking supervision (IMF 1998b). Similarly, IMF pressure for capital account liberalization and constitutional reform to enforce this for all member countries is intended to enhance its capacity to control financial policies beyond the present conditionality imposed on countries requesting last-resort lending or Enhanced Structural Adjustment Facilities (ESAFs).

However, the IMF has relatively little experience in financial surveillance and has made serious mistakes in its emergency policy packages in East Asia (FitzGerald 1998). The BIS hosted the International Association of Insurance Supervisors (IAIS) in 1996, but has not yet managed to extend its mandate beyond banking towards other global financial intermediaries. Although this gives the BIS the potential to supervise non-bank financial intermediaries as well as banks, the political will to exercise this power still depends on whether the US will have enough foresight to cede authority to a truly multilateral institution. There are few signs of the US changing its perception as yet, and with Europe preoccupied with the initiation of European Monetary Union and Japan embroiled in its own financial crisis, there is insufficient momentum for international pressure to resolve the impasse.

8.4   CONTRARY RESPONSES

8.4.1 Mutual Regulatory Recognition

The US alternative to financial regulation rests on mutual regulatory recognition. Under this arrangement, foreign banks, security houses and the like would be permitted to operate in the US only if their domestic regulatory authorities have been certified to be competent. For instance, doubts regarding the competence of Korean bank regulators would lead to the refusal to grant or renew licenses for operation in the US to Korean bank subsidiaries.

However, there are two problems inherent in this approach. First, this system could be used as a form of disguised protection for US banks. These would be tempted to lobby for excessively strict controls to be placed on foreign banks, particularly in view of the increased competition unleashed by the ongoing liberalization process.[12] Second, this approach would also increase the extraterritorial power of the US Securities and Exchange Commission (SEC) and the Federal Reserve and oblige them to extend their supervisory powers overseas dramatically. Thus, it would expose US monetary authorities to claims from US investors if there happened to be a crisis in an emerging market whose regulatory system had been certified competent.

This approach nevertheless has two principal attractions. One is that it provides a very powerful incentive for the regulatory authorities of leading emerging market economies to act in a more rigorous and transparent manner. The other is that it avoids both the diplomatic complications of constructing multilateral supervisory arrangements through, for instance, the IMF or the BIS, and the anticipated opposition of an increasingly isolationist Congress to greater pooling of US economic sovereignty toward international institutions. Therefore this approach is implicit in many multilateral trade agreements and the 'mutual recognition agreements' (MRAs) upon which most bilateral treaties on services trade are based.

8.4.2 Regional Monetary Co-operation

Reassessment of regional rescue arrangements has led to the emergence of an alternative form of international financial regulation. For instance the rescue packages assembled for Thailand, Indonesia and South Korea were sponsored by the IMF but reflected US policy objectives. In this case, the Clinton administration sought to simultaneously protect US investors in the region while maximizing pressure on East Asian countries to open their financial services markets to US banks and insurance companies. In doing so, it exploited and even to some extent, inspired the Fund's attempts to make emergency financing for countries in the region conditional upon capital market liberalization. Consequently, the reluctance of East Asian governments to cede ownership of domestic financial intermediaries to foreign investors has renewed interest in regional arrangements for monetary co-operation.

At least in the short term, however, the US administration has successfully sidelined proposals to create an Asian Monetary Fund with an emergency financing facility independent of the IMF. Although Washington is anxious to ensure that regional monetary arrangements do not undermine the IMF's role by circumventing the conditionality attached to the Fund's own lending, the US Congress nevertheless remains unenthusiastic about enhanced international financial co-operation, even if centred on the IMF.

Financial turbulence in Latin America has also reinforced the perceived need for greater monetary co-ordination. Within the NAFTA, the US Congress has been reluctant to establish formal institutional mechanisms, although in the wake of the 1995 peso crisis, the three central banks became engaged in closer operational co-ordination in practice. In the Mercosur, although there do exist institutional forums for economic co-ordination, tariff harmonization and infrastructure provision have dominated capital flows issues. Fortunately, financial market integration has stimulated greater interest in the harmonization of financial regulatory rules and macroeconomic co-ordination (FitzGerald & Grabbe 1997).

Although the European Union itself does not have a policy for intergovernmental financial regulation and relies on MRAs, once the European Central Bank settles down, it will be a major player in international finance among the developed countries (FitzGerald & Grabbe 1997). Presumably a 'global G3' of quasi-autonomous central banks such as the EBC, the Federal Reserve and the Bank of Japan will emerge in the longer run, once Japan addresses its domestic problems and is able to focus toward international issues. The current move to include Russia, China, Brazil and India in the OECD also implies a greater capacity for regulatory co-ordination.

8.4.3   An International Credit Insurance Corporation?

The third alternative to global bank regulation is an 'International Credit Insurance Corporation' (ICIC) as a sister institution to the IMF (Soros 1997a). This institution would monitor and guarantee international loans, and evaluate the risks involved in investing in a particular country. Borrowers would be required to provide details of all public and private loans to the ICIC and thus to the market, and on the basis of this information, the ICIC would set a strict ceiling on the amount of credit it was prepared to insure.[13] By guaranteeing international loans 'for a modest fee', the ICIC could generate over time the resources required to cover normal risks, as does any other insurance system. However, its initial capitalization would consist of SDRs issued for this purpose, which would 'render its guarantees watertight' from the start. Although the issuance of SDRs might potentially add to the global money supply, it would not be inflationary because the SDRs would only be drawn under conditions of a major international default. Should a country exceed the safe borrowing limits, the ICIC would then cease its guarantees, thus preventing excessive inflows. However, it is unclear whether loans to private banks and corporations in emerging markets would be insured in addition to sovereign risk, but given the nature of recent crises, the former would have to be included.

Essentially, the ICIC appears to be a combination of an export credit guarantee scheme and an official ratings agency with a capitalization comparable to the existing Bretton Woods institutions. Insurance schemes such as the Multilateral Investment Guarantee Agency (MIGA) already exist, of course, but their scope is extremely limited by the assets covered (direct investment) and by their small market share, and so they are marginal to global financial crises. Similarly, export credit guarantee schemes are confined largely to supporting credit (not market) risk to national capital goods exporters (DAC 1998). In any case, they are in secular decline.

The ICIC, however, faces two technical[14] difficulties that threaten its viability. First, the existing private ratings agencies and the intergovernmental agencies (such as the IMF) that are responsible for monitoring have a poor record in assessing national debt solvency, and one need only to look at the Mexican, East Asian and Russian crises for dramatic evidence. It is not yet clear how the ICIC would be able to gather more and better information than that which is presently available, assess this information more effectively, or downgrade countries without causing panic. Second, any insurance scheme involves risk pooling (which assumes low covariance between clients' risk) as a mechanism to prevent adverse selection and moral hazard. However, adverse selection would arise because preceding a crisis, the major borrowers already enjoy access to international capital markets at prime rates, so that the client base of the ICIC would draw from poor, insolvent countries. Similarly, moral hazard would arise in complex negotiations (equivalent to IMF conditionality) between the ICIC and countries requesting access to or avoiding exclusion from the scheme. Finally, the problem with major financial crises lies precisely in that they are highly contagious and affect a number of countries or a whole region at once (in other words, these countries or regions share high-risk covariance). Clearly, this would leave the ICIC dangerously exposed.

Nevertheless, the funding of this scheme (or of any other last-resort lending program) through the issue of SDRs is extremely attractive. First, in view of the scale of capital availability required (presumably at least US$100bn), sufficient funding would be virtually impossible to raise from the budgetary resources of the member governments but could be provided in the form of a conditional right to issue SDRs immediately in a crisis situation. Certainly, this would have made intervention in the Mexican, East Asian and Russian crises more rapid and, hence, more effective. Second, as noted above, the effect of adding liquidity to the world economy through a major SDR issue would not be inflationary but rather stabilizing, since major international crises involve large-scale asset deflation. Moreover, these loans could be repaid quickly by central banks or replaced by longer-term borrowing in the post-crisis recovery.

8.5 AN ALTERNATIVE APPROACH TO CAPITAL VOLATILITY

8.5.1 International Investment Rules

Over the past decade, developing countries have embarked on an unprecedented unilateral liberalization of their investment regimes and made significant strides toward stability, transparency and objectivity in policymaking to enhance the credibility of the new economic regime, including central bank independence and accession to international agreements. International investment agreements, for example, aim to 'lock in' this liberalization, thereby encouraging investor confidence in regulatory environments. International agreements – such as bilateral investment treaties, double taxation treaties, regional trade agreements and certain WTO provisions – also build investor confidence by 'locking in' policy commitments over time (WTO 1997). In particular, there is a close relationship between trade and investment agreements at the bilateral, regional and multilateral levels.

The accelerating trend towards bilateral, regional and multilateral arrangements for investment regulation (UNCTAD 1997) reflects a shift in emphasis from national rights to foreign investment control and norms for corporate conduct. These new agreements are usually based on general standards of treatment coupled with norms on specific matters such as the expropriation, compensation and transfer of funds and the mechanisms for international dispute settlement.

A Multilateral Agreement on Investment (MAI) was under negotiation at the OECD between developed countries with the prospect of accession for developing countries in 1993-99 (FitzGerald et al. 1998). It was based on existing bilateral arrangements in general and NAFTA provisions in particular and contained strong guarantees of property rights and investor recognition. Membership of the MAI would have had strong positive effects in stabilizing short-term flows by encouraging investors to shift away from liquid assets towards fixed investment and by reducing banks' uncertainty regarding the sovereign risk involved in lending. Furthermore, the MAI would have prevented neither appropriate measures to ensure monetary and fiscal stability nor control of short-term capital flows for balance of payments purposes, and would have provided more security for longer-term direct investment. However, the MAI negotiations broke down in 1999 due to opposition from the EU over US insistence on the liberalization of public services provision. It was also fatally flawed by the exclusion of developing countries from the negotiations, which were the main objects of the new discipline. A similar approach will be taken up in the WTO, with the added advantage that developing countries will be directly represented, in the 'Millennium Round', which is planned to start in 2002.

However, the reduction of capital flow volatility to developing countries through international investment rules faces two major shortcomings. First, taxing international capital to provide fiscal resources for social investment will prove difficult and unpopular. Second, working off the existing sovereign debt overhang increases uncertainty regarding national solvency. Unless these problems are resolved, it is difficult to see how international investment rules can stabilize capital flows to developing countries.

8.5.2 Global Capital Taxation

Global capital taxation offers another approach to capital flow control. Most developed countries enter bilateral tax agreements among themselves, but unfortunately not with many developing countries. Moreover, both the MAI and foreseeable WTO arrangements on investment fail to address international investment taxation. Only with implementation of a multilateral tax agreement (possibly drawing from the model treaty proposed by the OECD) would the legal framework of international investment be complete. A multilateral tax agreement would not only improve the fiscal revenue position of developing countries and reduce the attractiveness of tax incentives to foreign investors, but would strengthen efforts to combat money laundering and financial fraud as well by stabilizing financial flows.

However, from an individual country's point of view, corporate profits are difficult to tax for two reasons. First, capital is characteristically mobile, and as such, high tax rates can drive it abroad or deter the investment from occurring in the first place, leading to downward fiscal competition between developing countries and a lower average tax rate. Second, companies can accrue profits in the lowest tax jurisdictions ('tax havens') by arranging their international transactions appropriately, companies can accrue profits in the lowest tax jurisdictions, which reduces the tax burden on capital. In both cases, to the extent that the tax revenue would have been used for social infrastructure investment or effective poverty relief,[15] there is a clear loss in global welfare.

To be sure, effective multilateral taxation of corporate profits (or perhaps of dividends, if it is desired to promote the reinvestment of profits within firms) has become a topic of increasing concern to developed countries in recent years, with active proposals from the OECD for a multilateral tax treaty. In addition, there are current moves to establish withholding taxes in major financial centers in order to reduce the tax loss on the profits generated there. In order to strengthen this process of fiscal capture, it will become necessary to eliminate tax havens and, at the very least, deny the benefits of international investor protection to firms registered there.

If such a multilateral tax treaty were to include developing countries, it would confer a number of advantages. First, it would prevent wasteful tax competition between developing countries in order to attract foreign investors. Second, as all tax paid in developing countries is deductible against tax liability in (developed) home countries, increased effectiveness in tax collection by developing countries would be a net transfer between the treasuries of home and host country – far more effective than the present system of development assistance. Third, this would provide a stable source of long-term funding for the public investment in education, health and infrastructure that developing countries require.

Such an approach would have several advantages over proposals for a so-called 'Tobin tax' on short-term financial transactions.[16] A turnover tax would have little effect on speculative flows, because at any feasible rate it would imply a penalty of marginal importance compared to the prospective losses from maintaining asset-holdings in a currency under attack. In addition, it would be very difficult to collect in view of the complexity, speed and substitutability of cross-border currency transactions, leaving aside the problem of offshore transactions. In contrast, multilateral corporate taxation can be based on the statutory requirement to present accounts in some jurisdiction in order to satisfy shareholders. The other apparent attraction of the Tobin tax is to provide resources for international development assistance in general and for the UN in particular. However, aside from the fact that there are easier forms of raising international taxation,[17] the major barrier is clearly political: the unwillingness of national legislatures to devote more funds to aid or, *a fortiori*, to the United Nations. In contrast, a multilateral corporate tax agreement already has considerable support among developed countries; it only requires the co-ordination of existing bilateral tax treaties and would not require a new instrument. It would also deliver resources to developing country governments rather than to an international body, and not require, in principle, a new international bureaucracy to administer it. The alternative is for national tax systems to be gradually forced back on the taxation of the immobile factor of production: labour.

8.5.3 International Sovereign Debt

One of the essential reasons for the volatility of capital flows is doubt about the solvency of particular developing countries, as we saw in Chapter 6. It is evident that the failure of traditional structural adjustment programs to revive private investment, both foreign and domestic, on a sustainable basis is closely connected to persistent sovereign debt overhang. Similarly, the failure of recent IMF interventions in East Asia and Mexico are related to the failure to recognize and correct private debt problems. In the commercial world, of course, insolvent companies are placed under new management and the unserviceable debt is written off by the creditors. There is, however no equivalent in international sovereign debt matters (Eichengreen & Portes 1995).

In fact, the process of financial intervention in developing countries by the Bretton Woods institutions has led to the transfer of sovereign debt from commercial creditors to the IFIs themselves. Once so refinanced, it has become almost impossible to write off. The current HIPC (Heavily Indebted Poor Countries) initiative (DAC 1998) is both insufficient in scale and too lengthy in process to make a substantive contribution to the reduction of investor uncertainty. The main reason given for not cancelling this debt is one of 'moral hazard'.[18] The other justification – that cancellation would reduce the IFIs credit ratings and thus ability to mobilize further development resources – is wholly implausible because the ratings depend not on the quality of lending but underwriting provided by the member governments. In other words, IFI borrowing on international capital markets is secured against fiscal receipts in *developed* rather than developing countries.

The concept of moral hazard in this context refers to the belief that if developing country sovereign debt is cancelled, than their governments – freed from the external constraint – will return to policies unamicable to the promotion of private investment. However, the existence of a large international public debt overhang in a considerable number of the poorer developing countries also represents a major constraint on further foreign investment on any significant scale – due to the uncertainty caused by the prospect of severe stabilization measures in order to meet debt service, or the sovereign risk inherent in debt default. This debt overhang is thus a major disincentive to private foreign investors, due to the uncertainty it causes. The accession of a country to an international investment arrangement and a multilateral tax agreement, if combined with a write-off of old debt, could guarantee *future* private debt and thus constitute a form of conditionality more conducive to private sector development than the present systems operated by the IMF and other international financial institutions.

8.5.4 'Missing Institutions'

Any long-term view of the development of international investment regulation as a means of underpinning an equitable flow of capital towards developing countries must logically confront these four issues. They underline the large gaps in the institutional arrangements which the experience of constructing orderly financial markets in developed countries suggests might be necessary to contain the negative effects of global financial instability on developing countries. However, the problem is not just how the existing arrangements might be improved. Rather the logical question is what a desirable structure would look like. The obvious approach is to determine what institutions have proved necessary in developed market economies. The lessons to developing countries include:

First, the need for core central banking functions of providing liquidity to the market, including last-resort lending under distress conditions in order to support otherwise sound banks and prevent contagion. This is the putative function of the IMF. At present, however, it has insufficient funds, is only empowered to lend to governments (or their central banks), and cannot deal directly with global or local banks.

Second, the need for collective provision of prudential regulation of financial intermediaries. This would not only prevent fraud but also discourage imprudent behaviour and protect vulnerable consumers of financial products. To some extent this service is provided by the Basle system, but it only covers major banks, leaving the greater part of global financial intermediaries still unregulated.

Third, the need for recognition of a small number of leading financial institutions ('market-makers') who in principle stand ready to buy and sell assets at the current price. These 'market-makers' create 'depth', encourage market stability, and may be called upon to take over the operations insolvent financial intermediaries when necessary. These institutions do not exist in the global market, although they could emerge as international banking and securities management becomes more concentrated. However, there is little indication of how they might be co-ordinated.

Fourth, the need for a sound and transparent legal system that secures contracts and provides for efficient dispute settlement between contracting parties and between financial intermediaries and the regulators. This does not exist at the international level; indeed, international investors have no status other than in municipal jurisdictions with little legal recourse in solving investment disputes other than essentially political mechanisms.

Notes

CHAPTER 1

1. I would like to thank the MacArthur Foundation for support to the research program at the Finance and Trade Policy Research Centre on which this book is based.

2. This is the perspective set out by the OECD countries (see DAC 1998, OECD 1998b).

3. The reasons are, of course, largely political. Nonetheless, it is striking how few (if any) libertarian advocates of an unregulated global economy are willing to mention, let alone propose, the free movement of labour. Incidentally, it is not clear that if immigration controls were lifted, there would in fact be an unmanageable (say, more than ten per cent) mass movement from South to North.

4. Wood (1994) lays this argument out in a neo-Ricardian trade framework.

5. Alternatively, we might consider that skilled labour has considerable externalities and thus there are scale economies from which individual members benefit beyond their own marginal product, and that skilled labour requires a specific 'social infrastructure' (such as education) for support, in which case we reach a formulation similar to that given here.

6. Supposing unitary elasticity between per capita income growth and relative poverty, then per capita incomes would have to double over 20 years, or grow at four per cent per annum in order to reach the DAC target of halving the proportion (but not the number) of poor people in developing countries by 2020. However, this is far beyond the track record of poor countries and not far off that of pre-crisis East Asia. In contrast, since the poor receive only one per cent of world income, a transfer of one per cent of the income of industrial countries

174

(or one half of one per cent of world GDP) would double their average incomes immediately. However, clearly there is no support for social transfers of this scale, let alone for the build-up of social overhead capital on the scale required.

7. For a formal model of the 'asset value of citizenship' and a preliminary approximation of its financial valuation, see FitzGerald & Cuesta-Leiva (1998).

CHAPTER 2

1. Whereby individuals are assumed to maximize the present value of their utility subject to a budget constraint that is equal to their current net worth plus the present value of their expected income over the rest of their life.

2. Econometric results indicate, however, that differences in age structure and income growth are the only significant variables (see Dean, Durand, Fallon & Heller 1990, Bosworth 1993).

3. However, the US savings rate in the 1980s was not really low if measured as the change in the real market value of assets; once capital gains on direct investment are included, the current account deficit is an illusion (see Barro 1989). The reverse could be said of the Japanese surplus in the 1990s.

4. This conclusion is hardly surprising once the ambiguous implications for wealth and income in the overlapping-generations model are taken into account (see Blanchard & Fischer 1989).

5. It is interesting to note that all discussion of national savings is in terms of rates (for instance, domestic saving as a proportion of GDP). This method implies acceptance of Ricardian (or perhaps even Keynesian) savings propensities rather than the strictly neoclassical funds market, which would involve the tracking of absolute amounts.

6. Hutchinson (1992) also points out that the concept of a long-run 'balanced budget' should go beyond the simple cross-cyclical view to include contingent liabilities such as welfare entitlements. This would imply that existing measures of the private savings offset overstate the extent to which the private sector actually incorporates the government's budget constraint in its decision making.

7. Indeed, cross-section studies of private savings behaviour indicate that real interest rates are not a significant determinant. Furthermore, the

effect of demographic factors on saving varies greatly across countries for no readily explicable reason (see Aghevli et al. 1990 and Bosworth 1993).

8. The global current account discrepancy – which approximately equals the current account discrepancy in the IMF balance of payments statistics – is of the order of US$100bn in 1990 (IMF 1992a). This figure is relatively small in comparison with estimated global saving of US$5 trillion in 1991 (IMF 1992b). However, it is still large in comparison with the investment–savings balances (or the current account balances) of major economies such as the US or Japan, thus making empirical discussion of international capital flows difficult. On this accounting problem, see Vos (1989) and de Jong, Vos, Jellema & Zebregs (1993).

9. See de Jong, Vos, Jellema & Zebregs (1993) for the 'World Accounting Matrix' methodology, developed from Vos (1989), based on Stone's original proposals for SAM matrix balancing according to the relative reliability of statistical sources. In the case of the US and the UK, such balancing produces a major reduction in the current account deficit once the flows are reconciled.

10. Whereas under the Bretton Woods system of fixed exchange rates, capital flows were still relatively small and taking place between central banks, so that savings and investment still moved together in most large economies. This arrangement was purposeful and aimed to avoid some of the issues that had arisen under the Gold Standard (see Moggridge 1992).

11. In the neoclassical view, which forms the basis for IMF stabilization policy, a fall in public sector savings can lead to a rise in private savings, because the increase in the public sector borrowing requirement drives up interest rates. If the public sector's borrowing requirement is constrained in a closed economy, private savings can increase through an increase in the money supply and the subsequent real balance effect. In the small open economy, the effect is felt through an inflow of foreign savings in the monetary approach to the balance of payments.

12. For a model of international debt adjustment that traces the impact of the source of aid finance, see Vos (1994).

13. Indeed, the analysis of the demands and supplies of different categories of assets, both foreign and domestic, a central contribution of the application of portfolio theory to understanding the implications of international capital movements (see Brainard & Tobin 1992).

14. Brainard & Tobin (1992) supply the concept of 'home bias' as a form of liquidity preference in this approach, but the model itself remains a theory of one country's capital account and does not allow for interaction between portfolio preferences of various countries.

15. However, when capital markets and domestic monetary policies become 'misaligned', enormous short-term capital flows are generated and exchange rates come under intense pressure until the short-term rates adjust accordingly. Whether this lack of independence in domestic monetary policy is considered to be good or bad depends on one's opinion of governments' ability to make sound macroeconomic judgements, but certainly lack of monetary policy independence has left autonomous central banks with very little real maneuvering room.

16. The IMF admits this explicitly (see Goldstein & Mussa 1993).

17. In this respect, the effect of interest rates on capital flows appears to have an advantage over its effect on trade. A dramatic surge in exports would allow for current account adjustment whilst avoiding asset adjustment, but exchange rates fail to affect trade flows sufficiently or rapidly enough. In practice, the response of exchange rate adjustment to domestic interest rate differentials only allows for a margin of risk of no greater than five percentage points.

18. The fall in personal savings rates in OECD is due, in part, to demographic factors.

19. For instance, to finance the infrastructure requirements of Eastern Europe, Asia and Latin America.

Chapter 3

1. This chapter is based on my own research originally published as a chapter in Arestis & Sawyer (1997).

2. Similarly, Keynesian theory has much to contribute toward the integration of welfare criteria such as employment and sustainable growth into macroeconomic analysis, but this falls outside the scope of this chapter.

3. However, this anomaly can be explained theoretically in terms of the externalities captured either by foreign investors from human capital and infrastructure provision or by asymmetric information and agency problems (see Lucas 1990).

4. Indeed, addressing important issues such as shock transmission, segmentation in international trade and finance, market regulation by discretion versus rules, global economic co-ordination, or aid as a response to global market failure and global social security entitlement, would probably have to refer to recent work on global hegemony (see Walter 1993). Legal scholarship on the regulation of banks and other financial intermediaries would help clarify the rules within which agents operate, and the feasibility of containing systemic risk on a global scale, including the scope for international fiscal and regulatory legislation from which developing countries might benefit.

5. See IMF (1987) for canonical statements. Khan, Montiel & Haque (1990) present an interesting attempt to synthesize the analytical approaches of the World Bank and the Fund.

6. It is worth noting that Dornbusch chose the 'Australian' over the 'Scandinavian' version of the model. The former has neoclassical microeconomic foundations while the latter has fixed technological coefficients and does not require full-employment assumptions. The latter version is possibly of more relevance to most developing economies.

7. A separate but related question is why this model gained such widespread acceptance among policymakers in developing countries. Although their role in the formulation of economic doctrine should not be underestimated, the power of influence of the Bretton Woods institutions is unlikely to have been entirely responsible for the model's dissemination. The model's predominance is more likely due to the lack of a coherent and viable alternative policy model coupled with the need to maintain credibility in global capital markets (including aid agencies).

8. To be sure, the neo-structuralist theory of development macroeconomics shares close parallels the post-Keynesian critique of macroeconomics applied to industrial economies (see FitzGerald 1993).

9. Bacha (1990) develops the familiar 'two-gap' model still used by the World Bank to illustrate that the burden of the external debt determines which of the three gaps (savings, foreign exchange or budgetary) will bind, and to conclude that policies based on a single macroeconomic theory can easily have perverse effects.

10. Bevan, Collier & Gunning (1990) even subtitle their influential text 'a neoclassical approach to structuralism.'

11. Wood (1994) argues that *ex-post* rates of return are consequently similar in industrialized and developing countries.

12. Measured savings differ from changes in net worth because changes in asset values are not included in standard definitions of income and thus excluded implicitly from savings once consumption is subtracted. Hicks' definition of income equates it to the maximum value that a household (or other economic unit) can consume during a given period while remaining as well off as it was at the beginning of the period (see Hicks 1946). For discussion of the application of national accounting procedures at the global level, see Vos & de Jong (1995).

13. This is the case because saving rates vary widely over space and time.

14. Here the use of 'forced savings' to finance higher public investment levels through inflationary and real balance effects is excluded as being (at best) a Kaldorian rather than a Keynesian proposition.

15. Although this idea quite possibly originated from Pasinetti rather than from Keynes, it seems to fit into the same category. Incidentally, despite efforts to test the validity of the respective multipliers empirically that have failed to support the proposition, it continues to reemerge.

16. Rather than establishing complex schemes for sterilizing exogenous shocks, there is a case for adopting the old-fashioned rule of treating positive external shocks as temporary and negative, using the Keynesian approach to probability as the logical response to uncertain information about the future.

17. Including the Tinbergen-Kaldor proposal for a commodity-based currency reserve system that was put forward at the first UNCTAD Conference in 1964 as an explicit scheme to reduce volatility. I am indebted to Hans Singer for this point.

18. Arguably, the equivalent of the reduction of debt by a capital levy in the Treatise, as proposed in UNCTAD (1993).

19. This issue is highly relevant to Latin America and Southern Europe. The hope that the UK might escape this fate by leaving the ERM proved illusory for the simple reason that of all global capital markets, the bond markets are the most efficiently integrated.

CHAPTER 4

1. This chapter is concerned with the group of semi-industrial economies defined by Chenery that roughly correspond to 'middle-income countries' in World Bank terminology. This group includes most of Latin America and Asia in addition to Eastern Europe, but excludes much of Africa and aid-dependent economies in general (FitzGerald 1993).

2. For discussion of the data, see Pfeffermann & Madarassy (1992), Fitz-Gerald & Sarmad (1990), Serven & Solimano (1992), also Chapter 5.

3. Edwards & van Wijnbergen (1989) offer a general summary; Addison (1989) and IMF (1987) are the canonical texts. For an interesting attempt to synthesize these models, see Khan, Montiel & Haque (1990). Tanzi (1991) examines the standard view on the public finance aspects.

4. As it does in the 'Cambridge' approach, although demand for financial assets is based on a criteria of stock adjustment of privately held financial assets to the level of the autonomous component of GDP, rather than monetary flow concepts (see Godley & Cripps 1983).

5. This chapter does not consider the highly relevant issue of capital flight directly. Rather, capital flight should be considered an issue of financial asset substitution (primarily by rentier households) rather than as a direct portfolio trade-off between fixed investment and foreign currency. In other words, the private investment decision is assumed to be separate from the composition of financial wealth, as in McKinnon (1973) and Dornbusch (1980), as well as the more explicitly Keynesian Odagiri (1981).

6. On the 'crowding-in' effect, see Taylor (1983), Bacha (1990) and Pradhan, Ratha & Sarma (1990); Khan & Reinhart (1990) and Sarmad (1990) offer differing viewpoints on the relative contributions of public and private investment to aggregate growth.

7. Further, the World Bank's condition of loans to parastatal corporations on tariff and other reforms cannot be viewed as a commercial transaction because the service of the loan remains the responsibility of the central government.

8. At best, MNCs financial strategy aims to minimize the cost of capital rather than maximize shareholder wealth (see Grimwade 1989, Eitman & Stonehill 1979).

9. Indeed, 'even owner-managers often seem to be more interested in the growth of the firms than they do in the income they withdraw from it' (Penrose 1959).

10. In practice, there is a continuum of medium-size (competitive) firms down through the scale to microenterprises as defined here; the separation is for the purpose of discussion alone.

11. This assumes prudential behaviour by banks or their regulators, which is often conspicuously absent in LDCs.

12. Chamberlain (1990) argues this for the USA.

13. The effect of relative price changes will have a different effect on the microenterprise than it would on companies. A decline in real wages is unlikely to directly affect microenterprises using family labour.

14. Excepting remittances from overseas employment, which might be considered as the result of a household 'investment'.

15. 'Involuntary balances' arising from the rationing of consumption goods in an administered economy are excluded from consideration here, since this can only be of transitional importance and usually rapidly reduced by inflation on market liberalization.

16. This shift is seen as desirable, however, because the formal sector is assumed to use the funds more efficiently, thereby raising the growth rate (see Galbis 1977).

17. In fact, much of the 'boom' on LDC capital markets seems to have been related to the offer of public sector bonds at high interest rates to avoid monetary emission limits. In turn, this may affect not only the financial asset portfolios but also the incomes of rentier families in our model.

18. Mayer sees relationships between German and Japanese banks and clients as superior and leading to higher industrial investment rates. Although German and Japanese loan officers appear to rely on much the same criteria used elsewhere (standard financial ratios plus assessment of firm management), firms – particularly large and medium firms – are subjected to a much more intensive process of subsequent monitoring. However, Mayer's position probably underestimates the capacity of industrial clients to lead banks astray in many cases, in not only the US and the UK, but also in Mexico and the Philippines.

19. The same holds in international capital markets, where the spread of rates charged to different sovereign borrowers, even when including commissions, in no way reflects the risk of default.

20. FitzGerald (1993) sets out a possible Kaleckian macroeconomic model with a financial sector, firms and households.

21. Vos (1997) offers intertemporal and international comparison and improve macrofinancial modelling.

CHAPTER 5

1. I would like to thank Giorgio Perosino for assistance with the research upon which this chapter is based.

2. The standard neoclassical assumptions are that (i) factors and goods markets are perfectly competitive; (ii) production functions are continuous so that factors are good substitutes; (iii) production is characterized by constant returns to scale; (iv) goods and factors are homogeneous; and (v) economic agents are rational and have perfect information. The set of assumptions specific to the trade theory underlying the HOS model are that (i) trading partners have different given factor endowments but the same technology; (ii) goods can be ordered in terms of factor intensity; (iii) factors are perfectly mobile across sectors but immobile across countries; (iv) for a small economy, the international prices of goods are given; and (v) trading partners have similar demand structures (see Krugman & Obstfeld 1991: 40–54, 68–81).

3. If factor owners expect that the change in prices will be temporary, they will not reallocate labour and capital between sectors. Their failure to do so will hamper the adjustment process and force the government to fulfil those very expectations by reversing the reform in order to avoid losing political support and stave an unemployment or foreign exchange crisis (see Buffie 1984).

4. For an overview of the debate on these issues in the 1980s, see Rodrik (1989). In particular, Edwards & van Wijnbergen (1986) survey heterodox approaches to how different kinds of capital market restrictions may affect the desirable speed of liberalization.

5. For empirical evidence of this phenomenon in Latin America, see FitzGerald (1996).

CHAPTER 6

1. This chapter is based on my own research originally published as a chapter in Griffith-Jones, Montes & Nasution (2001).

CHAPTER 7

1. I would like to thank Andrew Hurrell, Frances Stewart, Laurence Whitehead and Ngaire Woods for helpful comments on an earlier draft of this chapter.

2. See BWC (1994) for a 'blue-ribbon' institutional critique of prevailing arrangements, and Helpman & Krugman (1989) for a New Keynesian theoretical critique.

CHAPTER 8

1. 'Unless we review our concept of markets, our understanding of markets, they will collapse, because we are creating global markets, global financial markets, without understanding their true nature. We have this false theory that markets, left to their own devices, tend towards equilibrium' (see Soros 1997b).

2. Because depositors in (say) pension funds cannot know the eventual value of the asset acquired when they retire, they can only rely on the current return on the fund in question. This encourages short-termism by fund managers in order to gain market share, a bias which is exacerbated by the system of quarterly bonuses as a form of remuneration.

3. Financial liberalization means that in an economy such as Mexico, the entire domestic money supply is, in effect, a contingent foreign exchange claim on the central bank, because bank deposits can be converted into dollars on demand (see FitzGerald, forthcoming).

4. It is sometimes suggested that as such agencies have emerging market governments as clients for the rating of new issues, they are reluctant to downgrade them, although there is no reliable evidence of this.

5. The assessment of whether the current account deficit of a particular country reflects longer-term debt solvency – and thus of the exchange rate risk and the probability of a policy shift that could affect asset values – not only depends on the current payments and debt situation, but on the expected rate of growth, the expected world interest rate and what investors will regard as an acceptable debt ratio as well.

These are all matters of economic (and political) judgement rather than statistical information.

6. Most notably the Barings bank in 1995 and Long Term Capital Management (LTCM) in 1998.

7. The direct and indirect costs of the 1982 banking crisis in Chile may have amounted to 30 per cent of GDP while the total costs of the crisis in Venezuela in 1995 has been estimated at around 20 per cent of GDP (Caprio Jr., Hunter, Kaufman & Leipziger 1998). The 1995 collapse of the Mexican banking system exposed its fatal weaknesses arising from hasty privatization and financial deregulation.

8. Nearly all emerging markets have adopted the Basle Committee's eight per cent minimum ratio as the standard for regulating their banking systems. However, emerging markets are subject to far greater financial volatility than developed countries. Indeed, an eight per cent risk–asset ratio may be too low to guarantee capital adequacy. Bank regulators in a number of emerging markets have adopted a higher standard – Singapore applies a 12 per cent minimum ratio – but at present there is no obligation for them to do so.

9. These include the standards and procedures for authorization, the supervisory authority's ability to gather information about the banks and banking groups it authorizes, and the powers available to the supervisory authority to take action against authorized institutions which breach their authorization requirements.

10. The Principles reflect generally accepted best practice in the G10 countries and include: (i) clear definitions of the permissible activities for institutions authorized as banks and controls on the use of the term 'bank' in the name of an institution; (ii) powers for the licensing authority to set criteria for authorization and rejection of applications from institutions that fail to meet the set standards; (iii) supervisors must have powers to evaluate the controlling interests of banking institutions and to reject proposals of transference of significant ownership stakes to other parties; (iv) supervisory authorities must ensure that banks maintain adequate capital and risk management systems; (v) supervisors must require banks lending to related companies and individuals to do so on an arm's-length basis to prevent abuses arising from connected lending; (vi) banks must institutionalize procedures to prevent their intentional or unintentional use by criminal elements, including 'know-your-customer' rules.

11. This group was comprised by representatives from Chile, China, the Czech Republic, Hong Kong, Mexico, Russia and Thailand. Brazil, Hungary, India, Indonesia, Korea, Malaysia, Poland and Singapore were also associated with the group's work.

12. Recent and ongoing changes in US banking legislation will undoubtedly have a major impact on this process.

13. 'Up to those amounts the countries concerned would be able to access international capital markets at prime rates. Beyond these, the creditors would have to beware' (Soros 1997a).

14. Leaving aside the likelihood of political opposition to such a scheme in the US Congress as evidenced by the 2000 Meltzer Report.

15. It might be argued that a higher international tax on global capital would reduce the rate of global investment. However, modern macroeconomic theory indicates that the effect of tax on savings is indeterminate due to 'Ricardian equivalence'. Further, the 'hurdle rate' of return for investment is far more responsive to uncertainty than tax rates, such that there is a potentially positive trade-off between the two.

16. The case for such a tax is set out in ul Haq, Kaul & Grunberg (1996). Arestis & Sawyer (1998) identify reasons for why such a tax would not reduce volatility.

17. A tax on international air travel, for instance, could be collected easily through the airlines themselves as a condition for international certification.

18. The concept of moral hazard originates in accident insurance, where once insured, car-owners may be careless of damage to their vehicle unless there is a minimum claim or no-claims bonus. Whether this notion can be applied rigorously to major macroeconomic crises where the outcome (for instance, a bailout) is uncertain seems very doubtful.

Statistical Appendix

Table A.4   World saving, 1986–2000 (% of GDP)

	1975-79	1980-84	1985-89	1990-94	1995-99	2000
World	24.8	22.8	23.0	22.7	23.5	23.8
Industrial economies	22.8	21.4	20.6	20.5	21.8	21.9
Private	21.1	20.8	19.8	19.8	20.2	18.7
Public	1.7	0.6	0.8	0.8	1.6	3.2
United States	20.3	18.9	16.4	15.3	17.9	18.2
Private	19.0	19.2	16.6	15.7	16.0	13.4
Personal	6.6	7.1	5.3	5.0	3.0	-0.1
Corporate	12.4	12.1	11.3	10.7	13.0	13.5
Public	1.3	-0.3	-0.2	-0.4	3.4	4.8
European Union	22.2	20.0	20.6	19.4	20.8	21.3
Private	20.7	20.0	20.9	21.4	21.1	19.2
Personal		9.3	7.6	7.9	7.4	5.2
Corporate		10.7	13.0	11.5	13.4	16.1
Public	1.5	0.0	-0.3	-2.0	-0.3	2.1
Japan	32.4	30.8	32.7	33.3	30.4	29.0
Private	29.1	26.7	26.0	25.0	28.0	30.1
Personal				20.3	18.2	
Corporate				4.7	9.8	
Public	3.3	4.1	6.6	8.3	2.5	-1.1
Less developed countries	26.5	23.2	23.5	25.2	26.5	26.7
Countries in transition	33.6	32.7	29.4	26.6	21.4	23.8

Source: Derived from IMF 1992b, 1993, 1997, 1998b, 1999, 2000.
Note: Calculations for personal and corporate savings based on IMF 1992b, 1993, 1997, 1998b, 1999, 2000 using data on US saving from Bureau of Economic Analysis 2001, Japan saving from ESRI 2001, EU personal and corporate savings derived using composition of UK private saving from National Statistics 1985, 1990, 2001 as a proxy.

Table A.5 The structure of global capital accumulation, 1999 (%)

	Number of countries	GDP[a]	Exports[b]	Saving[c]	Investment[d]	Private investment[e]	Public investment[e]
World	184	100.0	100.0	100.0	100.0	73.6[f]	26.4[f]
Industrial economies	28	57.4	77.6	53.1	53.4	77.1[f]	22.9[f]
USA	1	21.9	14	17.3	19.6	81.8[g]	18.2[g]
Japan	1	7.6	6.7	9.3	8.4	69.8[f]	30.2[f]
EU	15	20.3	39.3	18.1	17.9	84.9[h]	15.1[h]
ROW	156	42.6	22.4	46.9	46.6	62.8[g]	37.2[g]
Net creditors	9	21.1	2.0	18.4	18.6		
Net debtors	119	35.8	16.2	39.5	39.4		
Official financing	45	2.1	0.9	1.5	2.0		
Private financing	46	29.8	13.1	34.8	34.0		
Diversified financing	28	2.8	1.7	2.1	2.3		
Transition economies	28	5.8	4.4	5.5	5.1		
Developing countries	128	36.8	18.0	40.5	40.2		
Africa	51	3.2	1.8	2.2	2.8		
Asia	27	21.2	8.3	28.5	26.7	59.6[g]	40.4[g]
Middle East & Europe	17	4	3.4	3.6	3.7		
Western Hemisphere	33	8.4	4.5	6.2	7.2	70.9[f]	29.1[f]

Source: Derived from IMF 2000, public and private investment derived from World Bank 2000.
Notes: The estimates of country group shares in world investment and saving are derived by weighting the respective rates for each country grouping by their share in world GDP. IMF estimates for world investment and saving are not in balance, as they should be by definition. In Balanced Accounts, the error (which corresponds to six-tenths of a percent of world GDP and is attributable mainly to unreported investment income) is included with income and saving in Industrial Economies. The resulting shares are recalculated in accordance to the methodology in Vos & de Jong 1995).

[a] % of World GDP. [b] % of World exports of goods and services. [c] % of World saving. [d] % of World investment. [e] % of Gross Domestic Investment. [f] 1996. [g] 1997. [h] United Kingdom, 1996.

Table A.6 *Global saving and investment, 1999 (% of GDP)*

	Saving	Private saving	Public saving	Investment	Private investment	Public investment	Saving – investment
World	23.2			23.2 (22.2 [a])	16.3 [a]	5.9 [a]	0.0
Industrial Economies	21.7	18.9	2.8	21.9	18.1	3.8	-0.2
USA	18.5	14.4	4.0	21.1	17.7	3.3	-2.6
Japan	28.6	28.2	0.4	26.1	18.1	8.0	2.5
EU	20.9	19.5	1.4	20.7	18.3	2.4	0.2
ROW	25.8			25.7 (25.8 [b])	16.2 [b]	9.6 [b]	0.1
Net creditors	20.4			20.7			-0.3
Net debtors	25.9			25.9			0.0
Official financing	16.9			22.5			-5.6
Private financing	27.4			26.8			0.6
Diversified financing	17.7			19.5			-1.8
Transition economies	22.3			20.5			1.8
Developing countries	25.8			25.7			0.1
Africa	16.4			20.3			-3.9
Asia	31.5			29.6 (27.0 [c])	16.1 [c]	10.9 [c]	1.9
Middle East & Europe	21			21.5			-0.5
Western Hemisphere	17.3			20.1 (21.9 [b])	15.5 [b]	6.4 [b]	-2.8

Source: IMF 2000, public and private investment derived from World Bank 2000.
Notes: Fund estimates for world investment and saving are not in balance, as they should be by definition. In Balanced Accounts the error, which corresponds to some 0.6 % of world GDP and is mainly attributable to unreported investment income, is included with income and saving in Industrial Economies. The resulting shares are recalculated in accordance to the methodology in Vos & de Jong 1995).
[a] 1996. [b] 1997. [c] 1998.

Table A.7   Nominal and real long-term world interest rates, 1970–98

	Nominal long-term interest rates				
	United States	United Kingdom	Germany	France	Japan
1970	6.6	8.6		8.6	
1971	5.7	7.9		8.4	
1972	5.6	8.4		8.0	
1973	6.3	10.6		9.0	
1974	7.0	14.2	10.4	11.0	8.2
1975	7.0	13.2		10.3	
1976	6.8	13.6		10.5	
1977	7.1	12.0		11.0	
1978	7.9	12.1		10.6	
1979	8.7	12.9		10.8	
1980	10.8	13.9		13.8	
1981	12.9	14.9		16.3	
1982	12.2	13.1		16.0	
1983	10.8	11.3		14.4	
1984	12.0	11.1		13.4	
1985	10.8	11.0	7.0	11.9	6.4
1986	8.1	10.1	6.2	9.1	5.0
1987	8.6	9.6	6.2	10.2	4.4
1988	9.0	9.7	6.5	9.2	4.7
1989	8.6	10.2	7.0	9.2	5.1
1990	8.7	11.8	8.7	10.4	7.0
1991	8.2	10.1	8.5	9.5	6.3
1992	7.5	9.1	7.8	9.0	5.3
1993	6.5	7.5	6.5	7.0	4.3
1994	7.4	8.2	6.9	7.5	4.4
1995	6.9	8.2	6.9	7.7	3.4
1996	6.8	7.8	6.2	6.5	3.1
1997	6.7	7.0	5.7	5.7	2.4
1998	5.7	5.5	4.6	4.8	1.5
1999	6.1	5.1	4.5	4.9	1.7

Table A.7 *(continued)*

	United States	United Kingdom	Germany	France	Japan
	Real long-term interest rates				
1970					
1971	0.6	-1.4		2.0	
1972	1.3	0.3		1.0	
1973	0.6	3.0		0.5	
1974	-1.9	-0.6	3.2	-0.8	-10.4
1975	-2.2	-10.9		-2.4	
1976	1.0	-1.4		-0.6	
1977	0.5	-1.5		1.6	
1978	0.7	0.5		0.4	
1979	0.3	-1.4		0.8	
1980	1.5	-4.6		2.4	
1981	3.2	3.2		4.7	
1982	5.7	5.3		4.0	
1983	6.6	5.6		4.9	
1984	8.0	6.3		6.0	
1985	7.3	5.1	5.0	6.1	4.2
1986	5.8	6.8	3.3	3.8	3.2
1987	5.5	4.2	4.5	7.1	4.3
1988	5.4	3.4	5.0	6.0	4.0
1989	4.6	2.5	4.8	5.9	3.0
1990	4.7	3.8	5.1	7.3	4.5
1991	4.4	3.2	3.6	6.4	3.6
1992	4.9	4.9	2.7	6.9	3.5
1993	4.0	4.6	2.7	4.6	3.7
1994	5.2	6.5	4.3	5.7	4.2
1995	4.6	5.6	4.7	5.9	4.1
1996	4.7	4.4	5.1	5.0	4.6
1997	4.8	4.0	4.8	4.3	2.1
1998	4.5	2.4	3.4	3.9	1.2
1999	4.6	2.5	3.6	4.6	2.6

Source: OECD 1997, 2000.
Notes: Definition of long-term interest rates: United States: US Government bonds ('composite' over 10 years); United Kingdom: 20-year government bonds; Germany: 7-15 year public sector bonds; France: public and semi-public sector bonds; Japan: 10-year central government bonds. Real interest rate (R) calculated by deflating nominal interest rate (N) by the ratio of the GDP implicit price index for current year $(P_{(t)})$ to that of previous year $(P_{(t-1)})$ using the formula:

$$R = \left\{ \left(\frac{N}{100} + 1 \right) \bigg/ \frac{P_{(t)}}{P_{(t-1)}} - 1 \right\} * 100 .$$

Table A.8   *Sources and uses of funds in developing countries, 1994–99*
             (% of GDP)

	1974-81	1982-89	1990-95	1996-98
Saving	26.6	22.7	25.7	26.6
Investment	25.9	24.5	27.4	27.3[a]
Private investment [b]	..	14.0	16.4	17.5
Public investment [b]	..	10.5	11.0	10.2
Net lending	0.7	-1.8	-1.7	-0.7
Current transfers	1.0	1.0	1.2	1.2
Factor income	-0.6	-2.1	-1.7	-1.3
Resource balance	0.3	-0.7	-1.2	-0.6
Acquisition of foreign assets	3.7	0.5	2.2	3.3
Change in reserves	1.7	0.2	1.4	1.2
Other (private)	2.0	0.3	0.8	2.0
Acquisition of foreign liabilities	4.7	2.3	3.9	3.2
Net borrowing	0.7	1.8	1.7	1.4

Source: Derived from IMF 1992b, 1996, 2000, public and private investment derived from World Bank 2000. First seven rows as in source; remaining rows calculated as balancing items.

[a] In 1996-97, the figure was 27.7%.

[b] 1996-97.

References

Addison, D. (1989) 'The World Bank Revised Minimum Standard Model', World Bank Staff Working Paper Series No. 231, Washington DC: The World Bank.

Aghevli, B.B. et al. (1990) 'The Role of National Saving in the World Economy: Recent Trends and Prospects', IMF Occasional Paper Series No. 67, Washington DC: International Monetary Fund.

Aizenman, J. & N.P. Marion (1996) 'Volatility and the Investment Response', NBER Working Paper Series No. 5841, Cambridge MA: National Bureau of Economic Research.

Alam, A. (1994) 'The New Trade Theory and Its Relevance for Developing Countries', Policy Research Working Paper No. 1274, Washington DC: The World Bank.

Arestis, P. & M. Sawyer (1998), 'What Role for the Tobin Tax in Global Governance?' London: University of East London & University of Leeds (mimeo).

Arestis, P. & M. Sawyer (ed.) (1997) *The Relevance of Keynesian Economic Policies Today.* London: Macmillan Press.

Asimakopulos, A. (1991) *Keynes's General Theory and Accumulation.* Cambridge: Cambridge University Press.

Bacchetta, P. (1992) 'Liberalization of Capital Movements and of the Domestic Financial System', *Economica.* 59(236): 465-74.

Bacha, E. (1990) 'A Three-Gap Model of Foreign Transfers and the GDP Growth Rate in Developing Countries', *Journal of Development Economics.* 32(2): 279-96.

Barro, R.J. (1989) 'The Ricardian Approach to Budget Deficits', *Journal of Economic Perspectives.* 3(2): 37-54.

Barro, R.J. (1991) 'Economic Growth in a Cross Section of Countries', *Quarterly Journal of Economics.* 106(2): 407-43.

Barro, R.J. & X. Sala-i-Martin (1995) *Economic Growth.* New York: McGraw Hill.

193

Baumol, W.J. (1967) *Business Behaviour, Value and Growth*. New York: Harcourt, Brace & World.

Baumol, W.J. et al. (1994) *Convergence of Productivity: Cross-National Studies and Historical Evidence*. Oxford: Clarendon Press.

BEA (2001) 'Table 5.1. Gross Saving and Investment', Bureau of Economic Analysis, <http://www.bea.doc.gov/bea/dn/nipaweb/>, 22 June.

Bevan, D. et al. (1990) *Controlled Open Economies: A Neoclassical Approach to Structuralism*. Oxford: Clarendon Press.

BIS (1994) Sixty-Fourth Annual Report. Basel: Bank for International Settlements.

BIS (1998) Sixty-Eighth Annual Report. Basel: Bank for International Settlements.

Blanchard, O.J. & S. Fischer (1989) *Lectures on Macroeconomics*. Cambridge MA: MIT Press.

Blinder, A.S. (1987) 'Credit Rationing and Effective Supply Failures', *Economic Journal*. 97(386): 327-52.

Bosworth, B.P. (1993) *Saving and Investment in a Global Economy*. Washington DC: Brookings Institution.

Bourguinon, F. et al. (1989) 'Macroeconomic Adjustment and Income Distribution: A Micro-Macro Simulation Model', OECD Technical Paper Series No. 1, Paris: Organisation for Economic Cooperation and Development, Development Centre.

Brainard, W.C. & J. Tobin (1992) 'On the Internationalization of Portfolios', *Oxford Economic Papers*. 44(4): 533-65.

Brewer, T.L. (1993) 'Foreign Direct Investment in Emerging Market Countries', in L. Oxelheim (ed.), *The Global Race for Foreign Direct Investment: Prospects for the Future*. London: Springer.

Browning, M. & A. Lusardi (1996) 'Household Saving: Micro Theories and Micro Facts', *Journal of Economic Literature*. 34(4): 1797-855.

Brownlie, I. (1990) *Principles of Public International Law*. 4th ed. Oxford: Clarendon Press.

Bryant, W.K. (1990) *The Economic Organization of the Household*. Cambridge: Cambridge University Press.

Buffie, E.F. (1984) 'Financial Repression, the New Structuralists, and Stabilization Policy in Semi-Industrialized Economies', *Journal of Development Economics*. 14(3): 305-22.

Buiter, W.H. (1988) 'Death, Birth, Productivity Growth and Debt Neutrality', *Economic Journal*. 98(391): 279-93.

BWC (1994) Bretton Woods: Looking to the Future. Commission Report, Staff Review, Background Papers. Washington DC: The Bretton Woods Commission.

Caprio Jr., G. et al. (1998) 'Preventing Bank Crises (Keynote Speech)' in G. Caprio Jr., W. Hunter, G. Kaufman & D. Leipziger, conference sponsored by the Federal Reserve Bank of Chicago and Economic Development Institute of The World Bank, The World Bank, Lake Bluff, IL, 11 June 1997.

Chamberlain, T. (1990) 'Capital Structure and the Long-Run Survival of the Firm: Theory and Evidence', *Journal of Post-Keynesian Economics*. 12(3): 404-23.

Ciocca, P. et al. (1996) *The High Price of Money: An Interpretation of World Interest Rates*. Oxford: Clarendon Press.

Clark, R. (1985) *Industrial Economics*. Oxford: Blackwell.

Cohen, S.I. & J.M.C. Tuyl (1991) 'Growth and Equity Effects of Changing Demographic Structures in the Netherlands: Simulations within a Social Accounting Matrix', *Economic and Financial Modelling*. 8(2): 3-15.

Corden, W.M. (1971) 'The Effects of Trade on the Rate of Growth', in J. Bhagwati (ed.), *Trade, Balance of Payments and Growth: Papers in Honor of Charles P. Kindleberger*. Amsterdam: North Holland.

Corden, W.M. (1993) 'Protection and Liberalization: A Review of Analytical Issues', *Protection and Liberalization: A Review of Analytical Issues*, Washington, DC: International Monetary Fund,

DAC (1998) *Development Assistance Report 1998*. Paris: Organization for Economic Cooperation and Development.

Dailami, M. & M. Giugale (1991) 'Reflections on Credit Policy in Developing Countries: Its Effect on Private Investment', World Bank Country Economics Department Series No. 654, Washington DC: The World Bank.

Dale, R. (1992) *International Banking Deregulation: The Great Banking Experiment*. Oxford: Blackwell.

D'Arista, J.W. & S. Griffith-Jones (2001) 'The Boom of Portfolio Flows to 'Emerging Markets' and Its Regulatory Implications', in S. Griffith-Jones, M. Montes & A. Nasution (ed.), *Short-Term Capital Flows and Economic Crises*. Oxford: Oxford University Press.

Davidson, P. (1986) 'Finance, Funding, Saving, and Investment', *Journal of Post-Keynesian Economics*. 9(1): 101-10.

Dawson, T.C. (2001) 'A Letter to "Drop the Debt". May 3, 2001', International Monetary Fund, <http://www.imf.org/external/np/vc/2001/050 301a.htm>, 28 May.

de Jong, N. et al. (1993) 'Trade and Financial Flows in a World Accounting Framework: Balanced WAMs for 1989-90', ISS Working Paper Series on Money, Finance, and Development No. 52, The Hague: Institute of Social Studies.

Dean, A. et al. (1990) 'Savings Trends and Behaviour in OECD Countries', *OECD Economic Studies*. 14: 7-58.

Devlin, R. et al. (1995) 'Surges in Capital Flows and Development: An Overview of Policy Issues', in R. Ffrench-Davis & S. Griffith-Jones (eds), *Coping with Capital Surges: The Return of Finance to Latin America*. Boulder: Rienner.

Dixit, A.K. (1989) 'Intersectoral Capital Reallocation under Price Uncertainty', *Journal of International Economics*. 26(3/4): 309-25.

Dixit, A.K. & R.S. Pindyck (1994) *Investment under Uncertainty*. Princeton NJ: Princeton University Press.

Dixon, M. (1993) *Textbook on International Law*. London: Blackstone.

Domenech, R. et al. (2000) 'The Effects of Budget Deficit on National Saving in the OECD', *Economics Letters*. 69(3): 377-83.

Dornbusch, R. (1980) *Open Economy Macroeconomics*. New York NY: Basic Books.

Dornbusch, R. (ed.) (1993) *Policymaking in the Open Economy: Concepts and Case Studies in Economic Performance*. New York NY: Oxford University Press for The World Bank.

Drake, P.J. (1980) *Money, Finance and Underdevelopment*. Oxford: Robertson.

Dunning, J.H. (1992) 'Governments, Markets, and Multinational Enterprises: Some Emerging Issues', *International Trade Journal*. 7(1): 1-14.

Dutt, A.K. (1990) *Growth, Distribution and Uneven Development*. Cambridge: Cambridge University Press.

Dutt, A.K. (1990-1) 'Interest Rate Policy in LDCs: A Post Keynesian View', *Journal of Post-Keynesian Economics*. 13(2): 210-32.

Dutt, A.K. (1995) 'Interest Rate Policy, Growth and Distribution in an Open Less-Developed Economy: A Theoretical Analysis', in P. Arestis & V. Chick (eds), *Finance, Development and Structural Change: Post-Keynesian Perspectives*. Aldershot: Edward Elgar.

Edwards, J. et al. (1986) *Recent Developments in Corporate Finance*. Cambridge: Cambridge University Press.

Edwards, S. (1988) 'Terms of Trade, Tariffs and Labour Market Adjustment in Developing Countries', *The World Bank Economic Review*. 2(2): 165-85.

Edwards, S. (1993) 'Openness, Trade Liberalization and Growth in Developing Countries', *Journal of Economic Literature*. 31(3): 1358-93.

Edwards, S. (1996) 'A Tale of Two Crises: Chile and Mexico', NBER Working Paper Series No. 5794, Cambridge MA: National Bureau for Economic Research.

Edwards, S. & A. Cox-Edwards (1994) 'Labour Market Distortions and Structural Adjustment in Developing Countries', in S. Horton, R. Kanbur & D. Mazumdar (eds), *Labour Markets in an Era of Adjustment. 1.* Washington DC: The World Bank.

Edwards, S. & S. van Wijnbergen (1986) 'The Welfare Effects of Trade and Capital Market Liberalization', *International Economic Review.* 27(1): 141-48.

Edwards, S. & S. van Wijnbergen (1989) 'Disequilibrium and Structural Adjustment', in H.B. Chenery & T.N. Srinivasan (eds), *Handbook of Development Economics. 2.* Amsterdam: North-Holland.

Edwards, S. & C.A. Végh Gramont (1997) 'Banks and Macroeconomic Disturbances under Predetermined Exchange Rates', *Banks and Macroeconomic Disturbances under Predetermined Exchange Rates,* Cambridge MA: National Bureau for Economic Research,

Eichengreen, B. (1994) 'History of the International Monetary System: Implications for Research in International Macroeconomics and Finance', in F. v.d. Ploeg (ed.), *The Handbook of International Macroeconomics.* Oxford: Blackwell.

Eichengreen, B. & A. Mody (1998) 'Interest Rates in the North and South: Is There a Missing Link?' *International Finance.* 1(1): 35-57.

Eichengreen, B. & R. Portes (eds) (1995) *Crisis? What Crisis? Orderly Workouts for Sovereign Debtors.* London: Centre for Economic Policy Research.

Eitman, D.K. & A.I. Stonehill (1979) *Multinational Business Finance.* Reading, Mass: Addison-Wesley.

Ellis, F. (1988) *Peasant Economics: Farm Households and Agrarian Development.* Cambridge: Cambridge University Press.

Engen, E.M. et al. (1996) 'The Illusory Effects of Saving Incentives on Saving', *Journal of Economic Perspectives.* 10(4): 113-38.

ESRI (2001) 'System of National Accounts', Economic and Social Research Institute, Cabinet Office, Government of Japan, <http://www5.cao.go.jp/2000/g/1215g-sna-e/esnamenu.html>, 26 June.

Fazzari, S.M. et al. (1988) 'Financing Constraints and Corporate Investment', *Financing Constraints and Corporate Investment,* Washington DC: Brookings Institution.

FED-NY (1985) *Annual Report 1985.* New York NY: Federal Reserve Bank of New York.

FitzGerald, E.V.K. (1990) 'Small-Scale Industries under Adjustment Programmes: Some Analytical Considerations', in F. Stewart, H. Thomas & T. de Wilde (eds), *The Other Policy: The Influence of Policies on Technology Choice and Small Enterprise Development*. London: Intermediate Technology Publications.

FitzGerald, E.V.K. (1993) *The Macroeconomics of Development Finance: A Kaleckian Analysis of the Semi-Industrialized Economy*. London: Macmillan Press in association with the Institute of Social Studies.

FitzGerald, E.V.K. (1996) 'The "New Trade Regime", Macroeconomic Behaviour and Income Distribution in Latin America', in V. Bulmer-Thomas (ed.), *The New Economic Model in Latin America and Its Impact on Income Distribution and Poverty*. Basingstoke: Macmillan.

FitzGerald, E.V.K. (1998) 'Caveat Creditor: The Implications of the Asian Crisis for International Investment Regulation', in UNCTAD (ed.), *The Asian Financial Crisis*. Geneva: United Nations Conference on Trade and Development.

FitzGerald, E.V.K. (forthcoming) *Global Financial Regulation and the Emerging Markets*. Oxford: Oxford University Press.

FitzGerald, E.V.K. et al. (1998) 'The Development Implications of the Multilateral Agreement on Investment', *The Development Implications of the Multilateral Agreement on Investment*. London: Department for International Development, 21 March.

FitzGerald, E.V.K. & J. Cuesta-Leiva (1998) 'The Asset Value of a Passport: A Model of Citizenship and Income Determination in a Global Economy', QEH Working Paper Series No. 1, Oxford: Queen Elizabeth House.

FitzGerald, E.V.K. & H. Grabbe (1997) 'Financial Integration: The European Experience and Lessons for Latin America', *Integration and Trade*. 1(2): 75-111.

FitzGerald, E.V.K. et al. (1994) 'External Constraints on Private Investment Decisions in Developing Countries', in J.W. Gunning (ed.), *Trade, Aid and Development: Essays in Honour of Hans Linnemann*. London: Macmillan.

FitzGerald, E.V.K. & G. Mavrotas (1994) 'The Implications of Recent Changes in International Capital Flows for Structural Adjustment, Private Investment and Employment Creation in Developing Countries', ILO Occasional Paper Series (Interdepartmental Project on Structural Adjustment) No. 23, Geneva: International Labour Organisation.

FitzGerald, E.V.K. & G. Mavrotas (1997) 'The Employment Impact of External Capital Flows in Developing Countries', ILO Employment and Training Papers No. 5, Geneva: International Labour Organisation.

FitzGerald, E.V.K. & K. Sarmad (1990) 'Public and Private Sector Capital Account Behaviour in Less Developed Countries, 1970-88', ISS Working Paper Series on Money, Finance and Development No. 36, The Hague: Institute of Social Studies.

FitzGerald, E.V.K. & R. Vos (1989) *Financing Economic Development: A Structural Approach to Monetary Policy*. Aldershot: Gower.

Ford, R. & D. Laxton (1999) 'World Public Debt and Real Interest Rates', *Oxford Review of Economic Policy*. 15(2): 77-94.

Frankel, J. (1992) 'Measuring International Capital Mobility: A Review', *American Economic Review*. 82(2): 197-202.

Galbis, V. (1977) 'Financial Intermediation and Economic Growth in Less-Developed Countries: A Theoretical Approach', *Journal of Development Studies*. 13(2): 58-72.

Gersovitz, M. (1988) 'Saving and Development', in H.B. Chenery & T.N. Srinivasan (eds), *Handbook of Development Economics*. Oxford: North Holland.

Gibson, H. & E. Tsakalotos (1994) 'The Scope and Limits of Financial Liberalization in Developing Countries', *Journal of Development Studies*. 30(3): 578-628.

Godley, W. & F. Cripps (1983) *Macroeconomics*. Oxford: Oxford University Press.

Goldberg, L.S. (1993) 'Exchange Rates and Investment in United States Industry', *Review of Economics and Statistics*. 75(4): 575-88.

Goldsmith, R.W. (1975) *Financial Structure and Development*. New Haven CT: Yale University Press.

Goldstein, M. & M. Mussa (1993) 'The Integration of World Capital Markets', IMF Working Paper Series No. 95, Washington DC: International Monetary Fund.

Greenaway, D. (1993) 'Liberalizing Foreign Trade through Rose-Tinted Glasses', *The Economic Journal*. 103(416): 208-22.

Greenwald, B.C. & J.E. Stiglitz (1990) 'Asymmetric Information and the New Theory of the Firm: Financial Constraints and Risk Behaviour', *American Economic Review*. 80(2): 160-65.

Greenwood, C. & H. Mercer (1995) 'Considerations of International Law', in B. Eichengreen & R. Portes (eds), *Crisis? What Crisis? Orderly Workouts for Sovereign Debtors*. London: Centre for Economic Policy Research.

Griffith-Jones, S. (2001) 'Causes and Lessons of the Mexican Peso Crisis', in S. Griffith-Jones, M. Montes & A. Nasution (eds), *Short-Term Capital Flows and Economic Crises*. Oxford: Oxford University Press.

Griffith-Jones, S. et al. (ed.) (2001) *Short-Term Capital Flows and Economic Crises.* Oxford: Oxford University Press.

Grimwade, N. (1989) *International Trade: New Patterns of Trade, Production and Investment.* London: Routledge.

Grossman, G. & E. Helpman (1991) *Innovation and Growth in the Global Economy.* Cambridge MA: MIT Press.

Grubel, H.G. & P.J. Lloyd (1975) *Intra-Industry Trade.* London: Macmillan.

Gurley, J.G. & E.S. Shaw (1960) *Money in a Theory of Finance.* Washington: Brookings Institution.

Hallwood, P. & R. MacDonald (1994) *International Money and Finance.* 2nd ed. Oxford: Blackwell.

Heller, P.S. (1975) 'A Model of Public Fiscal Behaviour in Developing Countries: Aid, Investment and Taxation', *American Economic Review.* 65(3): 429-45.

Helpman, E. & P.R. Krugman (1989) *Trade Policy and Market Structure.* London: MIT Press.

Hicks, J.R. (1946) *Value and Capital: An Inquiry into Some Fundamental Principles of Economic Theory.* 2nd ed. Oxford: Clarendon Press.

Hill, J. (1994) *The Law Relating to International Commercial Disputes.* London: Lloyd's of London Press.

Hirschliefer, J. & J.G. Riley (1992) *The Analytics of Uncertainty and Information.* Cambridge: Cambridge University Press.

Horton, S. et al. (eds) (1994) *Labour Markets in an Era of Adjustment.* Washington DC: The World Bank.

Hutchinson, M.M. (1992) 'Budget Policy and the Decline of National Saving Revisited', BIS Economic Papers No. 33, Basel: Bank for International Settlements, Monetary and Economic Department.

IADB (1996) *Economic and Social Survey Progress in Latin America 1995.* Washington DC: Inter-American Development Bank.

IMF (1987) 'Theoretical Aspects of the Design of Fund-Supported Adjustment Programs: A Study', IMF Occasional Paper Series No. 55, Washington DC: International Monetary Fund.

IMF (1991) 'Determinants and Systemic Consequences of International Capital Flows: A Study', IMF Occasional Paper Series No. 77, Washington DC: International Monetary Bank.

IMF (1992a) *Report on the Measurement of International Capital Flows.* Washington DC: International Monetary Fund.

IMF (1992b) *World Economic Outlook 1992.* Washington DC: International Monetary Fund.

IMF (1993) *World Economic Outlook 1993*. Washington DC: International Monetary Fund.

IMF (1994) *World Economic Outlook 1994*. Washington DC: International Monetary Fund.

IMF (1995) *World Economic Outlook 1995*. Washington DC: International Monetary Fund.

IMF (1996) *World Economic Outlook 1996*. Washington DC: International Monetary Fund.

IMF (1997) *World Economic Outlook 1997*. Washington DC: International Monetary Fund.

IMF (1998a) *Toward a Framework for Financial Stability*. Washington DC: International Monetary Fund.

IMF (1998b) *World Economic Outlook 1998*. Washington DC: International Monetary Fund.

IMF (1999) *World Economic Outlook 1999*. Washington DC: International Monetary Fund.

IMF (2000) *World Economic Outlook. October 2000*. Washington DC: International Monetary Fund.

Jones, W.R. (1956) 'Factor Proportions and the Heckscher-Ohlin Theorem', *Review of Economic Studies*. 24: 1-10.

Jones, W.R. (1965) 'The Structure of Simple General Equilibrium Models', *Journal of Political Economy*. 73: 557-72.

Jones, W.R. (1971) 'A Three Factor Model in Theory, Trade and History', in J. Bhagwati et al. (eds), *Trade, Balance of Payments and Growth*. Oxford: North Holland.

Kapstein, E.B. (1994) *Governing the Global Economy: International Finance and the State*. Cambridge MA: Harvard University Press.

Kay, J.A. (1991) 'Economics and Business', *Economic Journal*. 101(404): 57-63.

Keesing, D.B. (1966) 'Labour, Skills and Comparative Advantage', *American Economic Review*. 56: 249-58.

Kenen, P.B. (1965) 'Nature, Capital and Trade', *Journal of Political Economy*. 73(5): 437-60.

Keynes, J.M. (1980) *The Collected Writings of John Maynard Keynes*. London: Macmillan.

Khan, M.S. et al. (1990) 'Adjustment with Growth: Relating the Analytical Approaches of the IMF and the World Bank', *Journal of Development Economics*. 32(1): 155-79.

Khan, M.S. & C.M. Reinhart (1990) 'Private Investment and Economic Growth in Developing Countries', *World Development*. 18(1): 19-27.

Kindleberger, C.P. (1988) *The International Economic Order: Essays on Financial Crises and International Public Goods*. New York NY: Harvester Wheatsheaf.

Kindleberger, C.P. (1996) *Manias, Panics, and Crashes: A History of Financial Crises*. 3rd ed. Basingstoke: Macmillan Press.

Kirkpatrick, C. et al. (1984) *Industrial Structure and Policy in Less Developed Countries*. London: Allen and Unwin.

Kitchen, R.L. (1986) *Finance for the Developing Countries*. London: Wiley.

Komiya, R. (1967) 'Non-Traded Goods and the Pure Theory of International Trade', *International Economic Review*. 8(2): 132-52.

Kregel, J.A. (1985) 'Budget Deficits, Stabilization Policy and Liquidity Preference: Keynes's Post-War Policy Proposals', in F. Vicarelli (ed.), *Keynes's Relevance Today*. London: Macmillan.

Kregel, J.A. (1994) 'The Viability of Economic Policy and the Priorities of Economic Policy', *Journal of Post-Keynesian Economics*. 17(2): 261-77.

Krueger, A.O. (1990) 'The Relationship between Trade, Employment and Growth', in G. Ranis & R. Schultz (eds), *The State of Development Economics*. Cambridge MA: Blackwell.

Krugman, P.R. & M. Obstfeld (1991) *International Economics: Theory and Policy*. New York: Haper Collins.

Lasok, D. (1994) *Law and Institutions of the European Union. 6th*. London: Butterworths.

Leff, N.H. (1978) 'Industrial Organization and Entrepreneurship in the Developing Countries: The Economic Groups', *Economic Development and Cultural Change*. 26(4): 661-75.

Leibfritz, W. et al (1996) 'Aging Populations, Pension Systems and Government Budgets—How Do They Affect Saving?' in OECD (ed.), *Future Global Capital Shortages: Real Threat or Pure Fiction?* Paris: OECD.

Lindbeck, A. (1997) 'Incentives and Social Norms in Household Behaviour', *American Economic Review*. 87(2): 370-77.

Lluch, C. et al. (1977) *Patterns in Household Demand and Savings*. New York: Oxford University Press for The World Bank.

Loayza, N. et al. (2000) 'Saving in Developing Countries: An Overview', *The World Bank Economic Review*. 14(3): 393-414.

Lucas, R.E. (1990) 'Why Doesn't Capital Flow from Rich to Poor Countries?' *American Economic Review*. 80(2): 92-6.

Lydall, H. (1979) *A Theory of Income Distribution*. Oxford: Clarendon Press.

Mankiw, N.G. (1991a) 'The Allocation of Credit and Financial Collapse', in N.G. Mankiw & D. Romer (eds), *New Keynesian Economics*. *2*. Cambridge MA: MIT Press.

Mankiw, N.G. (1991b) 'Imperfect Competition and the Keynesian Cross', in N.G. Mankiw & D. Romer (ed.), *New Keynesian Economics*. *1*. Cambridge MA: MIT Press.

Masson, P.R. et al. (1990) 'Multimod Mark II: A Revised and Extended Model', IMF Occasional Paper Series No. 71, Washington DC: International Monetary Fund.

Matsuyama, K. (1987) 'Current Account Dynamics in a Finite Horizon Model', *Journal of International Economics*. 23(3/4): 299-313.

Mayer, C. (1987) 'The Assessment: Financial Systems and Corporate Investment', *Oxford Review of Economic Policy*. 3(4): i-xvi.

McKibbin, W.J. & J. Sachs (1991) *Global Linkages: Macroeconomic Interdependence and Cooperation in the World Economy*. Washington DC: Brookings Institution.

McKinnon, R.I. (1973) *Money and Capital in Economic Development*. Washington DC: Brookings Institution.

McKinnon, R.I. (1988) 'Monetary and Exchange Rate Policies for International Financial Stability: A Proposal', *Journal of Economic Perspectives*. 2(1): 83-103.

Meade, J.M. (1951) *The Balance of Payments*. London: Oxford University Press.

Melitz, J. & C. Bordes (1991) 'The Macroeconomic Implications of Financial Deregulation', *European Economic Review*. 35(1): 155-78.

Michaely, M. et al. (1990) *Liberalizing Foreign Trade in Developing Countries: The Lessons of Experience*. Washington DC: The World Bank.

Michaely, M. et al. (eds) (1991) *Liberalizing Foreign Trade*. Oxford: Blackwell.

Minsky, H.P. (1982) 'The Financial-Instability Hypothesis', in C.P. Kindleberger & J.P. Laffarque (eds), *Financial Crises: Theory, History, and Policy*. Cambridge: Cambridge University Press.

Moggridge, D.E. (1992) *Maynard Keynes: An Economist's Biography*. London: Routledge.

Morris, J.H.C. & P.M. North (1984) *Cases and Materials on Private International Law*. London: Butterworths.

Muscatelli, V.A. & D. Vines (1989) 'Macroeconomic Interactions between North and South', *Journal of Development Studies*. 27(3): 146-66.

Mussa, M. (1974) 'Tariffs and the Distribution of Income: The Importance of Factor Specificity, Substitutability and Intensity in the Short and Long Run', *Journal of Political Economy*. 82: 1191-204.

Mussa, M. (1978) 'Dynamic Adjustment in the Heckscher-Ohlin-Samuelson Model', *Journal of Political Economy*. 85(5): 775-91.

Mussa, M. (1994) 'Improving the International Monetary System: Constraints and Possibilities', IMF Occasional Paper Series No. 116, Washington DC: International Monetary Fund.

Nakagawa, S. (1999) 'Why Has Japan's Household Saving Rates Remained High Even During the 1990s', Economic Research Division, Research and Statistics Department, Bank of Japan, <http://www.boj.or.jp/en/down/siryo/99/ron9907a.pdf>, 26 June.

Neary, J.P. (1978) 'Short-Run Capital Specificity and the Pure Theory of International Trade', *Economic Journal*. 88(351): 488-510.

NS (1985) *Financial Statistics*. London: HMSO.

NS (1990) *Financial Statistics*. London: HMSO.

NS (2001) *Financial Statistics*. London: HMSO.

Obstfeld, M. (1994) 'International Capital Mobility in the 1990s', CEPR Discussion Paper Series No. 902, London: Centre for Economic Policy Research.

Obstfeld, M. (1995) 'International Currency Experience: New Lessons and Lessons Relearned', *Brookings Papers on Economic Activity*. 1: 119-96.

Odagiri, H. (1981) *The Theory of Growth in a Corporate Economy*. Cambridge: Cambridge University Press.

OECD (1991) 'Systemic Risks in Securities Markets', *Financial Market Trends*. 49: 13-18.

OECD (1997) *Historical Statistics 1960-1995*. Paris: Organisation for Economic Co-operation and Development.

OECD (1998a) *Maintaining Prosperity in an Ageing Society*. Paris: Organisation for Economic Co-operation and Development.

OECD (1998b) *Open Markets Matter: The Benefits of Trade and Investment Liberalisation*. Paris: Organization for Economic Cooperation and Development.

OECD (2000) *Historical Statistics 1970-1999* CD-ROM. Paris: Organisation for Economic Co-operation and Development.

Ohlin, B. (1933) *Interregional and International Trade*. Cambridge MA: Harvard University Press.

Orr, A. et al. (1995) 'Real Long-Term Interest Rates: The Evidence from Pooled Time-Series', *OECD Economic Studies*. 25: 75-107.

Penrose, E. (1959) *The Theory of the Growth of the Firm*. Oxford: Blackwell.

Pfeffermann, G. & A. Madarassy (1992) 'Trends in Private Investment in Developing Countries', IFC Discussion Paper Series No. 14, Washington DC: International Finance Corporation, The World Bank.

Pindyck, R.S. & A. Solimano (1993) 'Economic Instability and Aggregate Investment', Policy Research Working Paper Series No. 1148, Washington DC: The World Bank Policy Research Department.

Pradhan, B.K. et al. (1990) 'Complementarity between Public and Private Investment in India', *Journal of Development Economics*. 33(1): 101-16.

Reinhart, V. & B. Sack (2000) 'The Economic Consequences of Disappearing Government Debt', *Brookings Papers on Economic Activity*. 2: 163-209.

Reisen, H. (1996) 'Managing Volatile Capital Inflows: The Experience of the 1990s', *Asian Development Review*. 14(1): 72-96.

Rodrik, D. (1989) 'The Credibility of Trade Reform – a Policymaker's Guide', *World Economy*. 12(1): 1-16.

Rojas-Suárez, L. & S.R. Weisbrod (1995) 'Financial Fragilities in Latin America: The 1980s and 1990s', IMF Occasional Paper Series No. 132, Washington DC: International Monetary Fund.

Samuelson, P. (1948) 'International Trade and Equalization of Factor Prices', *Economic Journal*. 58: 163-84.

Samuelson, P. (1949) 'International Factor Price Equalization Once Again', *Economic Journal*. 59: 181-96.

Samuelson, P. (1971) 'Ohlin Was Right', *Swedish Journal of Economics*. 73: 365-84.

Sarmad, K. (1990) 'Public and Private Investment and Economic Growth', Working Papers on Money, Finance and Development No. 34, The Hague: Institute of Social Studies.

Sawyer, M.C. (1985) *The Economics of Industries and Firms*. 2. London: Croom Helm.

Schrijver, N. (1997) *Sovereignty over Natural Resources: Balancing Rights and Duties*. Cambridge: Cambridge University Press.

Sen, P. (1994) 'Saving, Investment and the Current Account', in F. v.d. Ploeg (ed.), *The Handbook of International Macroeconomics*. Oxford: Blackwell.

Serven, L. & A. Solimano (1992) 'Private Investment and Macro-Economic Adjustment: A Survey', *The World Bank Research Observer*. 7(1): 95-114.

Serven, L. & A. Solimano (1993) *Striving for Growth after Adjustment: The Role of Capital Formation*. Washington DC: The World Bank.

Skott, P. (1988) 'Finance, Saving and Accumulation', *Cambridge Journal of Economics*. 12(3): 339-54.

Soros, G. (1997a) 'Avoiding a Breakdown: Asia's Crisis Demands a Rethink of International Regulation', *Financial Times*, Wednesday, 31 December. London.

Soros, G. (1997b) 'Society under Threat', *The Guardian*, Friday, 31 October. London.

Stewart, F. (1984) 'Recent Theories of International Trade: Some Implications for the South', in H. Kierzkowski (ed.), *Monopolistic Competition and International Trade*. Oxford: Oxford University Press.

Stewart, F. (1995) 'The Governance and Mandates of the International Financial Institutions', *IDS Bulletin*. 26(4): 28-34.

Stiglitz, J.E. (1994) 'Explaining Growth: Competition and Finance', in M. Baldassarri, L. Paganetto & E.S. Phelps (eds), *International Differences in Growth Rates: Market Globalization and Economic Areas*. New York NY: St Martin's Press.

Stiglitz, J.E. (1998) 'More Instruments and Broader Goals: Moving toward the Post-Washington Consensus' Wider Annual Lecture, United Nations University, Helsinki.

Stiglitz, J.E. & G.F. Mathewson (1986) 'New Developments in the Analysis of Market Structure: Proceedings of a Conference Held by the International Economic Association in Ottawa, Canada' in J.E. Stiglitz & G.F. Mathewson, Macmillan, Ottawa, Canada,

Stiglitz, J.E. & A. Weiss (1981) 'Credit Rationing in Markets with Imperfect Information', *American Economic Review*. 71(3): 393-410.

Stiglitz, J.E. & A. Weiss (1992) 'Asymmetric Information in Credit Markets and Its Implications for Macroeconomics', *Oxford Economic Papers*. 44(4): 694-724.

Tanzi, V. (1991) *Public Finance in Developing Countries*. Aldershot: Elgar.

Taylor, L. (1983) *Structuralist Macroeconomics: Applicable Models for the Third World*. Oxford: Clarendon Press.

Taylor, L. (1988) *Varieties of Stabilisation Experience: Towards Sensible Macroeconomics in the Third World*. Oxford: Clarendon Press.

Taylor, L. (1991) *Income Distribution, Inflation and Growth: Lectures on Structuralist Macroeconomic Theory*. Cambridge MA: MIT Press.

Taylor, L. (1992) 'Polonius Lectures Again: The World Development Report, the Washington Consensus, and How Neoliberal Sermons Won't

Solve the Economic Problems of the Developing World', *Bangladesh Development Studies.* 20(2-3): 23-53.

Tew, B. (1988) *The Evolution of the International Monetary System 1945-88.* 4th ed. London: Hutchinson.

Thomas, V. (1991) 'Trade Policy Reform', in V. Thomas, A. Chibber, M. Dailami & J. de Melo (eds), *Restructuring Economies in Distress: Policy Reform and the World Bank.* New York: Oxford University Press for The World Bank.

Tobin, J. (1982) 'Money and Finance in the Macroeconomic Process', *Journal of Money, Credit and Banking.* 14(2): 171-204.

Tobin, J. (1989) 'On the Efficiency of the Financial System', in C. Johnson (ed.), *The Market on Trial. Lloyds Bank Annual Review.* 2. London: Pinter.

Tobin, J. (1998) *Money, Credit and Capital.* Boston MA: McGraw-Hill.

Triffin, R. (1960) *Gold and the Dollar Crisis: The Future of Convertibility.* New Haven CN: Yale University Press.

Turner, P. (1991) 'Capital Flows in the 1980s: A Survey of Major Trends', BIS Economic Papers No. 30, Basel: Bank for International Settlements.

ul Haq, M. et al. (ed.) (1996) *The Tobin Tax: Coping with Financial Volatility.* Oxford: Oxford University Press.

UNCTAD (1993) *Trade and Development Report, 1993.* New York: United Nations Conference on Trade and Development.

UNCTAD (1997) *World Investment Report 1997: Transnational Corporations, Market Structure and Competition Policy.* Geneva: United Nations Conference on Trade and Development.

UNCTAD (2000) *Least Developed Countries Report 1999: Aid, Private Capital Flows and Debt.* Geneva: United Nations.

UNCTC (1992) *The Determinants of Foreign Direct Investment: A Survey of the Evidence.* New York NY: United Nations Conference on Transnational Corporations.

UNRISD (1995) *States of Disarray: The Social Effects of Globalization.* Geneva: United Nations Research Institute for Social Development.

van der Ploeg, F. (ed.) (1994) *The Handbook of International Macroeconomics.* Oxford: Blackwell.

Vos, R. (1989) 'Accounting for the World Economy', *Review of Income and Wealth.* 35(4): 389-408.

Vos, R. (1994) *Debt and Adjustment in the World Economy: Structural Asymmetries in North-South Interactions.* Basingstoke: Macmillan in association with the Institute of Social Studies.

Vos, R. (1997) 'External Finance and Structural Change', in K. Jansen & R. Vos (ed.), *External Finance and Adjustment*. Basingstoke: Macmillan Press.

Vos, R. & N. de Jong (1995) 'Trade and Financial Flows in a World Accounting Framework: Balanced Matrices for 1985-90', *Review of Income and Wealth*. 41(2): 139-59.

Walter, A. (1993) *World Power and World Money: The Role of Hegemony and International Monetary Order*. New York: Harvester Wheatsheaf.

WB (1994) *World Debt Tables 1993-4*. Washington DC: The World Bank.

WB (1995a) *Global Economic Prospects and the Developing Countries*. Washington DC: The World Bank.

WB (1995b) *World Development Report 1995*. Washington DC: The World Bank.

WB (1997a) *Global Development Finance 1997*. Washington DC: The World Bank.

WB (1997b) *Private Capital Flows to Developing Countries: The Road to Financial Integration*. Oxford: Oxford University Press for The World Bank.

WB (2000), 'World Development Indicators CD-ROM', Washington DC: The World Bank.

Williamson, J. & M.H. Miller (1987) 'Targets and Indicators: A Blueprint for the International Coordination of Economic Policy', Political Analyses in International Economics Series No. 22, Washington DC: Institute for International Economics.

Williamson, O.E. (1975) *Markets and Hierarchies*. New York: Free Press.

Williamson, O.E. (1985) *The Economic Institutions of Capitalism*. New York: Free Press.

Wood, A. (1975) *A Theory of Profits*. Cambridge: Cambridge University Press.

Wood, A. (1994) *North-South Trade, Employment and Inequality: Changing Fortunes in a Skill-Driven World*. Oxford: Clarendon Press.

Woodford, M. (1991) 'Self-Fulfilling Expectations and Fluctuations in Aggregate Demand', in N.G. Mankiw & D. Romer (eds), *New Keynesian Economics*. 2. Cambridge MA: MIT Press.

WTO (1997) *The Relationship between Trade and Foreign Direct Investment*. Geneva: World Trade Organization.

Index